Government Audit:

An Effective Tool for the Anti-Corruption Struggle

in the New Era of China's Governance

Zhao Yang, Zhang Yanzhe, Zhang Jian, Zou Bowen

Paths International Ltd

Preface:

From a global perspective, corruption, which emerges repeatedly, is a cancer of the world. For the past few years, China has been intensifying its crackdown on corruption, as it not only weakens the purity and pioneering nature of the CPC, but undermines the interests of the people. The breeding and contagion of corruption will severely affect the modernization of national capacity for governance and be detrimental to the stability and unity of the Chinese society. Therefore, driven by the will of the state, the efforts of anti-corruption have been strengthened continuously, and a system of tackling corruption has been constructed incrementally in order to give full play to the role of discipline inspection departments, judicial organs and state audit. Among them, the importance of state audit cannot be underestimated. When struggling against corruption, the state audit can reveal corrupt behaviors through trails and prevent as well as curb the latent corruption cases in the meanwhile.

The 4th Plenary Session of the 19th Central Committee of the CPC pointed out that China shall insist on a long-term anti-corruption strategy, namely "establishing and boosting an integrated mechanism of dare not, cannot and do not want to be corrupt". This can also be deemed as China's basic policy fighting against corruption. Since the 18th National Congress of the CPC, the Party has changed its approach from taking temporary solutions to seeking for permanent cure when concerning anti-corruption, and the administering thinking of exploring corruption via practice has been developed and further ameliorated, but the general guideline never alters. "Dare not to be corrupt" asks the state to take cases of corruption seriously and punish the relevant stakeholders with no mercy, namely tries to curb corruption through punishment. "Cannot be corrupt" lays emphasis on supervision, namely attempts to suppress corruption from the perspective of specific institutional arrangement by improving the supervision system and combining the inner-party supervision with outer-party supervision. "Do not want to be corrupt" centers on ideological education, namely endeavors to eliminate corruption in terms of individual thoughts by setting up lofty ideals and firm beliefs as well as improving political consciousness and the Party spirit. The integration of the "Three-No" mechanism fully demonstrate the importance, arduousness and protracted nature of the struggle against corruption.

Xi Jinping, General Secretary of the CPC, has pointed out that with the purpose of strengthening the Party construction and state-building, the primary task is to limit the abuse of power by relevant institutions through building a clean and honest government, consolidating its institutional construction, and ameliorating the supervisory mechanism of state governance. As a general condition and necessary guarantee for the development of China's economic construction, the state audit can be simultaneously in favor of supervising and promoting the balance of the financial revenues and expenditures of government departments as well as the construction of a clean government.

Liu Jiayi, former Auditor-General of the State Audit Office, mentioned in the "audit-immune system theory" that the state government shall serve as the "immune system" of a state, and undertake its due obligations of forecasting risks, discovering problems precisely and putting forward proposals of mobilizing national resources, so as to eradicate corruption at its most fundamental, ward off the invasion of "disease" indefinitely, promote and improve the functions and mechanism of state governance, and at the same time establish a line of defence for China's economic security and stability. The "audit-immune system theory" believes that China's state audit must step into a new stage to predict and evaluate the potential risks. Under the guidance of General-Auditor Liu, the core of the state audit is to clarify the major issues in economic operation, encourage the normal performance of the macro-economy, make clear the fundamental interests of the overwhelming majority of the people; improve people's living standards and build a harmonious society, promote the construction of a clean government and expose serious violations of laws and regulations; boost the establishment and implementation of administrative responsibility mechanisms and increase the efficiency of government administration.

Centering on the basic principle, the system of corruption harness contains many aspects. From the perspective of governing subjects, there shows the trend of diversified development. In addition to specific organs of the Party and the state, other social organizations and news media have also gradually participated in audit activities. From the point of view of governing objects, illegalities and violations against laws for personal gains of civil servants and administrative staff in Party and government Offices and SOEs have also been included in the scope of review, for such behaviors will lead to losses in state-owned assets. Judging from governing measures, what matters most is the construction of legal systems, which can struggle against corruption on the track of rule of law, and in the meanwhile, methods of supervision and prevention shall also be employed to seek both temporary and permanent solutions to corruption. In eyes of objectives of governance combined with the basic policies of corruption harness, what of the most significance is the realization of the "Three No" mechanism. Along with the continuous exposure of corruption, China is also constantly exploring new approaches and means to cope with the nasty disease, and the system of corruption harness will also be optimized and ameliorated incrementally.

According to its fundamental cause, what incur corruption are the excessive concentration of power, non-democratic decision-making and deficient supervision. China now has three forms of audit: pre-audit, concurrent audit (or follow-up audit) and post audit. Among them, the function of "immunization" of the state audit is reflected in pre-audit, which can dig out corruption in due course, effectively prevent the occurrence of crime of corruption, bring the possibility of corruption down, and make administrative behaviors more open and transparent.

State audit can play a "revealing role" in preventing corruption mainly because its scope of work involves all public resources, property and assets. In the process of audit inspection, auditors scrutinize economic problems first, clues of cases of corruption then, and finally violations against laws and regulations. Currently speaking, most corruption problems are economically illegal and are therefore reflected and recorded in economic activities and financial accounts. Via careful investigation, auditors can find traces of corruption, such as embezzlement and bribery. Numerous cases discovered through audit over the past few years have shown that audit institutions can able to identify economic crimes qualitatively and quantitatively and provide clues for relevant institutions to further investigate and punish corruption.

In addition to correcting problems of corruption, state audit shall also analyze the causes of corruption in depth and put forward audit suggestions for the construction of a clean government. On the one hand, audit institutions can discover the defects in their internal control system and table corresponding suggestions to reduce the risks in audit. On the other hand, state audit can point out defects and loopholes in the systems themselves, therefore can issue initiatives to legislation departments and the government in order to improve the regulations, ameliorate the internal management system of the government, standardize the mechanism of financial revenues and expenditures, and reduce the possibility of the abuse of power for personal gain.

Generally speaking, most corruption cases involve economic interests, such as defrauding of state subsidies and embezzlement of funds, and such illegal acts will inevitably lead to the loss of state-owned assets and damage the interests of the public. According to the report it issued, the State Audit Office investigated more than 1300 units in 2014, and more than ¥300 billion were recovered. Many corruption cases also involved huge economic interests over the past few years. By dint of the ability of the state audit, China can detect and stop corruption in time, so as to better protect the national assets. By virtue of collecting audit trails and investigating auditees in due course, the State Audit Office and other audit institutions have restored huge economic losses each year, not only ensuring the security of state-owned assets, but sounding the alarm for more auditees. In a manner of speaking, the recovery of economic losses is both the achievement of corruption harness and the important embodiment of the performance of state audit.

Intensifying the struggle against corruption is a major issue of the administration of the CPC and the government. As a part of great significance of China's macro-management and economic supervision, state audit bears a mission in the battle of anti-corruption. Based on limited research, this book discusses the role and functions of state audit in anti-corruption as well as existing problems, and raises five measures to strengthen the state audit supervision in the meanwhile. The construction of a clean government, as a long-term and sophisticated systematic project, requires the participation of various departments and sectors. State audit shall be conscientious in anti-corruption, seriously review and cope with economic corruption, play its special role in supervision and investigation, and achieve the purpose of purifying the social and economic environment.

Content

Contributors:

Dr. Yang ZHAO: is Associate Professor of Northeast Asian Research Center of Jilin University.

Dr. Yanzhe ZHANG: is Associate Professor of Northeast Asian Research Center of Jilin University.

Dr. Jian ZHANG: is Doctor in Economics and Assistant Professor of Management School at the Changchun Institute of Technology.

Mr. Bowen ZOU: is Research Student of Northeast Asia Studies College at Jilin University.

This book is published with the financial support by the project of Center of integrity studies at Jilin University (2018LZY008)

Chapter One: The History of China's State Audit System

Centering on Financial Audit for Financial and Economic Discipline (1983-1993)

Establishing the National Audit Office of the PRC in 1983

It is a common practice for most of the countries in the world, or more than 150, exactly, to establish audit institutions for domestic audit supervision. Moreover, the institutional setup of audit agencies is almost always stipulated in the constitution, which is the fundamental law of a country with the highest status in the legal framework and strictest procedures for amendment. Endorsed by the constitution, the stability of audit supervision system and the legal status of audit agencies are ensured up to the hilt, which means that audit agencies cannot be repealed ad arbitrium. Practice at home and overseas has shown that the performance

1

of audit supervision is of great significance to ensure the authenticity, legality and effectiveness of financial revenues and expenditures.

After its founding, there was no audit institution in China for up to 34 years before the official establishment of the National Audit Office of the People's Republic of China, a department of the State Council at the ministerial-level, on 15th September, 1983, according to Paragraph 1, Article 91, of the Constitution of the PRC (1982). The establishment marked the end of the history of China without an audit institution.

Mainly Supervising the Authenticity and Legality of Financial Revenues and Expenditures

In 1984, the 3rd Plenary Session of the 12th Central Commission of the CPC issued the "Determination of the Central Commission of the CPC on Economic Restructuring", which nailed down the targets of building a "socialist planned commodity economy" or "socialist commodity economy". The 13th National Congress of the CPC held in 1987 held that the operating mechanism of the "socialist planned commodity economy" should, on the whole, be a mechanism of "state regulating the market, and the market guiding enterprises". In 1992, the 14th National Congress of the CPC formally defined the target of building "socialist market economy" in which "the market plays a basic role in the allocation of resources".

With the acceleration of opening to the outside world, the reform breathed new life into the national economy, enabling China's rapid economic recovery and development. In the meanwhile, however, due to the incomplete reform measures and the unsound legal mechanism, the economic sphere also witnessed some serious violations of financial discipline, in view of which during the economic transition, state laws made clear and compulsory regulations on financial audit. As an annual audit item, departments in charges are required to submit a report to the NPC standing committee.

In line with the requirements of the social and economic environment in this period, the main duties of audit institutions were to enforce financial and economic disciplines, maintain the economic order, and serve the government in improving the economic supervision. Therefore, the audit work at that time mainly emphasized the authenticity and legality of financial revenues and expenditures, especially the implementation of the supervision, focusing on the establishment and maintenance of a good economic order.

Relevant Legislation

Paragraph 1, Article 91, of the Constitution of the PRC (1982) provided that "the State Council shall establish audit institutions to exercise supervision through auditing over the financial revenues and expenditures of all subsidiary departments under the State Council, local governments at various levels, as well as state-owned public institutions and enterprises", and the Paragraph 2 stipulated that "audit institutions, under the leadership of the Premier of the State Council, shall independently exercise their supervision through auditing in accordance with the law, and are not subject to interference by other administrative organs, public organization and individuals". The provisions in the constitution were later reflected in the Audit Law of the PRC, the Article of which stated that "the National Audit Office is established by the State Council and takes the charge of the audit work of the whole country under the direct leadership of the Premier, with the audit general as the chief executive".

Centering on Special Funds Audit to Promote Macro-Control (1994-2002)

Promulgating the Audit Law of the PRC in 1994

At the beginning of 1992, Deng Xiaoping first preliminarily put forward the strategic conception of establishing the socialist market economic system in his Southern Talks. In October 1992, the 14th National Congress of the CPC officially set the target of establishing a socialist market economic system, and truly began the course of the market economy in China. Launched in 1994, the reform in the finance and taxation, financial system and foreign exchange management deepened China's economic reform and achieved the goal of initially establishing a market economic system by the turn of the century.

To follow the trend of deepening economic reform, the Audit Law of the PRC was promulgated on 31st August, 1994 and came into force on 1st January, 1995. The Audit Law provided that governments and departments at all levels as well as state-run financial institutions, enterprises and public institutions should establish and improve their internal audit systems in accordance with relevant state regulations under the guidance and supervision of audit agencies.

Role of the Audit Law

Practices have shown that the promulgation and implementation of the Audit Law, with the purpose of establishing and improving China's audit supervision system, ensuring audit agencies to perform their duties in line with laws and regulations, strengthening the audit supervision, and promoting the robust and orderly development of national economy, has played a role of great significance in the following several aspects: first, bringing the overall audit work into the legal track. Regulations on audit supervision in the Constitution of the PRC and the Audit Law, the Enforcement Regulations of the Audit Law issued later on the strength of the Audit Law of the PRC, as well as work specifications and auditing standards, etc., together make up a relatively thorough system of audit laws and regulations, incrementally directing China's audit supervision into the orbit of legal rationality. Second, offering the audit work with a good legal environment. The Audit Law is the concrete representation of regulations on the content of audit

5

supervision in the constitution, which explicitly stipulates the principle of audit supervision, the responsibility and jurisdiction of audit agencies and auditors, audit program and legal liability, and provides the audit agencies with legal safeguard. Third, being both relative steady and aggressive in legislation. Compared with the Audit Regulations issued in 1988, the Audit Law not only maintains the continuity and stability of the audit supervision system, but also focuses on adopting to the needs of social and economic development as long as the reform in the financial system. With insightful perspectiveness, core concepts of the Audit Law fit closely to the international conventions.

Issuing the Enforcement Regulations of the Audit Law

The 15th National Congress of the CPC held in 1997 proposed the target of "establishing the basic economic system for the joint development of economies of various types of ownership". The amendment of the constitution approved in 1998 explicitly stipulated that the implication of China's basic economic system was "the mutual development of economies of different types of ownership, with the public ownership as the main subject". Thus, China launched its work of adjusting and improving the structure of ownership of the national economy on the strength of the principle of "Three Benefits", namely "to the benefits of developing socialist productive forces, to the benefits of enhancing the overall national strength, and to the benefits of raising people's living standard".

To further play a basic role in resource allocation, the market required the reform in management methods. On the one hand, the market economy demanded the government to withdraw from the fields of microeconomic activities and market competition and supersede the national economic management by administrative instructions directly with macro-control by virtue of fiscal, financial, legal and other means. On the other hand, it was the government's duty to rearrange the interest pattern among the central government, local governments at all levels, administrative departments, public institutions and enterprises by macroeconomic policies, and incrementally eliminate the obstacles to the establishment of a socialist market economic system. To meet the requirements, the State Council issued the Enforcement Regulations of the Audit Law.

Mainly Promoting the Implementation of Macro-Control Policies

In the process of China's economic transition, government's functions have gradually shifted from too much responsibility for economic affairs under the planned economy to "macro-control, provision of public services, management of state-owned assets and supervision over economic operation", which objectively required the finance, as the economic behavior of the government, should also be transformed from construction finance to public finance. To establish and ameliorate the public finance framework was an objective requirement of the socialist market economy system and an inherent need for the transformation of the government functions. Due to the transformation of government functions and the adaptation to the requirements of public finance, the allocation of financial funds and the mode of expenditure have also changed. In line with this, the budget administration system should also be reformed. Therefore, the responsibility and target of state audit has also changed from "maintaining financial discipline".

Some departments and enterprises violated the macroeconomic policies severely for their own interests of local departments and political cliques during the period of economic transition, seriously affecting the macro-control of China's national economy. Therefore, the government tried to adapted the manner of working to changes in economic environment. During that period, the main responsibility of the state audit institutions was to promote the implementation of macro-control policies. To this end, audit agencies mainly carried out audit works of finance, taxation, banking, key industries and special funds, so as to supervise the performance and provide reference for the formulation of macro-control policies.

Strengthening Supervision and Monitoring (2002-present)

Emphasizing the Importance of Audit in Law-Based Administrative Supervision

Entering the 21st century, China incrementally established the macroeconomic management system and the form an economic structure of multiple-ownership in the wake of the deepening of economic reform, the growth of the share of the private economy, and the increasingly significant roles of commodity markets and factor markets in the allocation of resources. People's living standards have been generally improved as the rapid growth of China's economic aggregate, but in the meanwhile, there appeared some lawlessness in the administrative field of the government, and economic corruption has been a vital political issue concerning the survival of the party and the country.

In 2002, the report delivered to the 16th National Congress of the CPC clearly stated in the discussion on the reform of the political system that "we should strengthen and restriction and supervision over power, establish a power operating system with a logical structure, scientific configuration, strict procedures and effective constraints, reinforcing the supervision on exercise of power from the perspectives of decision-making and implementation......and give full play to the role of judicial organs and functional departments such as institutions of administrative supervision and audit", which put forward new higher requests to the audit work. The Outline for Comprehensively Promoting the Performance of Law-Based Administration issued by the State Council in March 2004 pointed out that "specialized supervisory organs of supervision and audit should earnestly perform their duties and strengthen the supervision on administrative acts", emphasizing the important role of audit institutions.

Issuing the Measures for Quality Control of Audit Projects of Audit Institutions

Along with the deepening of China's reform and opening up, great progress has also been made in constructing a democratic and legal social system in the meanwhile, and the strategy and concept to running a state have also transformed from "rule of man" to "rule of law", with a qualitative leap. The core and key of law-based governance is the administration in accordance with the law, and the good governance requires the government and its departments to properly exercise their administrative functions and powers in line with the law and manage the assets of the country befittingly. On 26th May, 2004, the National Audit Office issued the Measures for Quality Control of Audit Projects of Audit Institutions (trial), which pointed out that audit institutions could encourage the government and its departments to bring their power exercise to the open public and guide the administrative power to protect and seek welfare of the all citizens by providing detailed audit results and administrative decision-making reference, regulating the audit behavior, improving the audit quality and clarifying audit responsibilities via audit works with transparency, fairness and efficiency.

Officially Promulgating the Revised Audit

Law of the PRC

The historical task of constructing new socialist countryside proposed in 2005 and the judgement of establishing the harmonious socialist society put forward in 2006 marked the success during that period. The constant changes of the objective audit environment have brought the most significant reform to China's state audit system. on 1st June, 2006, the revised Audit Law of the PRC, which was promulgated on 28th February in that year, came into force. The revision of the Audit Law was a big deal in the development of China's audit works, financial and economic activities and the establishment of democracy and the rule of law. The promulgation and enforcement of the law, on the one hand, were conducive to encouraging audit institutions to perform their duties in accordance with the law, further strengthen the supervision and better maintain the financial and economic order, and urging the government to correctly line the statutory duties; on the other hand, were beneficial to audit institutions to further standardize audit behaviors in line with the law, strengthen the audit quality control, ensure the impartiality and authenticity of audit results, constantly improve the quality and level of audit works, and spur the long-term development of China's audit activities. Based on the spirit of the constitution, the Audit Law took into full consideration the legal system of socialist market economy. In the process of formulating the Audit Law, core ideas of the Administrative Review Law, Administrative Litigation Law, Administrative Penalty

Law, Budget Law, Accounting Law and Commercial Bank Law were fully taken into account and connected with, ensuring the unification of the legal system. Combining with the mature experience and practices that audit institutions had explored and formed during that period, the audit supervision system was further ameliorated, and moreover, the rearranged scope and newly added methods of audit supervision fully reflected the needs of development of China's social economy and audit work. When audit institutions were given the necessary means of supervision, strict procedural requirements were set appropriately, which not only stipulated the relief channels of auditees, but also shaped the error correction system of audit institutions themselves and specified legal responsibilities that auditors shall bear when violating the confidentiality obligation. The above-mentioned regulations fully embodied the spirit of standardizing and restricting audit power in accordance with the law, promoting audit in line with the law, and safeguarding the legitimate rights and interests of the auditees.

Studying and drawing lessons from beneficial experience of foreign audit legislation, the revised Audit law improved the efficient use of public funds as one of the major goals of state audit supervision, cancelled opinion of auditors, transformed auditing reports from internal business documents of audit institutions to legal instruments released to the public, and stipulated corresponding report review procedures. The regulations all reflected the connection with the international audit practice, which was conducive to the development of China's performance audit and the improvement of audit results announcement system. With a certain forward looking, the Audit Law adhered to the principle of keeping pace with the time and maintaining stability. The revised Audit Law maintained the framework structure and basic content of the original one, and only solved some practical problems in the current audit work, thus maintaining the relative stability and continuity of the law. The initial Audit Law has a total 51 articles, and in the revision, 29 articles were modified, 5 more were newly added, 1 was deleted, 1 was emerged to another, resulting in 54 articles in the aggregate. The revision that time mainly focused on 4 aspects, namely improving the audit supervision system, strengthening audit supervision responsibility, enhancing audit supervision methods and standardizing audit supervision behavior.

Calling for Strengthening the Responsibility Audit of Leading Cadres by Report of the 17th CPC National Congress

Ranking the 3rd in the world, China's total import and export volume reached $2.17 trillion. Reform and Opening Up has not only improved the material standards of living of the Chinese people, but also raise people's demand for non-material goods. The market mechanism driven by profit-oriented competition would, of course, invigorate the whole economic society, but leading cadres, who were also "economic men", would inevitably prioritize their own selfish interests when contradicting with public advantages. Therefore, it was urgent to strengthen the responsibility audit of government officials.

From the perspective of developing socialist democracy, the report delivered to the 17th National Congress of the CPC in 2007 further proposed to "focus on strengthening the supervision over leading cadres, especially major ones, the management and allocation of human resosurces, financial resources and materials, and key positions, and establish systems of inquiry, accountability, economic responsibility audit, blame-taking resignation and deposition". As a specialized economic supervision department, the State Audit Office shall, and should be able to play an important role in reinforcing the restriction and supervision on power and promoting the law-based administration of the government. Since the promulgation of the Temporal Provisions released by the General Office of the CPC Central Committee and the General Office of the State Council on economic responsibility audit, audit institutions at all levels have adhered to the principle of "being active but prudent, working within the capacities, improving the work quality and guarding against risks", closely combined with actual, actively explored and innovated working methods, established and improved the work system, comprehensively encouraged the economic responsibility audit on leading cadres. A series of remarkable results have been achieved so far. At present, economic responsibility audit for leading cadres at and below the county level enterprise leaders has been widely carried out, the same work at the department level and ministerial level have also been promoted gradually and expanded continuously.

The newly revised Audit Law of the PRC has officially defined the economic responsibility audit of party and government leading cadres as a statutory duty of audit institutions. Thus, it can be seen that the State Audit Office would play an increasingly important role in strengthening the supervision and management of cadres, preventing and punishing corruption, promoting the law-based governance and constructing a harmonious socialist society.

Current Situation of China's Government Auditing System

Status quo of Relevant Legislation

China's constitution issued in 1982 formally established the national audit system, and since then, China's national audit legislation officially kicked off. To ensure the smooth progress of the audit work, the State Council successively formulated the Temporary Provisions on Audit Work of the State Council, Audit Regulations of the PRC, Audit Law of the PRC and Enforcement Regulations of Audit Law. From the constitution to laws then to specific enforcement regulations, China's legal system of national audit had been preliminary established. In 2006, the standing committee of the NPC overhauled the Audit Law. After the implementation of the newly revised Audit Law, the

National State Office has issued audit standards in the form of order 1, Order 2, Order 3, order 5 and another 1 basic principle and 15 specific regulations in succession, with the purpose of better guiding audit work. From the Constitution, to Audit Law, Enforcement Regulations and Audit Regulations, China formed an integrated legal system of national audit step by step.

The Juridical Status by the Constitution

As the fundamental law of China's legal system, the constitution is the basis of China's legislation, and no law may contravene the basic principles of the constitution. Article 91 and 109 of the constitution specifically stipulate the state audit system and establish the administrative audit mode in China, and the constitution also makes clear provisions in Article 62, 63, 80 and 86 concerning the nature of audit institutions, the position of chief executives of audit institutions, and the appointment and removal of leaders concerned. The constitution clearly proposes China's administrative power to establish audit institutions at all levels and the audit system, provides constitutional basis for relevant laws such as the Audit Law and ordinances formulated by the State Council such as Enforcement Regulations on the Audit Law, and lays the legislative foundation as well as the juridical status of China's state audit system. The constitution was amended in 1988, 1993, 1999 and 2004, but the content of audit system remained unchanged.

The Content and Scope of Audit Law

The Audit Law of the PRC was passed by the standing committee of the NPC in 1994 and came into force on 1st January, 1995. After the implementation of the Audit Law, the standing committee of the NPC amended the law in 2006 in light of the problems encountered in the continuous development of China's economic construction and society, and the newly revised Audit Law came into effect on 1st June of the same year. Since the revision of the audit law was more consummate, China's audit system has been better protected by the law. Compared with the audit law before revision, there were 34 amendments to the original law in 2006, focusing in improving the law and functions.

As the basic law of China's state audit, the content of the Audit Law makes detailed and complete provisions on the state audit system. With regard to China's audit system, of course, there are also relevant provisions in some other ways in addition to provisions of the audit law, especially those concerning economic management such as the Budget Law and the Accounting Law. China's audit institutions are, by nature, state administrative organs, therefore, the Administrative Review Law, Administrative Penalty Law, Administrative Procedure Law, State Compensation Law and other laws governing the supervision and management of state administrative activities are also applicable to audit works. These laws, together with the constitution and the audit law, constitute China's legal system of state audit.

The Working Standards of Auditing Standards

After the revision of the Audit Law, the State Council also amended the Enforcement Regulations of the Audit Law to further interpret the content and provisions of the Audit Law. in the meanwhile, professional and technical characteristics of audit supervision require more complete and detailed rules to guide the audit activities, with the purpose of strengthening audit supervision. In 2010, the Meeting of Audit Generals of the State Audit Office adopted the National Auditing Standards of the PRC, which made clear the requirements that audit institutions and auditors shall follow the requirements of the standards when performing their duties, and stipulated that the assessment of audit quality should also be based on the standards. In China, the "auditing standards" is a systematic concept composed of three levels: the first is the "basic standards", which could be divided into 5 parts, including general principles, general standards, operation standards, report standards and auditing report handling standards. The second is the "specific auditing standards". On the strength of the basic standards which includes general standards and auditing standards specifically guiding the audit work in a certain field, the State Audit Office has formulated 15 specific standards in accordance with the basic requirements of the audit work. The third is the operation guidance of professional audit which was formulated in order to guide and regulate the specific audit work and put forward reasonable audit programs as well as requirements for the specialized fields of given industries. Operating guidelines, such as the Enterprise Financial Audit Guideline, are instructive documents with strong guidance and operability as well as a certain degree of constraining force.

The National Auditing Standards was a set of departmental regulations formulated in accordance with the Audit Law and the Enforcement Regulations of the Audit Law by the State Audit Office. Although it legal effect is lower than that of laws, it can still restrain and guide audit institutions and auditors to a certain extent. Professional Audit Operation Guide was designed for rationality and convenience of audit programs, with the purpose of better regulating the process of audit work, improving the efficiency of audit supervision, and guiding auditors to a certain degree.

Functions and Power Reference of Government Audit

First, government audit is responsible for audit activities, namely the audit of financial revenue and expenditure of local governments of all levels in China within the legal bounds, with the purpose of ensuring the authenticity and dependability of audit supervision, maintaining the robust operation of the national financial system, guaranteeing the service efficiency of China's financial funds, promoting the construction of a clean and honest administration, boosting the steady progress in harmonious society and national economy, making corresponding overall auditing reports for relevant social institutions and different administrative agencies at all levels and taking charge of the results. In the meanwhile, government audit is also in charge of the rearrangement and rectification of auditees.

Second, government audit shall also participate in drafting national audit laws, compiling the national audit regulations related to the draft, formulating strategies of government audit, regulating related statutes of government audit, supervising specific work of audit activities, organizing and enacting special auditing plans on the development related to government audit and different public institutions and enterprises, arranging the annual audit programs, evaluating, verifying and investigating necessary items of audit, and offering corresponding suggestions and countermeasures in line with the results.

Third, the State Audit Office shall submit the comprehensive financial budget of the government and state institutions to the Premier of the State Council and auditing reports on the situation of financial revenue and expenditure of other units within the jurisdictional limits of state laws. Entrusted by the State Council, the State Audit Office is obliged to provide government auditing reports of national financial budget and other specific affairs to the standing committee of the NPC, and to supervise over the rectification when there would be problems in auditing reports. The State Audit Office shall also be responsible for the report submitted to the State Council and publishing the results of auditing reports to the public, related subsidiary departments of the State Council and provincial governments of auditees.

Fourth, the State Audit Office shall make auditing decisions according to government auditing reports within the laws and propound suggestions and punishments to competent departments of auditees when directly facing the following audit issues: first, performance conditions of budget audit in accordance with comprehensive central financial budget and the income and expenditure situation of other finance, performance conditions of budget audit in accordance with comprehensive financial budgets of different central departments, direct subsidiaries included, and the situation of their final accounts. Second, financial budget, final account, and financial revenue and expenditure of other projects of departments of provincial governments, as well as the government audit related to the use of special central government fiscal transfer payments. Third, government audit on comprehensive financial revenues and expenditures of social enterprises and institutions employing fiscal funds. Fourth, government audit on funds for engineering projects, especially the ones invested by the central government or mainly conducted by the central government. Fifth, audit on the specific income and expenditure situation of People's Bank of China and the Administration of Exchange Control, state-run large and medium-sized enterprises and financial institutions, and the gain and loss of possessors of financial institutions and enterprises dominated by state-holding capital in line with relevant regulations. Sixth, audit on the income and expenditure situation of social funds entrusted to be managed by superior departments in charge. Seventh, audit on the income and expenditure situation of international aids and loans.

In addition, China's government audit also has the following functions: conducting government audit on persons in charge of relevant auditees and leading cadres of related provincial departments in accordance with the law; comprehensively analyzing and auditing the implementation of policies formulated in line with the law, and auditing the revenues and expenditures of state-owned assets subsumed to budgetary management; supervising the actual performance of government audit decisions and the revision of problems emerged in auditing reports, presiding over administrative review and administrative litigation raised in audit activities, and assisting relevant departments in the investigation and handling of major cases; supervising and guiding the internal audit of the government and auditing reports issued by social audit institutions according to correlative laws and regulations, and undertaking other tasks assigned by the State Council.

Organization and Management System of Government Audit

As the supreme audit institution of China's government audit, the State Audit Office is immediately at the mercy of the State Council and has its headquarters in Beijing. It accepts orders from the Premier and delivers its reports to the State Council. Audit institutions at all levels have adopted a system of dual leadership and responsibility. Article 109 of the constitution stipulates that "audit institutions are responsible to People's government at the corresponding level and audit institutions at the next higher level". Article 8 of the Audit Law stipulates that "audit institutions of People's governments of provinces, autonomous regions, municipalities directly under the central government, cities divided into districts, autonomous prefectures, counties, autonomous counties, cities without districts and municipal districts are responsible for the audit work within areas of competence under the leadership of provincial governors, chairmen of autonomous regions, mayors, governors, county magistrates and audit institutions of the next higher generation respectively", and Article 9 further makes it clear that "local audit institutions at all levels are responsible for governments at the corresponding levels and audit institutions at the next higher level and obliged to deliver auditing reports. Auditing businesses are under the leadership of superior audit organs".

Auditor general, as the supreme leader of the State Audit Office, is appointed and dismissed in accordance with the relevant procedures and content of the constitution, directly nominated by the Premier of the State Council, terminally determined by the NPC or its standing committee, and appointed by the state president. With the term of office of 5 years, one can be reelected as the auditor general. Generally speaking, auditor general cannot be replaced optionally, but Article 15 of the Audit Law states that "the NPC shall have the power to remove the auditor general from his office if got involved in illegal criminal activities, got criminal punished, receives disciplinary sanction because of violation of laws or dereliction of duties and is no longer fit to be the person in charge of the State Audit Office, or is unable to perform his duties for long due to health problems". The deputy auditor general is appointed directly by the State Council. According to relevant regulations, the appointment and removal of heads of local audit institutions at various levels shall be decided by local people's congresses and opinions of the audit institutions at the next higher level shall be solicited in advance.

China implements a civil service system in government audit. In view of the particularity of audit work, relevant auditors ae required with competent professional literacy, decent moral traits and qualified aptitude. In general, auditors must pass the strict professional technical grade examinations, which can be classified into the primary, the intermediate and the advanced, i.e., the examinations for audit assistants, auditors and senior auditors. Occupational requirements of primary and intermediate auditors can be obtained mainly by passing the relevant unified state examination, and the qualification of senior auditors can be obtained only by passing the state examination and the title examination of the Senior Audit Committee.

In the process of government audit carried out by audit institutions, sufficient audit funds must be guaranteed, which is significant to ensure the smooth and effective operation of government audit and the audit supervision in accordance with the principle of independence. There is no regulations on specific use cases of funds of administrative departments in China's laws. Different from the relation with other administrative organs, there is objectively a relationship of supervision and management between audit institutions and local civil services, allowing for that audit institutions are mainly responsible for revenues and expenditures of funds of local civil service. According to Article 11 of the Audit Law, expenditures of audit institutions of the Chinese government shall be included in the budget and borne by local governments at the corresponding level.

Framework of China's State Auditing Agencies

The constitution, or Article 91 and 109 of the constitution, exactly, is the basis for the establishment of China's organizational system of state audit supervision. According to relevant regulations in the constitution and the Audit Law, the State Audit Office was established under the leadership of the State Council as China's supreme audit institution, with the purpose of exercising audit supervision on central departments and local governments and guiding the audit activities of local audit agencies which adopt dual leadership, that is, led by audit agencies at higher levels and people's governments at the same level.

Central Audit Institution

The State Audit Office, as China's central audit agency, is a subordinate agency of the State Council under the direct leadership of the Premier and established in 1983 according to the Constitution of the PRC (1982). Auditor general, the chief executive of the State Audit Office, is nominated by the Premier and appointed by the NPC. So far, 21 internal agencies and 9 directly affiliated public institutions included, the State Audit Office has established 20 Beijing-based audit bureaus in resident agencies of major departments and 18 specially appointed local administrative bodies in line with the jurisdictional limits of the Audit Law and the Enforcement Regulations of the Audit Law.

In March 2018, the First Session of the 13th National People's Congress adopted the Plan for Institutional Reform and Functional Transformation of the State Council, which further expanded the functions of the State Audit Office. After the reform, functions such as project investigation, financial supervision and prosecution as well as the economic responsibility audit of leading cadres of state-run enterprises, which used to be part of the term of reference of the NDRC, the Ministry of Finance and the State-owned Assets Supervision and Administration Commission (SASAC) respectively, were put under the administratio0n of the State Audit Office, further strengthening and improving China's audit supervision. Predictably, functions and the scope of supervision of the State Audit Office will be further strengthened and expanded after the reform which not only ameliorates China's audit system and declares audit institutions' status of "economic police", but also facilitates the independence of audit institutions, enhances their role in the framework of national governance and promotes the development of China's democratic politics.

Local Audit Institutions

China' local audit institutions at all levels follow a system of dual leadership, which means led by audit institutions at the nest higher level and people's governments at the same level. When necessary for work, local audit institutions could launch specially assigned agencies to undertake the audit supervision work within the corresponding scope as authorized by superior organs. According to laws, China established and improved audit institutions at all levels by the mid-1980s. So far, more than 3,000 audit institutions have been set up nationwide, with more than 100,000 auditors employed. In 2015, the General Offices of the Central Committee and the State Council jointly issued the Framework of Opinions on Some Major Problems to Improve the Audit System, with the purpose of formally reform the leadership system of national audit supervision. According to its requirements, the document focused on further strengthening the leadership over subordinate audit institutions and weakening the interference from local governments on audit independence, besides making further efforts to specify the responsibility and scope of audit supervision. In addition to stipulating that the appointment and removal of main leaders of provincial audit institutions shall be approved by the State Audit Office, the document also focused on the polit reform of line management in audit institutions in 7 provinces, Shandong and Jiangsu included. In polit areas, audit institutions below the provincial level shall adopt the model of line management, and the personnel appointment and removal as well as financial budgets of audit organs at the municipal and county level shall be managed uniformly by provincial audit institutions. It is foreseeable that line management will be introduced to audit institutions across the whole countries once the pilot work finishes, and moreover, there are every reason to believe that the ultimate direction of the reform should be the line management of audit institutions from the central government down to the county level. Then audit institutions will be in the same management mode as disciplinary inspection, supervision, taxation and other systems, with the management running from the central government to grassroots organs vertically, and in this way, the independence and function of audit supervision can be guaranteed to the utmost.

Organization Structure and Leadership System of

Audit Institutions

The current organization structure and leadership system of China's audit institutions are as shown in the following figure: in addition to audit institutions at all levels in mainland China, audit offices have also been set up in Hong Kong and Macao, and there are also corresponding audit institutions in Taiwan, China.

China's Audit Supervision System

Audit work covers state audit supervision, internal audit supervision inside work units and social audit supervision. There are significant links and similarities among the above-mentioned three in terms of the specific nature of the business and audit techniques, but they are fundamentally different in essence. As part of the state power, state audit exercises the right of supervision on behalf of the country and the government; internal audit is the self-restraint of an institution; and social audit is a kind of intermediary social service provided by professional audit institutions. The object of study in this paper is the state audit supervision system. The definition of state audit is different at home and overseas, and the specific systems vary from place to place, but the understandings of fundamental theoretical basis and its characteristics of state audit supervision systems are almost the same.

Theoretical Basis of Audit Supervision System

From patterns of manifestation, audit is the supervision of state institutions on other state institutions, and state audit is in nature the function and power bestowed by audit institutions in accordance with the constitution and related laws, with the purpose of performing supervision over government sectors to ensure the safety of public funds; while in essence, the audit system is mechanism of power restriction, by restraining the financial power at first, audit institutions are required to publish and report the audit results then in line with relevant regulations, and in this way, people's supervision over audit institutions can be realized. Therefore, the power source of audit supervision is the people, and in other words, audit supervision is people's rights reflected in the structure of state power and acted by audit institutions.

First, as a major approach of government supervision, state audit represents the force of state and the rights of people, and the mode as well as scope of the exercise of power shall be determined by the constitution and other laws. In modern states, subordinating to legislative power, juridical power or executive power, the power of audit does not exist independently. According to power at the next higher level, different patterns of audit supervision have been formed, including legislative mode, juridical mode and administrative mode. There are also some countries, of course, adopted the so-called independent audit supervision mode, but whatever the specific operating pattern, the state audit belongs to the state supervision essentially.

Second, the power of audit supervision is endowed by the people. Fundamentally speaking, all power of the state and the government is bestowed by the people, and they shall exercise specific functions and powers in line with the will and entrustment of the people. As part of the state supervision, state audit is nothing more than the expression of people's supervisory power. Just because of this, the state audit supervision must be responsible to the people, and accept the supervision of the people. However, at the present stage there is a misunderstanding that the state audit is only accountable to the state. Take China as an example. Before 2003, China's audit reports were not disclosed to the public, even editions after extensive deletions and revisions. That was typical of being accountable to the state rather than the people. Since 2004, China has formally carried on the system of audit result publicity, which was not only a reform of specific audit supervision system, but a sign that audit institutions truly realized that its power was entrusted by the people and its works shall be held accountable to the people.

Third, the oversight of auditing is the restriction and supervision on power. How to supervise and restrain the power has been a both unfailing and worth-pursuing topic in national governance, and the original intention of the birth of audit supervision system was to better solve the problem, which is also the main responsibility of the state audit supervision. Different from the modern system, audit supervision in ancient China mainly aimed at regulating behaviors of individuals as a tool to administrate officials in order to prevent them from corruption and misfeasance. With the development of audit supervision system, main subjects of the audit system of modern countries has changed from individuals to financial revenues and expenditures. For instance, Article 2 of the Audit Law of the PRC stipulates that financial activities of departments of the State Council, local governments, state-run enterprises and financial institutes must be audited, and the priority of audit supervision has been given to affairs rather than individuals. However, no matter for affairs and individuals, audit supervision is, in essence, a mechanism of power restriction and supervision, and from this perspective, audit supervision has never transformed its nature regardless of changes in audit targets. In recent years, some scholars have put forward the "contract concept of the nature of state audit".

In the face of the concept, it is the people that entrust audit institutions to supervise and regulate behaviors of the government, but fundamentally, it is still a mechanism of power restrain and supervision. State audit supervision refers to the inspection, examination and supervision with strong specialty and technicality over the budget enforcements of auditees. From the theoretical basis of state audit supervision and its differences with other modes of supervision, it has its own unique characteristics.

Independent Status of Audit Supervision System

The modes of audit supervision adopted by various countries in the world are different, which have been mentioned above and will not be repeated here, but for different modes, there independent status is also diverse. However, the location of the audit supervision system determines that independence, which means audit institutions' power to exercise their audit supervision separately without being disturbed by external inference, is the most essential characteristic and fundamental requirement. The root of the independence lies in the fact that audit supervision comes from people's power: people has the will to supervise the use and management of their taxation contributed to the government as they paid it, but being short of relevant skills, it is unrealistic for individual citizens to directly wield their rights of supervision. Therefore, the supervisory power is entrusted to specific state organs eventually, that is, audit institutions are required to exercise effective supervision over various powers of the country on behalf of themselves. The constitution clearly stipulated the independence of China's audit institutions. Independence is the lifeline and prerequisite of the system of state audit supervision, without which the audit work will count for nothing. Although China adopts the mode of administrative audit supervision, its independence is still lightly insufficient. However, both the Constitution and the Audit Law have made specific provisions to guarantee the independent status of audit supervision, which can be mainly reflected in the following aspects on the stage:

First, the relatively independent mechanism setting. Directly controlled by the Premier of the State Council, audit works of the State Audit Office shall not be intervened by any other administrative sectors in the central government, and local audit agencies at all levels are also led by principal persons in charge of the government, being independent of auditees. The relatively independence of audit institutions ensures smooth implementation of audit supervision.

Second, the relatively independent audit work.

Audit institutions independently discharge their duties in accordance with the powers and functions bestowed by the Constitution and the Audit Law, and draw up plans on audit works, carry out audit examination, make final audit conclusions, issue audit reports and put forward treatment suggestions on their own. The independence of audit work offers the fair and objective working achievements of audit works with the premise and foundation.

Third, the relatively independent personnel arrangement. Principal leaders of audit institutions are nominated by heads of government and appointed by the standing committee of the NPC at the corresponding level, and the Audit Law specially stipulates that local governments must seek for opinions of audit institutions at the next higher level before determining the appointment and removal of persons in charge. Local governments have no power to make such decisions by itself. The relative independence of personnel arrangement can minimize the interference of local governments to audit work.

Fourth, the relatively independent administrative funds. The operation funds of audit institutions shall, in line with provisions of the Audit Law, be included in the state budget and guaranteed by financial funds without restraints of auditees. Ensuring the administrative funds by law can provide material guarantee for audit institutions and their independence, prevent them from being restrained by others due to lack of money, and facilitate them to carry out audit work independently.

Compulsory Functions and Powers of Audit

Supervision System

According to differences in the object and nature of supervision, audit can be divided into 3 categories: state audit supervision, supervision inside working units, and social audit supervision, whose specific status and distinctions are clearly stipulated in in Article 29 and 30 in the Audit Law. different from internal supervision and social audit supervision, state audit supervision represents the state power, with strong coerciveness in the exercise of its powers and functions.

First, the enforceability in its predominance. Established according to the Constitution, audit institutions wield the power of supervision on behalf of governments at all levels. The audit supervision must be carried out on the strength of the Constitution and other laws with strong legal coerciveness. In addition, the Audit Law states that the state audit shall guide, supervise and administrate internal audit and social audit. the provisions in the Audit Law lay the foundation for the state audit to occupy a dominating position in China's audit supervision system.

Second, the enforceability in discharging its duties. Audit institutions at all levels formulate plans and carry out audit works independently. The objects and scope of audit work shall be carried out by audit institutions according to provision in the Audit Law and audit work plans, and no other individuals or units shall have the power to interfere.

Third, the enforceability of the supervision authority. It is stipulated in both the Constitution and the Audit Law that auditees shall cooperate with audit institutions, and the provisions made in this respect guarantee not only the independence of audit institutions, but their enforceability in their work. In reality, of course, difficulty levels of works of audit institutions vary due to different facilitating conditions. However, according to laws, auditees are amenable and responsible to cooperate with audit institutions and accept their audit supervision.

Fourth, the compulsory punishment. Audit institutions are required to issue audit reports, mete punishments to auditees and send results of handling to auditees for compliance after completing all audit works. In the meanwhile, specific supporting measures have also been made in the Audit Law with the purpose of guarantee the authority and coerciveness of the state audit supervision.

Technical Expertise of Audit Supervision System

State audit supervision is in nature a kind of national supervisory power, which fundamentally belongs to administrative supervision. However, compared with legislative supervision, judicial supervision and other approaches of administrative supervision, state audit supervision has its unique characteristics in the whole system of state supervision, that is, the technical expertise in supervision.

The power of state supervision exercised on the strength of the constitution and other laws is derived from the state, which is fundamentally authorized by the people. The uniqueness of audit supervision lies in that the technical means of audit come from accounting, and the main approach of audit supervision is "audit accounts". Although in the specific process of audit supervision, there are also methods such as talk and inquiry, but their content cannot be included in final audit reports as audit evidence. The major way to obtain evidence in the audit process is to check financial books and financial information, and the reliable evidences are all gathered by account auditing. It is just for this reason that audit supervision has its expertise, and the staff of audit supervisions should have solid foundation of financial knowledge. Radically, audit comes from accounting, or it should be mentioned that audit is higher than accounting, because it is the duty of audit supervision to identify problems in financial transaction, and the staff of audit institutions should not only carry out their work from the perspective of accounting, but examine their work out of the box of accounting treatment. However, in any case, auditors serve in audit institutions must be considerably skilled in accounting to be competent for the basic work of audit supervision. It is a distinct characteristic of audit to be inseparable with accounting, which also determines that audit supervision is a supervisory approach with technicality.

Specialized Objects of Audit Supervision System

According to the Audit Law, state audit supervision has a series of function, including supervising the implementation of government budget, the incomes and expenditures of government organs, public institutions and state-run enterprises, the management and use pf special funds, and the economic responsibilities of major leading cadres. However, it can be pointed out that fundamentally speaking, all functions of audit supervision have a certain economic attribute. In other words, audit supervision can be called "economic supervision".

Legislative supervision and judicial supervision respectively refer to the supervision of national legislature and judicial organs over administrative organs, with the purpose of ensuring administrative institutions to act in accordance with the Constitution and other laws while performing their duties. As an internal self-supervision of administrative organs themselves, audit supervision is distinct from legislative supervision and judicial supervision. Legislative organs have the power to invalidate government regulations formulated by administrative organs when they are contradictory to the Constitution and other laws; and judicial organs are authorized to call into account the illegal behavior of administrative organs and their employees in line with the law. No matter it is legislative supervision or judicial supervision, the objects and scope of supervision are quite extensive, that is, all powers and functions of administrative organs endowed by the Constitution and laws shall be supervised, but targets of audit supervision are relatively specialized by comparison. In fundamental respects, objects of audit supervision have the "economic attribute", which focuses on whether economic activities of the government are lawful and compliant. Even when audit supervision performs its functions to investigate misfeasance of auditees, all the unlawful acts basically belongs to the category of economic crimes. In this sense, audit supervision is essentially a kind of "economic supervision".

Integrating Range of Audit Supervision System

First, as an integrated institution of economic

supervision, audit supervision is quite different from business and taxation sectors. Professional economic supervision departments are merely responsible for the specific supervision over the given scope, while audit institutions, as the economic police, are authorized to supervise all aspects of the national economy, covering not only administrative organs, but state-run enterprises and financial institutions. Second, audit institutions focus on supervision rather than other business works. However, for business and taxation sectors focusing on economic administration, supervision is just a subsidiary work within the scope of their major work. Closely connected with auditees, business and taxation sectors are not always objective because of the mode of self-supervision, while for audit institutions specifically dealing with the supervision, there is no such problem. Third, audit institutions may supervise there economic administrative departments themselves and encourage them to perform their duties according to the law. In conclusion, audit supervision institutions only concentrate on supervision and investigation without other functions of economic administration, so as to encourage them to focus their energy and resources to supervision. In addition, audit institutions can also supervise other sectors of economic administration and ask them to accept and coordinate with the audit supervision. In this way can audit institutions coordinate all forms of audit supervision.

Main Features of China's State Audit System

First, audit departments are internal organs of the government instead of external organs aiming at the government. In fact, in the relationship of administrative subordination, audit institutions are led by the government and supervise its behaviors at the same time. At first, the priority of audit work was audit supervision and economic administration supported by the government and its head leaders in order to identify and correct all misfeasance timely, which contributed to the improvement of the administrative performance of all departments of the government. Later, with the continuous advancement of various economic construction, the National People's Congress, representing the interests of the whole people, shifted its attention to the effect of government departments' performance of fiduciary responsibilities and the struggle against power corruption, leading to the shift of focuses of audit work to the audit of budget, final accounts and other situation.

Second, audit institutions can exercise the power of audit treatment and punishment according to the laws. Laws require audit institutions to effectively supervise economic activities of auditees, and the implementation as well as correction of audit opinions and results shall also be made in the meanwhile. As one of the most important legal powers and law enforcement tools of audit institutions, the power of penalty refers to measures of corrections of rationalization in illegal behaviors of incomes and expenditures of auditees and quantitative punishment in accordance with laws.

Third, the audit system has distinct local characteristics. Allowing for China's vast territory, huge territory, wide differences in economic development, political situations and cultural background in different regions, audit institutions of local governments have established audit systems propitious to their own developments in line with local objective environments on the strength of the Constitution and the Audit Laws, with distinctive local characteristics.

Effect and Defect of China's State Audit System

China's state audit system has achieved a lot: First, China's legal and regulatory system has been incrementally improved. The current audit laws and regulations mainly include the Audit Law of the PRCC amended in 2006, the enforcement Regulations of the Audit Law, the Regulations on Economic Responsibility Audit of Leading Party and Government Officials and Leading Cadres of State-Run Enterprises, and Punishment Regulations of Financial Illegal Acts revised in 2010. According to the statistical data, 6 administrative laws related to audit formulated by the State Council, over 30 local audit regulations enacted by local NPC and its standing committee, and more than 200 local regulations, administrative rules and authority files drafted by the State Audit Office of the State Council and governments at the provincial level have been published since the release of the Audit Law of the PRC, leading to an increasingly perfect construction of state audit system with legislation and standardization.

Second, the government audit has made remarkable achievements. Since the establishment and implementation of the system of audit government in line with the law, the audit work of governments at all levels have scored outstanding accomplishments in the aspects of preventing the loss of state-owned assets, improving the efficiency of special government financial funds, and maintaining the operation order of financial institutions. In 2014, audit institutions tracked and audited all types of government-subsidized housing projects (Comfortable Housing Project for short) in urban areas throughout the whole country in the previous year, including shantytowns transformation, low-cost commercial residential buildings, low-rent housings and economically affordable housings. To sum up, audit institutions intensively examined and supervised the finance and investment, construction management and the implementation of related policies of the housing projects, investigated 33,500 units concerned and 272,500 households, recovered the stolen or embezzled money of ¥4.167 billion, deprived 29,000 households against regulations of their qualification as protected objects, recovered the allowance drawn illegally of about ¥17.1281 billion, cleaned up 16,500 illegally used and distributed affordable houses, re-applicated procedures of 23 land-use projects, and improved 724 provisions of related management systems and regulations. In China's audit of the implementation of budget of the central government and the incomes and expenditures of other financial projects in 2012, the fiscal performances of 18 provinces were tested in depth, promoting the rational division of the powers and responsibilities of governments at all levels, encouraging the further scientific formulation of standards on transfer payments, unearthing the problems of integrity and normalization in the respect of budget management, bringing all incomes and expenditures of government departments into budget, and speeding up the construction of the system of government financial reports.

Third, with the audit intensity increasing gradually, audit results are more and more transparent. The released results of audit announcements in recent years reflected the gradual improvement of the strength of China's government audit. Throughout the development process, there was only one case of audit results appeared in China' government audit reports in 2002, but by 2007, more than 10 cases involved multiple government administrative departments at different levels were exposed. In 2012, over 120 cases related to problems of financial budget in governments at all levels were pointed out in the process of the audit of national administrative departments, because of which more than 90 people were prosecuted for their criminal liabilities, over 1,000 people were directly expelled from the CPC. In the meanwhile, the degree of actual transparency of China's government audit is also improving. The government audit reports delivered in 2014 mainly involved 38 central departments as well as the executive conditions and final accounts of their 389 affiliated units. The 4th Plenary Session of the 18th Central Committee of CPC clarified the position of audit supervision from the perspective of power operation and the establishment of supervision system, requiring it to serve the reform of the party and the state as well as actively promote the complete coverage of audit supervision of leading cadres' performance on economic responsibilities, public funds and state-owned assets and resources.

However, the following defects in China's current state audit system cannot be neglected: China's administrative audit system in the current stage under the leadership of the government is determined by the characteristics of China's political climate at present. According to the Constitution, China implements the system of people's congress as the fundamental system of government. Wielding the legislative power of the state, the National People's Congress, which not only takes charge of law-making, but supervises the implementation of laws, is China's organ of supreme power. The State Council is both the executive institution of the ultimate authority and the supreme administrative organ. China's government audit chose the administrative pattern subordinating to the State Council, which was in line with the characteristics of political and economic environment at that time. However, with the development of the economic society, disadvantages of the pattern of audit government are manifesting themselves.

First, the supervision power of government audit is unreasonably limited. At present, it is quite hard for the government audit to play its role of impartial evaluation on economic responsibilities entrusted by the public, on some cases, on the contrary, it becomes a one-sided tool to safeguard the local or partial interests. Theoretically and legally, the government audit shall evaluate the financial revenues and expenditures of governments at the same level and state-run enterprises and institutions, so as to determine or remove the economic responsibilities of the government entrusted by the public. However, the current system of government audit organs makes the supervision power limited unreasonably. The administrative pattern determines that the audit and the corresponding personnel appointment and removal shall be under the leadership of the governments at the same level, leading to the result that audit institutions are loath to audit the projects directly arranged by administrative leaders. On the issue of options, audit institutions may intervene by superior leading cadres sometimes, and even think that instructions made by government of the same or higher levels are in de facto "protective umbrellas" in respect of obtaining evidences and explaining questions, greatly affecting the punishment and correct evaluation of audit reports. As a result, audit institutions are unable or unwilling to make the audit reports public, and are not very likely to strengthen the audit by feat of the power of media, but tend to pour oil on troubled waters on most cases and try to solve all the problems inside administrative organs. This practice, unfortunately, makes the role of audit supervision greatly reduced. It can be seen that government audit institutions are faced with many difficulties in supervising leading cadres, and sometimes even the audit supervision can be disturbed.

Second, the role of government audit to a large extent depends on how much priority given to by leading cadres of the government. Because of the insufficient recognition and weak legal sense in audit works of some leaders of local governments, audit supervision of the budget enforcement of governments at the same level is affected to a certain degree. In some situations, a few local governments and relevant leading cadres even intervene in the normal performance of audit supervision directly. The main reason is that the local governments are trying to hide the problems for fear that the exposure of defects may lead to joint liabilities and affect their political achievements. Therefore, they are incline to take risks to interpose the work of audit institutions with the purpose of preventing them from revealing problems. In some other cases, they even try to stop audit institutions from reporting the work conditions to the standing committee of NPC at the same level, and deliberately ask audit institution to delete some issues of major violation of laws and regulations. In particular, when the problems are found involved in the interest relationship between the central government and local governments, they are more likely to conceal some cases severely damaging the state interests out of the interests in their control areas, or avoid the important ones and dwell on the trivial. The more the grassroots the audit institutions are, the more prominent the phenomenon is. In addition, according to the Constitution and the Audit Law, the audit work shall be directly led by heads of governments at all levels, but in China the system has not been completely carried out yet. In many regions, the audit work is nominally under the direct control of government heads, but as a matter of fact, the top leaders rarely have any involvement in the audit work instead, and there are usually other leaders that are in charge of or assist in the audit work. On most cases, it is often the same leader that control the audit supervision and financial administration at the same time, which goes against the good running of audit institutions' supervision over financial departments.

Third, the quality and ability of local auditors, as well as the expenditures required are not guaranteed. Led by agencies at the higher next level in business, local audit institutions are also functional departments at the same time, and the appointment and removal, occupation mobility, rewards and punishment of their persons in charge are to a large extent decided by the government at the same level. Local governments are major leaders of audit institutions, and their choices cannot be contradicted by audit institutions at the same level. In the staffing of leading cadres, of audit institutions, due to the lack of particularity of audit work in some places, some cadres with no knowledge in audit are dispatched to audit institutions for operating posts without the consent of institutions at the next higher level, thus resulting in the aberration that many leaders in audit agencies are laymen. Audit institutions and financial departments are in the relationship of supervision, but at present, the expenditure of audit institutions is examined and approved by financial departments at the same level. therefore, audit institutions are inevitably affected and restrained, resulting in a weaker supervision of auditors over their fund suppliers objectively. Although the Audit Law and the Enforcement Regulations clearly stipulate the necessary expenditures of audit institutions with the purpose of fulfilling their responsibilities, and with the endorsement of the government at the same level, the funds shall be listed in financial budgets. However, from the actual situation, financial departments and audit institutions are just regarded as general administrative organs, which greatly affects the smooth development of audit work.

Fourth, the strength of the central audit office is seriously inadequate. According to the current relationship of financial subordination or the supervision over state-owned asset, the State Audit Office and its agencies have about 30,000 working units. In terms of sheer number, it accounts for less than 5% of the country's 800,000 auditees, which are holding 70% of China's financing volume or so. Therefore, it is necessary to strengthen the audit supervision over areas, sectors and funds of great significance. However, because of the understrength situation of China's central audit office at present, less than 3,000 units are actually audited every year, covering about merely 10% of the total. Many units of the central government have not been audited sine their establishment. Take the audit of central budget enforcement as an example. There are more than 100 first-class budget units, which can only be audited for about 50%, and the rate of audit involvement of second or third-class budget units are only 20%. Among more than 3,000 National Tax Bureaus above the county level, less than 5% can be audited, and only 20% of the 250 sub-offices of the customs system can be audited. The contradiction between the heavy tasks of audit works and the scarce working competence of audit institutions has been increasingly prominent since the instructional reform in the year of 1998.

Chapter Two: The Changes and Characteristics of China's Auditing Standards

The Changes and Characteristics of INTOSAI

General Situation of Current Criteria

Founded in 1953, International Organization of Supreme Audit Institutions (INTOSAI) is the most influential and authoritative professional organization in the field of global public audit. After joining INTOSAI in 1982, China participated in the 11th INTOSAI Conference for the first time after the establishment of auditing administration as well as all successive conferences afterwards. On 22nd October, 2013, the 21st INTOSAI Conference was held in Beijing. The conference approved Beijing Declaration as the only official document of achievement, which clearly defined the role and target of supreme audit institutions of all countries, namely promoting favorable management and global governance. Based on its strategic planning, INTOSAI sets up 4 basic goals, including professional standards, capacity building, knowledge sharing and example organization, among which the target of professional standards is to construct powerful, independent and integrated supreme auditing institutions and actively improve their governance by constantly updating and promoting the international criteria. Therefore, it is one of the most significant work objectives of INTOSAI to formulate and promulgate auditing criteria for supreme auditing institutions of all countries. Under INTOSAI, a committee of professional criteria is set for formulating auditing standards.

The criteria system consists of two parts: the first is the International Standards of Supreme Auditing Institutions (ISSAI), which aims to set basic principles for responsibility, general auditing criteria and auditing guidelines; the second is the guide of good governance (INTOSAIGOV), which is designed to promote the favorable governance in public sectors. There guidelines provide a basis for better work of supreme auditing agencies of all members.

The auditing criteria framework of INTOSAI includes documents of 4 levels, which are respectively orchestrated: the first level is the Declaration of Lima, which is regarded as the basis of government audit, regulating audit objectives, audit type, auditing independence, the relationship among supreme auditing institution, parliament, government and administrative departments, functions and power of supreme auditing agencies, method and progress of audit, as well as submitting reports to parliament and the public, with the digit segment of ISSAI 1-9. The second level consists of the Declaration of Mexico about the Independence of Supreme Auditing Institutions (approved by the 19th INTOSAI Conference in 2007), the Guideline on Independence of Supreme Auditing Institutions and Good Practice (article No.11 of Auditing Criteria of INTOSAI in 2007), Principles for Transparency and Public Responsibility and Code of Professional Ethics. Numbered ISSAI 10-90, Code of Professional Ethics regulates that auditing agencies and auditing officers should be honest, independent, objective, fair, professionally competent and able to keep professional secret. The third level, with the digit segment of ISSAI 100-900, is the Auditing Criteria, which includes 4 chapters except for preface and vocabulary: the first chapter contains the basic principles, determining 10 fundamental tenets of government audit; the second chapter includes general standards, which mainly regulate the qualification of auditing agencies and auditors; the third chapter, on-site audit rules, mainly standardize conducting audit and spot audit management; chapter 4 covers reporting standards, which defines the results of regular auditing and performance auditing as audit opinion and audit report respectively, and specifies the form, content, type, applicable conditions and expression; the fourth part consists of documents of audit guideline, which are mainly frequently-sued instructions of audit work, namely subsections and concrete content of basic auditing principles, such as Guide for Financial Auditing, Guide for Regularity Auditing, Guide for Performance Auditing and guides for other specific businesses, and their digit segment is ISSAI 1000-5999. In addition, there are also some favorable governance guideline parallel to the fourth level, which are mainly standards on internal governance and accounting formulated by INTOSAI for some public sectors, including guidelines of internal control and accounting criteria numbered as ISSAI 9000-9999. At present, a normalized criteria system of INTOSAI is still being enriched and improved to ensure its feasibility and perspectiveness.

Vicissitude Process of Criteria

With the development and improvement of international criteria of INTOSAI, the importance to auditing practice of the organization has been widely recognized in the world. The international criteria of INTOSAI are enacted based on the Lima Declaration, the Tokyo Declaration, statements and reports made by the organization at various conference as well as reports delivered for public conferences and auditing issues of developing countries by UN team of experts, on the strength of which auditing agencies of all governments have successively formulate their own auditing criteria. In 1984, INTOSAI established the Commission of Auditing Criteria, and over the years INTOSAI has formulated criteria of financial statement audit, compliance audit, performance audit, internal control and a series of guidelines to direct specific auditing works in succession, which were all approved by the general assembly or board of INTOSAI after extensive consultation, with the purpose of providing auditors with a framework of necessary procedures and methods when conducting audit works, including those of computer systems.

Issued in 1977, the Lima Declaration is the panoramic exposition of concepts and rules about audit, which has long been worshipped as the classical guideline and summary of state audit, including a statement of principles, a program of action, a joint statement on necessary measures to be taken by developing countries and measures to be taken by developed countries requested by developing countries, etc. The declaration contains 7 chapters and 25 articles in total, including general principles, independence, relationships with parliament, government and administrative machineries, functional authority of supreme auditing agencies, auditing methods, reports, exchanges of auditors and international experience. The Lima Declaration is closely bound up with the global context at that time. With the rise of developing countries, the effective use of public funds was one of the prerequisites for the proper management of public financial affairs and effectiveness of decision-making, and each country had to establish a supreme auditing agency whose independence was guaranteed by law. After the issue of the Lima Declaration, by establishing their own independent supreme auditing institutions, member states have in various degree maintained their stability and development and achieved the standards of the UN, In particular, such agencies have been playing a positive role in specific targets of auditing works, such as the effectual utilization of public funds, establishment of sound financial managing system, well-organized arrangement of government works and information spreading to authorities and the public by objective reports.

Determining 8 principles of auditing independence, issued in 2007, the Mexico Declaration, which reaffirmed the important demonstration of independence in the Lima Declaration and stressed the necessity of legal protection, is the guarantee of the independence of supreme auditing institutions. On the strength of the understanding in the Lima Declaration that state institutions can never absolutely be independent, the Mexico Declaration further realized that supreme auditing institutions should be bestowed with necessary functions and organizational independence to perform their duties. Therefore, it put forward 8 principles, including enacting proper and effective legal documents, impowering explicitly and being adequately cautious, obtaining information freely, rights and responsibilities of reports, autonomous decision-making on content and time of reports, effective tracking of audit recommendation and protected access to manpower, material and financial resources. The greatest contribution of the Lima Declaration and the Mexico Declaration was to determine independence as the first and most fundamental principle of supreme audit institutions. According to the resolution of the 19th INTOSAI Conference in 2007, principles of INTOSAI were summarized into a unified system, known as International Standards of Supreme Audit Institutions (ISSAIs).

The 20th INTOSAI Conference held in November 2010 in Johannesburg, South Africa approved the South Africa Declaration on International Auditing Principles of Supreme Audit Institutions, and officially published the first battery of ISSAIs. The Conference pointed out that "the approval of the International Auditing Principles of Supreme Audit Institutions offers INTOSAI with a series of proper and comprehensive international auditing criteria, guidelines and optimal practice of public sectors, which are of great significance to all member states. In the meanwhile, the implementation of the principles will be a complicated undertaking, and to address the problem INTOSAI provides a clear strategy to ensure the successful operation".

The 21st INTOSAI Conference held in 2013 in Beijing adopted the Article 12 of the International Standards of Supreme Audit Institutions: Values and Benefits of Supreme Audit Institutions — Playing a Crucial Part in Public Life, a series of basic auditing principles, the special auditing guideline on disaster relief and assistance, the Integrates Financial Accountability Framework (IFAF) and Exchange and Improving the Values and Benefits of Supreme Audit Institutions — Guideline of INTOSAI as well as other documents counting up to 12, including auditing principles, guidelines on favorable governance and official papers of INTOSAI, which made the results of INTOSAI in the field of values, basic principles and disaster relief public and greatly promoting the improvement of the system of international audit criteria. The amelioration emphasized the role of supreme audit institutions in raising efficiency of public administration, enhancing operational transparency and strengthening the accountability mechanism, for the first time clearly pointed out that the state audit is also a part of great significance in national governance in the perspective of national administration, fully affirmed the vital function of supreme audit institutions in maintaining national financial security and promoting favorable governance, and made it clear that promoting good administrative management is an important task and target of supreme audit institutions of all countries.

Characteristic Analysis on Vicissitude of Criteria

It is one of the momentous performance measures of INTOSAI to formulate and promulgate the state auditing criteria in the world. Member states of INTOSAI and external related bodies can further standardize auditing practices and play an important role in accountability by implementing ISSAIs for supreme audit agencies, and the organization also makes it a strategic priority to assist supreme audit institutions of all countries to fulfill its criteria. In the process of vicissitude of INTOSAI's international standards, there are following characteristics:

First, in terms of the orientation of guidelines, it has been emphasized that the guidelines for member states are designed and revised for playing a leading role from the very beginning to the present. INTOSAI respects the appeals of its member states to maintain their independence. When the Committee of Audit Standards was set up in 1954, it made it clear that member states could decide whether to adopt or how to implement the standards on their own in accordance their legal systems. After the revising of the Beijing Declaration in 2013, INTOSAI continued to advocate its member states and other parties concerned to actively reference the system of international auditing standards as a common framework for auditing work, propagandized the standard system of supreme audit institutions at the global, regional and national level, and zealously fed back as well as shared successful experiences and problems in the implementation of auditing criteria to continuously improve the audit mechanism.

Second, based on an abstract and comprehensive criteria system, INTOSAI incrementally formed an integrated mechanism with a series of specific details and maneuverability. As the first fundamental level, the Lima Declaration issued in 1977 merely offered abstract, theoretical and panoramic interpretation. The Mexico Declaration issued in 2007 was the second level, which on the basis of the Lima Declaration stressed how to specifically ensure the necessary functions and organizational independence to perform the obligation of supreme audit institutions, establishing the basic principle of independence. Compared with the first level, regardless of the overall comprehensiveness, the Mexico Declaration was more specific. The third and the fourth level, auditing standards and auditing guidelines, are more specific than the first and the second level, especially the fourth level, which was facilitate with better manipuility.

Third, taking INTOSAI Conferences as the platform, auditing standards were revised duly to maintain the perspectiveness of the content. So far, INTOSAI Conference has been held for 21 times, but only four of them referred to the revision of core contents of auditing principles, including independence of auditing agencies and professional ethics of auditors. In terms of content, INTOSAI tried to made the latest achievements public to improve the system of audit principles. For instance, the 12 auditing criteria approved at the 21st INTOSAI Conference were the results in the field of values of supreme audit institutions, basic audit principles of public sectors and disaster relief of the conference.

The Evolution and Characteristics in Each Stage of China's National Auditing Criteria

According to special events during the process, the evolution of China's national audit standards can be roughly divided into 4 stages since China resumed the establishment of national audit system after the Reform and Opening-up.

Infancy Stage (1983-1995)

At the early stage of its establishment, all work of China's national audit institutions was in exploration. Restrained by the development level at that time, China found it hard to carry out the audit work completely in accordance with scientific criteria, but could only raise claims by administrative instructions in form of working system, methods and regulations. The normative documents had the character of standards more or less. In September 1982, to further regulate the audit system and audit work, the preparatory group of audit institutions intended to issue Audit Regulations. To promulgate a makeshift, transitional law for the absence of a formal one in the period for revision, deliberation and release, the State Council transmitted the Notice of Request of Several Issues on Audit Works of Auditing Administration Endorsed by State Council, which regulated the tasks, authority, institutional setup and leadership relationships of audit institutions. To facilitate audit work, the State Council promulgated Provisional Regulations in August 1985 to clearly regulated audit procedure, audit report, audit conclusion, audit decision, request for review, legal obligation and protection of auditors and the legal liability of violating the Provisional Regulations. In October of that year, the Audit Administration issued the Trial Procedure of Audit Work, which explicitly stipulated procedures of audit works, work content, requirements and format of audit documents for each step. As the inheritance and improvement of the

Provisional Regulations and consisted of 9 chapters as well as 40 articles, the Audit Regulations announced in November 1988 was a relatively complete administrative law, which could be seen as the embodiment of the working regulation determined by the constitution. To cooperate with the implementation of the Audit Regulations, on 21st June, 1989, the Audit Administration published Detailed Enforcement Regulations of Audit Regulations (40 articles in total) as its No.1 order, which was the administrative statute with more pertinence and maneuverability. In addition, a series of general rules and regulations on audit work, such as Certain Regulations on Audit Work Procedures of the Audit Administration, were formulated.

The Audit Administration had commenced the preparation of the Audit Law since 1990. After revision, consultation and deliberation for many times, on 31st August, 1994, the 9th meeting of the Standing Committee of the 8th National People's Congress approved the Audit Law of People's Republic of China. Greatly replenished and arranged the content of Audit Regulations, the Audit Law contained 7 chapters and 51 articles, covering authority, jurisdiction, work procedures of audit agencies as well as relative laws. Besides, it also contained 3 basic principles of China's audit supervision, namely the principles auditing by law, audit independence and dual leadership of local audit agencies.

In addition to the above-mentioned normative documents, the Audit Administrative has also formulated a series of related regulatory frameworks on the strength of constantly summarizing successful experiences and referring to useful theories and methods from other countries because of its emphasis on the standardization of project audit. For instance, on the aspect of audit of foreign funded projects, the Audit Administration promulgated the Specification of Audit Work of Projects Relating to Loans from the World Bank (Trial) in 1986, and after 3 years of pilot tests the formal version was published officially in 1989, which offered detailed and clear provisions on how to standardize the content and format of external reports. In 1991, the Audit Administration issued the Notice on Improving Work Quality of Audit Projects of Loans from International Organizations and Foreign Aids, which put forward specific measures to ameliorate audit work reports. With the purpose of further upgrading the quality of external audit reports, the Audit Administration formulated the Complimentary Notice on Improving the Quality of Audit Notarization Projects of Loans from International Organizations and Foreign Aids as well as Improvement Suggestions on Overseas Audit Reports about Projects of Loans from International Financial Organizations in 1992 and 1993 in succession. In 1994, by dint of the special grant from the Asian Development Bank, the Audit Administration compiled the Audit Handbook of Projects Financed by International Financial Organizations. Which offered a set of high-quality auditing standards and universal auditing methods for the utilization of foreign capital. The above-mentioned normative documents in the use of foreign capital auditing all have the nature of standards.

In the infancy stage, national auditing standards

had the following features: the first was to advance in exploration. Allowing for the situation that China's auditing system was in the recovery phase at that time, regulations and systems of audit work were considerably defective, China had to try to "cross the river by feeling the stones". In addition, the complicated national condition in the early stage of Reform and Opening-up offered China no choice but to grope incrementally. The second was to carry out the work in a gradual way. From the Notice endorsed by the State Council, to Provisional Regulations, Audit Regulations and the Audit Law, with the status and level of the documents increasing gradually, China published legal instruments of audit work in an incremental way. The third was that auditing standards were reflected in various administrative regulations. In all documents relating to notice, rules, laws and enforcement regulations of audit work, there were always content about audit procedures, audit methods, audit quality control, audit legal responsibility and audit professional ethics. These administrative rules acted as audit standards before their final maturity.

Exploration Stage (1996-1999)

Before 1995, audit institutions had summarized a lot of experience in the management of audit work in practice, and the series of audit regulations formed on aspects of audit procedures and audit methods played a certain role in improving the quality of audit work. However, with the development of practice and the improved requirements for auditing standardization, audit regulations could no longer meet the need for audit works.

In 1995, the Audit Administration commenced the formulation of audit criteria. In 1996, the Planning Scheme of the Construction of Audit Work Standardization and the Implementation Plan of the Division of Audit Work Standardization Projects were formulated, in the end of September of the same year, the audit regulations drafted by the Audit Administration were issued across the whole country for consultation, and in November, 43 regulations were discussed and deliberated one by one. After the approval, related institutions successively released 38 regulations including the Basic Criteria of National Audit of PRC, which would come into force from 1st January, 1997. The specific content of the 38 regulations involved all main links of audit works, including criteria of standards, business and management. Criteria of standards covered regulations on basic principles of national audit, professional ethics of auditors and auditing evidence; criteria of business incorporated audit implementing measures of projects relating to state-run financial enterprises, national construction and administrative funds, as well as auditing measures of special audit investigation and computer-aided auditing, and criteria of management included specific works of divisions of scope jurisdiction limits, audit treatment and punishment, audit review, audit archives and audit statistics.

The reasons for the formulation and development of auditing standards were described in relevant documents and literatures during that period, mainly from the two perspectives of legal orientation and functions. In terms of legal orientation, as a manifestation of auditing legal standards and a major part of auditing legal system, auditing standards belong to inter-departmental audit rules. On the aspect of function, as the general regulatory instrument of the Audit Administration to organize the work of audit agencies across the whole country and the basic principles to guide audit activities and the management of audit business, auditing standards mainly regulate professional requirement and qualification of audit institutions and auditors. In addition, effectively restraining concrete behaviors of auditors and measuring the quality of auditing business, auditing standards are the most specific and exercisable rules of conduct to China's auditing institutions and auditors, which can in the meanwhile supervise social audit and internal audit services.

In the exploration stage of China's national audit standards, there were mainly two characteristics: the first was the combination of localization and internationalization. To a large extent, the style design and content of the 38 regulations were basically established based on the demand of general style framework and criteria system int eh field of national audit, which referenced international experiences and routines as well as the actual situation of China's national audit, especially the fact that the audit system with Chinese characteristics had not been established for long. The second was the clear and coherent levels. For the 38 audit regulations, the supreme audit institution adopted differential treatment in reviewing the drafts. Immature criteria that fell far from standards, belonged to administrative management works and were not published in normalized form shall be renamed as provisions, interim rules or measures, while mature audit codes of conduct were collectively called as audit regulations in order to facilitate the compilation of understanding, publicity and implementation. Therefore, among the 38 regulations, only some of them were standards, while the others were administrative regulations regardless of their nature of standards.

Developmental Stage (2000-2010)

Constructing a Relatively Integrated Standard System. With the development of auditing practice, problems gradually manifested themselves in the implementation of the 38 regulations: First, being half-baked, the system lacked some specific auditing regulations, such as auditing procedures and methods. Second, contents that did not belong to audit standards, such as provisions on certain aspects of the auditing work, should have been separated from the auditing system and issued in the form of regulations. Third, contents belonged to audit standards were not completely covered by the 38 regulations. Fourth, the lack of evaluation standards for practicing behaviors and the unclear responsibility of posts greatly increased the difficulties in quality control and risk management.

In November 1998, to set up a battery of audit standard system which could both meet the demand of China's national conditions and fully embody the general accepted auditing principles, the Audit Administration established the Commission for Demonstration and Revision of Drafts of Audit

Standard System, issued Suggestion on Strengthening the Construction of Standard Auditing Regulation System and Implementation Opinions on Constructing Auditing Regulation System, and put forward the idea that the 38 regulations should be further revised, replenished and improved. The system could be divided into three levels: basic criteria, specific criteria and guides of professional operation. Basic criteria mainly stipulated fundamental principles for audit institutions and auditors to carry out audit works, and put forward principled requirements on major links and factors of audit activities, linking the requirements of the Audit Law and other related regulations as well as specific audit standards. Specific Audit criteria were the standards to regulate major factors and main activities of the audit work, and also included professional auditing standards for standardizing auditing activities. Guides of professional operation were instructional documents guiding and regulating some certain specific aspects of national audit service. According to the content and nature of the regulations, auditing standards to be formulated were divided into 20 general auditing standards and 25 professional auditing standards. After 2000, the Audit Administration has successively issued 20 auditing standards including 4 National Auditing Standards of PRC in the name of the Audit Administration.

Background and Main Content of the Measures for Quality Control of Audit Projects Carried out by Audit Institutions

Allowing for problems of quality control in practice, such as the dereliction of duty as well as latent audit risks caused by the failure to point out serious violations of laws and disciplines, it was necessary to address the plights by normalization and better quality-control of the audit work. By adopting the method of process monitoring, audit institutions took major links of audit projects as a system of quality control to clarify the corresponding goals, steps, quality requirements and responsibility, so as to provide assurance for the audit work of high quality. In February 2004, the Audit Administration issued its 6th order, the Measures for Quality Control of Audit Projects Carried out by Audit Institutions (Trial), which regulated the quality control of audit program, audit evidence, audit diary, audit reports and auditing files, to pinpoint corresponding responsibility for quality control and implement the accountability rating system of quality of auditing projects, with the formats of audit diary reference, audit work papers reference and audit report covers, counting up to 8 chapters, 100 articles. So far, China had eventually formed the situation of coexistence of hierarchical auditing standards and quality control methods, while in the actual process of implementation afterwards, quality control methods in de facto replaced the auditing standards.

Main Characteristics of Criteria in That Phase. In the developmental stage of its national auditing standards, China not only constructed a relatively integrated auditing standards system, but also strived for a breakthrough in auditing quality control. Characteristics in that stage mainly included the following: First, China successfully constructed a relatively comprehensive system of audit standards.

According to preliminary assumption, the standard system included general audit standards and professional audit standards. The contents of the 20 initially released general standards, which laid a solid foundation for the in-depth development for the standards, were basically the embryonic form of single audit standards in the later period. Second, China constructed a system of quality control which was parallel to the audit standards. In order to implement the quality control and investigation system of the whole process of audit projects, China established a battery of integrated quality control systems, which clarified the work goals and quality requirements of the major links and in the meanwhile made elementary preparation and exploration for the further improvement of audit standards in line with the demand for the quality control. The importance of quality control was highlighted by the establishment of the quality control system parallel to the standards.

Improvement Stage (2010-Present)

With the continuous exploration and development of audit practice, the originally formulated national audit standards became more and more incommensurate with national auditing status, so the requirement of revision has been urgent. The main reasons included: First, changes in laws and regulations. The revised Audit Law and Enforcement Regulations of the Audit Law came into force on 1st June, 2006 and 1st May, 2015 respectively. As the major carrier of the Audit Law and its enforcement regulations, audit standards were also in need of corresponding revision to adapt the current situation. Second, the development of audit practice. In wake of the development of the economic society, the state audit was integrated with the overall situation of China's economic construction, and sound experiences as well as good methods should be fixed in the form of standards to guide the practice. Third, the continuous improvement of audit standards. Along with the higher requirements of auditing practice on the grounds of new developing situation, some provisions of the original standard system could not entirely acclimatize the actual economic conditions, and the disadvantages of the hierarchical standard system have been manifesting themselves.

On 15th July, 2008, the Audit Administration issued the Notice on the Establishment of the Advisory Group of Experts and the Revision Group of National Audit Standards, which marked the official launch of the revision of new audit standards. After two years of formulation, revision and opinion collection, the audit standards were revised mainly on the aspects of system structure, range of application, occupational requirements, business process and audit quality control. Going into effect on 1st January, 2011, the National Audit Standards was published as the 8th order of the Audit Administration.

Analysis on Changes in Main Content and Characteristics of China's National Auditing Standards

The National Audit Standards is an organic integrity composed by many parts which have passed through phases of uniparted rules and single regulations before finally becoming parts of the one-for-all system. This book selects 6 parts, including general standards, auditing evidence, auditing professional ethics, audit quality control, audit program and audit reports, for analysis. The reasons for the selection are: First, the 6 parts, which running through all developmental stages of audit regulations, can clearly reflect the overall evolution sequence; second, the 6 parts were designed as standards right from the start, the stage of exploration, development and improvement respectively placed particular emphasis on principled rules, basic and specific criteria, and normative regulations. Definitely, other parts, such as audit records and audit program, are not covered in this book.

General Standards

Status and Content of General Criteria in Standard System. From the perspective of existing records home and abroad, general criteria are not contained in all criteria systems. On some aspects the criteria system is listed separately. For instance, in the Generally Accepted Governmental Auditing Standards (GAGAS), general criteria monopolize Chapter 3, while contents aiming at assurance service are in Chapter 6, General Criteria, Field Work Criteria and Reporting Standards of Assurance Service. In some cases, criteria systems are not listed separately, but included in basic auditing standards. For example, in the framework of ISSAI, general criteria belong to the Chapter 2 in the 3rd level, Auditing Standards of Basic Audit Principles, with the full title of General Criteria of Government Audit and Significant Standards of Professional Ethics. In China's audit standards, general criteria belong to the 2nd chapter of Basic Standards. While under some circumstances, there is just no criterion in some standard systems, such as the International Auditing and Assurance Standards of the International Federation of Accountants (IFAC), Internal Auditing Standards of the Institute of Internal Auditors and Professional Practice Standards of Chinses Institute of Certified Public Accountants. In China's national auditing standards, general criteria belong to Chapter 2 in basic standards in the early period, while new criteria at present are reflected in each article in the 2nd chapter.

General auditing criteria usually contain the following 3 aspects: First, required qualification for audit institutions and auditors, including status (such as maintaining independence and staying away from conflicts of interests), capability (professional competence and follow-up education) and moral standards (integrity, objectivity, diligence, confidentiality, etc.). For example, the ISSAI put forward 8 principles for auditors' independence, the GAGAS emphasizes the absolute independence and decent working competence of audit institutions and auditors, and China's Basic Standards of Internal Audit proposes the importance of independence and objectivity. Second, the work attitude and quality (maintaining professional skepticism, making professional judgements, behaving in professional manners, etc.) that should be brought by independent status, decent work competence and good conducts. For instance, the ISSAI made 4 standards to highlight the significance of professional ethics, and the GAGAS emphasizes the importance of professional judgements in auditing works and the preparation of relevant reports. Third, to meet the qualification and quality requirements necessary to audit institutions and auditors, proper measures should be taken to ensure the quality control (recruitment, personnel training and business supervision), for example, the ISSAI adopts 5 policies and measures of quality control, and China's Internal Auditing Standards also established an effective system of quality control. Running throughout the entire business activity, these elements of general criteria are intended to lay primary foundation for the rest of the standards.

Evolution of General Standards. The analysis of changes in general criteria can be separated from 2 aspects, namely form and content. In terms of form, including carriers and clauses, because of the different modes of presentation in various periods, it is scattered in relevant documents in the embryonic stage, and in the later 3 periods it is reflected as a part of the standards. Therefore, the comparison between form and contents are mainly concentrated in the stages of exploration, development and improvement. In the matter of content, according to the previous overview, here mainly selects the contents of 5 aspects, namely vocational competence, independence, requirements of professional qualification, training and examinations, as shown in Table 1.

Table 1 Changes in General Criteria

Situation Changes	Infancy Stage	Exploration Stage	Developmental Stage	Improvement Stage
Carriers	Article No.13 of the Interim Provisions,	National Basic Auditing Standards	National Basic Auditing Standards	National Auditing Standards
Clauses	and part of the Audit Regulations on Loan Projects of the World Bank	Article No.6 to No.14 in Chapter 2	Article No. 6 to No.14 in Chapter 2	Article No.13 to No.25 in Chapter 2, Audit Institutions and Auditors
Vocational Competence	No specific rules	Having work experience and mastering professional knowledge of accounting, auditing and other relevant businesses.	Having work experience and mastering professional knowledge of accounting, auditing and other relevant businesses.	Processing necessary professional skills.
Independence	No specific rules	Shall not participate in administrative activities or business management of auditees, and voluntarily withdraw when	In Article No.9, the status of independence was raised for the first time, and other contents were basically remained	Article No.16 to No. 19 of the new regulations, including undermining independence, no participation in activities affecting independence and management, and

73

		there is an interested relationship.	unchanged.	cases of avoidance.
Requirements of Vocational Qualification	Adhering to principles, daring to struggle, being devoted to the duty and handling affairs impartially. Misfeasance, dereliction of duty, irregularities for favoritism and breach of confidence are firmly forbidden.	Shall be objective and fair, be practical and realistic, be integrity and public-spirited, and maintain a rigorous, prudent and conscientious professional attitude.	Shall be objective and fair, be practical and realistic, and maintain the due independence and professional prudence.	Scrupulously abiding by basic auditing professional ethics, such as righteousness, honesty, objectiveness, fairness, diligence, responsibility and confidentiality.
Training and Examination	No specific rules	Shall get approved after undergoing professional training to independently undertake audit operations.	Shall get approved after undergoing professional training to independently undertake audit operations.	Shall be equipped with professional knowledge, vocational competence and work experience relating to audit businesses.

Analysis on Characteristics of Changes in General Standards. There are 3 characteristics of changes in general criteria: Frist, it combined foreign experience with Chinese features. In terms of form, the general criteria of China's audit standards are similar to those of other countries. For example, just like what the ISSAI does, the general criteria are deemed as part of the basic standards. While on the aspect of contents, as many other countries do, it roughly includes contents such as independence, vocational competence, training and examination, and follow-up education, but there are also contents about political consciousness and political caliber which reflect Chinese features. Second, changes in auditing environment have led to new elements of occupational competency requirements. For instance, to qualifications of auditors, the exploration stage emphasizes the importance of accounting knowledge, which is related to the fact that at that time China's national audit mainly focused on eliminating errors, therefore the corresponding accounting knowledge were necessary for auditors to consult accounting books. With audit targets and methods also developing in wake of the evolution of audit as an independent discipline, merely mastering accounting knowledge was not enough for auditors any more, and other knowledges about law, computer science and management were also of great significance. In new standards, not only audit knowledge, but also knowledges of politics and policies corresponding to performance auditing and follow-up auditing are required to auditors. Third, the requirements for auditors are incrementally enhancing. For example, for the issues of recruiting auditors and the follow-up educations of audit institutions, audit institutions upgraded the standard from "training qualified" in the exploration stage to "passing the examination" in the developmental stage. Due to the reason that China's construction of audit as a discipline was just on the threshold at that time, it was necessary to emphasize the importance of training in the developmental stage for new recruits to meet the job requirements. In the developmental stage, with the increase in the scale of professional talents in accounting and auditing, the follow-up education can no longer be approved by the oversimplified "training qualified", and auditors needed good grades in examinations to approve their vocational competence. At present, auditors not only need to master the basic skills of accounting, but also to be able to analyze problems and propose feasible suggestions. Therefore, in the framework of new standards, auditors are required more in terms of overall qualities including "political caliber, professional knowledge and business proficiency".

Standards of Auditing Evidence

Status and Content of Auditing Evidence Criteria in the System of Audit Standards. As one of the major factors of audit businesses, auditing evidence, which directly relating to the quality of audit work, is the foundation for evaluating audit matters and drawing audit conclusions. Provisions and statements of audit evidence at home and overseas have their own unique characteristics. In some cases, audit evidence is stipulated separately according to nature of businesses, for instance, in the IFAC's system of international auditing and attestation standards, the international framework of authentication business and international auditing standards respectively specify the evidence and auditing evidence in detail. In some situations, depending on types of business sections, audit evidence is commonly determined by the requirements of audit institutions themselves and part of the audit evidence standards of CPA. For instance, based on the division of audit business, the GAGAS (2007 edition) regulates the audit evidence of audit business by specifically formulated standards according to related criteria and statements of financial audit and assurance service applying to American Institution of Certified Public Accountants (AICPA). Under some circumstances, audit evidence is just regulated in principle simply, such as the regulations on audit evidence in Basic Audit Criteria of the INTOSAI. Similar to international practice, China also adopts the method of "general regulations on audit evidence + special provisions on particular procedures and methods + individual specific provisions on other criteria" when arranging the layout of audit evidence.

Contents of audit evidence at home and overseas are also not exactly the same. In some cases, in the framework of IFAC's international assurance service, the contents of evidence include the overall requirements for obtaining evidence, professional skepticism, sufficiency, appropriateness and importance of evidence, risks of assurance service, procedures of evidence collection, as well as the quality and quantity of the available evidence. Chapter 7 of the GAGAS, Standards for Fieldwork of Performance Evidence, which makes general criteria on the sufficiency, appropriateness and overall evaluation of the audit evidence, regulates that auditors have to obtain enough and proper evidence to lay the foundation for auditing results and conclusions. In some cases, there are just some orientative statements, but the specific contents are reflected in other standards. For example, in the international auditing standards of the IFAC, audit evidence is reflected in 12 specific standards, including ISA500 Auditing Evidence, ISA505 External Confirmations and ISA540 Audit of Accounting Estimated. Under other circumstances, there are just some simple provisions, such as the Fieldwork Standard of the Basic Audit Standards at the 3rd level of the INTOSAI Criteria, which merely makes simple regulations audit standards. In terms of content, China also adopts the practice of general standards, including the definition, content and types of auditing evidence, auditing methods, coping approaches to special circumstances in the process of collecting evidence, as well as the evaluation, utilization, record and archiving of audit evidence. Besides, there are also special regulations on quality control, risk assessment and audit sampling in the meanwhile.

Vicissitude Course of Audit Evidence Criteria. Changes of audit evidence criteria can also be analyzed from the aspects of form and content. In terms of forms of audit evidence criteria, because of the different modes of presentation in different periods, in the infancy stage their carriers and provisions are not centrally reflected, but are just partially mentioned in some documents such as the Temporary Provisions and Auditing Standards. However, in the latter three stages, the forms of audit evidence are embodied as a complete standard or a part of standards. In terms of the content, this book mainly selects the definition, types, basic characteristics and audit methods of audit evidence, and the specific changes are as shown in Table 2. In addition to the above-mentioned five changes, there are also responses to special situations in the collection of audit evidence due to the changes in the evaluation, utilization, record and archiving of audit evidence with the vicissitude of audit practice.

Table 2 Changes in Standards of Auditing Evidence

Situation Changes		Infancy Stage	Exploration Stage	Developmental Stage	Improvement Stage
Form	Carriers	Article No.21 of the Auditing Provisions	Criteria of Auditing Evidence of Audit Institutions	Criteria of Auditing Evidence of Audit Institutions	the National Audit Standards
	Provisions		18 articles in total.	18 articles in total.	Article No.82 to No.100 in Chapter Four
Content	Definition of Auditing Evidence	No regulations	Proving the authenticity of auditing matters as the material of auditing results	Explaining the truth of auditing matters to form the supporting materials for the basis of auditing conclusions.	All facts providing a reasonable basis for auditing conclusions
	Types of Auditing Evidence	Relative documents and data of account and assets	Documentary evidence, physical evidence, audio-visual materials, evidentiary materials, export conclusions, record of inspection and other evidence	Documentary evidence, physical evidence, audio-visual or electronic data materials, oral evidence, expert conclusions, record of inspections and other evidence.	"Investigating and understanding the relevant information of auditees" and "Examining evidence obtained from the identified

					auditing matters".
	Basic Characteristics of Auditing Evidence	No regulations	Objectivity, relevance, sufficiency and rationality	Objectivity, relevance, sufficiency and rationality	Appropriateness and sufficiency
	Auditing Methods	Inspection of documents, data, cashes and material objects	Investigation, supervision on the stockpile, observation, confirmation, as well as the analytical review of recordings, videos, copying and calculation	Inspection, supervision, observation, inquiry, confirmation, calculation and analytical review.	Inspection, observation, inquiry, external investigation, recalculation, reoperation and analysis.

Analysis on Characteristics of Changes in Audit Evidence Criteria. By sorting out changes in main contents of audit evidence, it can be pointed out that there are 3 major characteristics in its vicissitude course: First, it reflects the development from paying attention to evidence itself to attaching importance to the effect of evidence. Audit evidence has undergone a transition from emphasizing the quality of evidence itself to focusing on the actual effect of evidence. In terms of definition, for instance, in the early stage, the statements such as "materials collected from......" and "evidence acquired by......" place particular emphasis on the existence of evidence, while "all facts obtained by......" stresses the effect of audit evidence, that is, to prove the truth of matter themselves.

Second, it reflects the development and changes of other disciplines on audit evidence. As the requisition of audit evidence needs both methods and carriers, the development of other disciplines can greatly impact the audit evidence. The first is the development of informatization. In terms of types of audit evidence, the upgradation from audio-visual evidence to electronic data evidence clearly reflects the development of information technologies from 1996 to 2000. In addition to auditing methods including records, videos, photographs and copies, which reflect the technological level in the earlies stage, the new standards cover the handling of electronic audit evidence. The second is the development of accountancy. For the characteristics of audit evidence, during the period from 1996 to 2000, audit regulations stressed the importance of "objectivity, relevance, sufficiency and legitimacy", while the new standards in 2010 merely put emphasis on "sufficiency and appropriateness". In the Auditing Standards of CPA in 2006, the characteristics of audit evidence were also summarized as "sufficiency and appropriateness", which were also the requirements on quality and quantity.

Third, it incrementally increased the weight of auditors' professional judgement. To the judgement of relevance of audit evidence, compared with the simple principled provisions in the audit standards from 1996 to 2000, the new standards in 2010 made regulations on relevant issues in detail in 5 cases, which stipulates that the increasing difficulty in the judgement of relevance requires further detailed regulations to strengthen the professional judgement in the development of audit evidence. Another example is that when it comes to appointing or engaging specialized audit institutions or auditors for audit evidence, neither the 1996 version nor the 2000 version of audit standards asks or the professional judgement of auditors, while it is indispensable in the new standards. In the meanwhile, the professional judgement of auditors is also necessary when taking external results have formed before as the audit evidence.

Standards of Code of Ethics for Auditing Profession

The code of ethics for auditing profession refers to the standards of conducts that auditors should follow in auditing activities, which reflects the special moral requirements of auditing profession, and is the standard to evaluate the appropriateness as well as rationality of auditing behaviors. Contents of code of ethics for auditing profession are not all named after the "code of ethics" in the auditing standard system at home and abroad. For instance, the international standard issued by the INTOSAI and the Handbook of International Auditing and Assurance Standards and Professional Ethics released by the IFAC refer the jargon as "code of ethics", while the GAGAS translates it as "ethical principles". The Association of Charted Certified Accountants (ACCA) of the UK issued Rules of Professional Conduct, and Japanese Institution of Certified Public Accountants (JICPA) promulgated Code of Conduct of JICPA. Relevant content in practice standards of Chinese Institution of Certified Public

Accountants and China's Internal Audit Standard System is known as "code of professional ethics".

Due to the disparate status of the code of ethics for auditing profession in auditing standards as home and overseas, there contents are naturally different. Some codes of ethics for auditing profession have their own complete systems, such as the Code of Ethics formulated by the INTOSAI (ISSAI30), including Preface, Integrity, Independence, Objectivity, Impartiality, Professional Confidentiality, Professional Competence and Glossary. The Code of Professional Ethics of the Institute of Internal Auditors in the IIA standard system includes 4 parts, namely Introduction, Applicability and Enforcement, Principles, as well as Rules of Conduct. As the soul running through all audit standards, some codes of ethics, instead of having their own system, are parts of the whole audit standards and the basis to practice all special audit works. For instance, the Governmental Code of Ethnic for Audit Profession of the GAGAS applies to all frameworks of the GAGAS (including general standards, fieldwork standards and reporting standards), covering the specific content of public interests, the utilization of information resources of the government with accuracy, integrity and objectivity, status and professional conduct. According to the Code of Ethics for Internal Auditors issued by China Institute of Internal Audit (CIIA), there are 13 moral requests, including abiding by standards and regulations, safeguarding the interests of China and the organization as well as professional honor, being good at interpersonal communication, etc. In terms of the expression of auditing professional ethics in China's

National Auditing Standards, the content consists of separate regulations as complete systems as well as portions of other regulations, while on the aspect of content, with lots of convergence, it basically refers to other standards at home and overseas.

In the analysis of carriers and clauses of auditing ethic codes, there is are discrepancies in modes of presentation in different periods. In the infancy stage, except for some relevant statements in Temporary Provisions and Auditing Standards, the criteria were not centrally reflected in a document, while in the later 3 periods they were reflected as complete standards or parts of regulations. Therefore, the comparison between the form and content were mainly concentrated in the later 3 stages. In terms of content, this book mainly selects the definitions and specific contents of auditing ethic codes. The specific changes are shown in Table 3.

Table 3 Changes in Codes of Ethics for Auditing Profession

Situation Changes		Infancy Stage	Exploration Stage	Developmental Stage	Improvement Stage
Form	Carriers	Article No.13 of Temporary Provisions and Article No.11 of Auditing Standards	The Code of Professional Ethics for Auditors of Audit Institutions	The Code of Professional Ethics for Auditors of Audit Institutions	National Auditing Standards
	Clauses		9 clauses in total	18 clauses in total	Article No. 25
Content	Definitions of Codes of Ethics for Auditing Profession	No regulation	Codes of professional conducts that auditors and audit institutions	Professional morality, professional discipline, professional competence	No regulation

		shall observe.	and professional responsibility of auditors and audit institutions.	
Content of Codes of Ethics for Auditing Profession	Auditing in accordance with the law, be loyal to the duty, adhering to principles, being objective and fair, being honest to the public, keeping the professional secret.	8 aspects, including upholding the 4 fundamental principles, studying hard, abiding by laws and regulations, being prudent in career, keeping professional secrets, being modest and prudent.	14 clauses of 4 aspects, including professional morality, professional discipline, professional competence and professional responsibility.	Abiding by laws strictly, being honest and straight-out, being objective and fair, being diligent and responsible, keeping professional secrets.

By sorting out changes in codes of ethics for auditing profession, the vicissitude course has the following characteristics: First, it reflects the development tendency of spiral rising in form. In the infancy stage, auditing ethic codes was scattered in some documents as recapitulative and inducive statements, presenting in a "general" form. In stages of exploration and development, with a more comprehensive system of content and more clauses, more single regulations appeared in a dispersive way, compared with the primary stage. In the stage of improvement, auditing ethic codes was just a single clause in the new standards with high summarization.

From a criterion to a clause, the "general" way is not only a turning back to the traditional way but also a refinement and sublimation, which is memorable and convenient. Second, it reflects the spirit of changing with the times in content. With distinct brands of time, professional ethics of audit has been formed incrementally in the long-term auditing practice. For instance, in the infancy stage, due to the less demanding and incomplete audit environment, the only requirement was "auditing by law". In the exploration stage, auditors were asked to "abide by laws and regulations". The requirements were expanded to "abiding by laws, regulation, regulatory frameworks, as well as disciplines of audit work and government integrity". Finally, the new standards put forward the concept of "being in line with laws strictly", which reflected the idea of law-based governance as well as higher requirements and implementation of auditing in accordance with laws and regulations.

Criteria of Audit Program

Audit program is the specific working arrangement designed by auditing teams with the purpose of achieving auditing goals and finishing auditing tasks smoothly. The scientificity and maneuverability of audit programs are directly related to the implementation quality and final effects of audit projects, and how to make a good audit program is the key content to be standardized and guided in the auditing standards of the INTOSAI and governments of all countries. In the Criteria of Field Audit in the 3rd level of INTOSAI's auditing standards, auditors are required to make specific plans (namely programs of auditing implementation) on some audit projects in order to implement the audit work economically and effectively as well as ensure the auditing quality, and in the meanwhile auditors' work matters are also specifically regulated. The GAGAS also explicitly requires auditors to fully scheme auditing projects and make job logging. Auditors are also, at the same time, asked to investigate and understand auditees as well as their environments, confirm the importance and evaluate the auditing risks according to professional judgement, and define the specific targets, scopes as well as methods of audit on this basis. The idea has been stressed that the audit program runs through the whole process of audit work, and auditors shall make continuous and dynamic adjustments to the formulated plans according to specific implementations of the audit work.

Allowing for the differences in frameworks of auditing standards at home and overseas, there are discrepancies in forms and contents of criteria of audit program. Some integrate audit programs and auditing plans. For instance, the Criteria of Audit of Budgeted Financial Statements issued by the IFAC covers the functions and temporal arrangements, the participation of key members of the project team on audit program, preliminary professional activities, schedule activities, job logging of audit program, as well as the supplementary consideration of initial audit engagement. Some bring the content of audit programs into auditing plans. For example, the planning audit work (namely the embodiment of audit work) of INTOSAI's Criteria of Field Audit covers a series of contents, including analysis on auditing environments, clarifying responsibilities, giving consideration to the interests of all parties, audit goals, tests of internal control, levels of importance, evaluations of internal audit, confirmation of audit methods, as well as proper record. Another example is the Field Criteria of Performance Auditing issued by the GAGAS, which regulates that auditors must fully plan and record the audit work. On this strength, by understanding and evaluating the risks and significance of audit works, there should be matters to be determined, including auditing standards, quantity and types of auditing evidence, audit resources and communications. In China's system of new auditing criteria, as part of audit program, auditing plan only includes specific plans of auditing implementation, while in the previous framework audit programs and auditing plans are strictly separated.

Vicissitude Course of Criteria of Audit Program. In the infancy stage, with all related contents scattered in some documents, there was no single file or regulation on provisions of auditing standards. For instance, the Temporal Provisions and the Trial Program of Audit Work issued in 1985, the Auditing Standards issued in enacted in 1988 and the Several Provisions of the Audit Administration on the Implementation of Audit Program promulgated in 1993 and other documents all involved regulations on establishment and implementation of audit programs. Due to the great discrepancies in the later 3 periods, this book only analyzes contents in stages of exploration, development and improvement. In addition, this book mainly selects

5 aspects of the vicissitude course of audit program criteria, including the scope of standards and regulations, the understanding off audit program, main contents of audit program, the attention to internal audit and internal control, as well as the concern on informatization. The specific changes are shown in Table 4.

Table 4 Changes in Criteria of Audit Program

Situation Changes		Exploration Stage	Development Stage	Improvement Stage
Form	Carriers	Criteria of Establishment of Audit Program of Audit Institutions	Audit Program Criteria of Audit Institutions	National Auditing Standards
	Clauses	18 clauses in total	18 clauses in total	Article No. 52 to 81 in Chapter 4
Content	Scope	Preparation, revision, review, approval and adjustments of programs.	Establishment, review, adjustment and implementation, including work plans and implementation plans.	Programs of audit implementation only.
	Understanding of Audit Program	Formulating work plans for specific audit works in order to successfully complete audit tasks and projects.	Specific arrangements designed for the audit work with the purpose of finishing audit tasks.	Investigating and understanding auditees and their related situations, assessing the possibility of important problems in auditees, determining auditing responses, and establishing auditing implementation plans.
	Main Content of Audit	Including the basis, basic	Audit work plan includes	Audit Implementation plan include auditing

89

	Program	situation, scope, content, goals, key points, implementation step, as well as predetermined dates of start & finish as well as division of labor.	content of 6 aspects, such as target, scope, object and division of labor, while audit implementation plan includes content of 8 aspects, such as basis, object, evaluation of importance, and division of labor.	goals, auditing scope, audit content and key factors and methods of audit works, and job requirements of audit work.
	Attention to Internal Audit and Internal Control	Paying attention to the related situation of internal control.	Paying attention to relevant internal control and its implementation, providing audit report materials issued by internal audit institutions and social audit agencies, teasing, analyzing and evaluating relevant internal control.	Understanding the 5 major factors of internal control, and testing the effectiveness of relevant internal control.
	Concern on Informatization	No regulation	Providing electronic data and data structure documents related to audit work.	Understanding the related information system and the situation of their electronic data, investigating the control of information system of auditees, evaluating auditees' degree of dependence,

				and checking their effectiveness as well as security.

Characteristics of Changes in Criteria of Audit Program. By sorting out changes in main contents of audit programs, the vicissitude course of audit program criteria has the following characteristics: First, in the process of revising and arranging audit program criteria, China regards referencing advanced experience at home and overseas and keeping Chinese characteristics as equally important. The previous analysis shows that in the Spot Auditing Criteria of the INTOSAI and the Field Standards of Performance Audit issued by the GAGAS, audit programs are all embodied in auditing plans, while under the framework of new standards, China makes its audit criteria geared to the international standards by bringing plans of audit work into audit programs and bringing audit implementation plans into regulations on field audit. in the meanwhile, in the vicissitude course of audit program, China has also persisted its unique characteristic, namely differential treatment between audit programs and audit plans, in systems of both old regulations and new standards.

Second, the vicissitude reflects the influence of changes in environment on audit works. The first is the effect of internal control. From the previous analysis, with the increasing attention to internal control and more related regulations, the theory of internal control has been developed from "3 factors" to "5 factors", following close on the development of theory and practice. The second is the impact of informatization. In the wake of the rapid development of informatization over the recent years, related contents on audit work have grown out of nothing, with more and more regulations on internal control of information system, security and timeliness of information system, and electronic data.

Third, China's audit institutions have paid enough attention to the maneuverability of spot audit. Generally speaking, the audit program is divided into work plans and implementation plans. By bringing work plans into audit program and limiting audit plans as audit implementation plans, China stresses the importance of spot audit. In the meanwhile, from the perspective of the development of program guidelines, specific regulations are incrementally specific and operable. In the new standards, there are 10 criteria of professional judgement, 8 factors of importance judgement, 6 situations to adjust schemes, 4 matters relating to approval of adjustment plans by the person in charge of audit institution.

Criteria of Audit Quality Control

Audit quality control refers policies and programs designed by audit institutions to ensure audit quality, which provide reasonable assurance for abiding by professional criteria, laws & regulations, and proper audit reports issued by audit institutions and auditors according to specific circumstances.

According to situation home and abroad, in some aspects, audit quality control is relatively centralized. For instance, in the International Audit and Assurance

Criteria System of the IFAC, the system of quality control standards exists as two independent parts: one is the international quality control standards, which is applicable to 4 types of businesses, including audit business, review business, other assurance business and related services; the other is the quality control aiming at the service of historical financial information. Chapter 3 of the GAGAS includes the contents of independence, professional judgement, competence and quality control, and among them, the systems of quality control and external peer review form the part of quality control together.

On some cases, content of audit quality control scatters in other parts of auditing standards. For example, audit quality control of the INTOSAI is reflects each level of its framework: in the second level, there are requirements on independence and regulations on professional ethics, which are of great significance to audit quality; in the third level, there are general standards and professional ethics, and in the fourth level there exists the guideline of audit control of historical financial information, which is specifically made for the audit quality control in this respect. In contrast, China has a broader understanding of the concept of quality control, which is not only reflected in basic standards, but also in some specific standards and methods aiming at quality control, and in some situations, there are single regulations compiled for the service of audit quality control.

Differences in the form of audit quality control can also significantly affect the content of quality control standards. In fact, there are obvious differences between specific contents of audit quality control at home and overseas. Some institutions or organizations only control auditing behaviors. For instance, aiming at quality control of historical financial information service, the IFAC has made policies and procedures for leadership responsibility for quality of service, professional ethical requirements, maintenance of relationship with clients, specific businesses, human resources, as well as implementation and supervision on businesses. Main content of quality control of the GAGAS covers 6 aspects, including leadership responsibility for quality of audit business, requirements on independence, laws and professional ethics, beginning, undertaking and continuing of audit and assurance business, human resources, implementing, recording and reporting of audit and assurance business, and the supervision on quality. In some aspects, audit organizations pay attention to both the control of audit behavior and factors influencing audit quality. For instance, the INTOSAI divides the content of audit quality control into 5 parts, including training and recruitment of personnel, compilation of handbooks and guidelines, supports to acquisition of experience and skills, personnel allocation, audit programs and their supervision, as well as effects and effectiveness of standards and procedures for internal evaluation. In China, both the content of promoting auditors to abide by the professional criteria, such as audit review and record filing, and the content of regulating auditors and auditing teams, such as regulations on audit programs, audit implementation and audit reports, are brought into audit quality control.

Audit quality control in China is broadly understood as actions influencing audit control and control over audit works. For instance, in the Methods of Quality Control over Auditing Projects of Audit Institutions (trial), all content regulating behaviors of auditors and audit agencies were regarded as content of quality control.

Vicissitude Course of Criteria of Audit Quality Control. With the deepening of the understanding of audit quality control and the changing of influencing factors, the carriers and content of regulatory documents of audit quality control are also making differences. In the infancy stage, with no specific documents of audit quality control, its related content was reflected in other documents, such as the Temporal Provisions, the Audit Regulations and the Audit Laws enacted in 1994, which all made regulations specifically on audit quality control, including issuing advice of audit, consulting opinions from auditees, examining audit reports. Since the vast gap between the infancy stage and the latter 3 stages, only the contents in the stages of exploration, development and improvement will be brought into consideration in the comparative analysis.

Table 5 Changes in Criteria of Audit Quality Control

Situation Changes		Exploration Stage	Development Stage	Improvement Stage
Form	Carriers	Regulations on Audit Review Works of Audit Institutions, Regulations on Audit Archives Work of Audit Institutions, etc.	Audi Review Standards of Audit Institutions, Temporal Provisions on	National Auditing Standards

			Quality Inspection of Audit Projects of Audit Institutions, Standards on Audit Archives Work of Audit Institutions, and Methods of Quality Control over Auditing Projects of Audit Institutions (trial).	
	Clauses	All	All	Article No.172 to No. 196 in Chapter 6
Content	Goals of Audit Quality Control	Strengthening the internal control and improving the management mechanism.	Standardizing audit behaviors, improving audit quality and clarifying audit responsibility.	Abiding by laws, regulations and these standards, drawing appropriate audit conclusions and making penalties according to laws.
	Key Factors of Audit Quality Control	The Criteria covers works about files, evidence, programs and reviews, without introduction.	In addition to criteria, the methods also include audit practice influencing audit quality and the control of audit practices.	5 aspects in total, including responsibility mechanism of responsibility, professional ethics, human resources, implementation of service, and quality inspection of audit work.

	Establishment of Hierarchical Quality Control	No specific establishment, but contents about review agencies, responsibilities of full-time review personnel, institutions of archives management and the responsibility of archives personnel.	Putting forward working procedure of audit program, quality control of audit evidence, audit diary, audit working paper, audit reports and audit archives.	Clearly proposing the establishment of hierarchical quality control for members of audit teams, chief auditors, group leaders, business departments, trial agencies, auditor generals and heads of audit institutions as well as their corresponding quality responsibilities at each level.
	Quality Inspection of Audit Projects	No clear illustration	Order No. 1 stipulates the jurisdiction, enforcement bodies, contents, methods and results of the inspection. Article No. 94 of the Measures requires that "all relevant departments of audit institutions shall strengthen the inspection on quality of audit projects".	Article No. 190 to No. 193 regulate the content, methods, key points and authority of quality inspection.

Characteristics of Changes in Criteria of Audit Quality Control. By sorting out changes in criteria of audit quality control, it can be seen that there are two major characteristics in the vicissitude course: First, it reflected the changes in the concept of quality control. In the exploration stage, measures to urge auditors to comply with professional standards were taken as the content of quality control, such as audit review and record archives; while in the stage of development, contents to regulate audit teams and auditors, such as regulations on audit programs, audit implementation and audit reports, were newly added as audit quality control. At present, in the stage of improvement, the framework of new standards embraces new contents including behaviors affecting audit quality and control over audit implementation.

Second, it embodies the Chinese characteristics while referencing foreign experience. Some regulations on audit quality control fully draw lessons from foreign practice. In addition to the two standards on quality control in the framework of international audit criteria, there is also a quality-control-specific regulation, namely the Codes of Ethics of Professional Accounts, which is the basis to guarantee the quality of the business, and can be regarded as quality control of generalized category. In new standards, as a key factor of the system of audit quality control, codes of audit ethics are playing their roles in the developmental stage and exploration stage of national audit standards in the form of norms and standards.

Criteria of Audit Report Standards

The audit report is the comprehensive reflection of

the quality of the audit work, and an important sign of the final completion of the audit work. From the practice at home and overseas, in spite of the quite different expressions, audit reports occupy a significant position in the system of audit standards. Some audit reports adopt a centralized approach, such as the audit report standards of the INTOSAI, which consists of 29 clauses, including general requirements, specific requirements for regular (financial) audit reports and performance audit reports, as well as requirements for auditors' auditing judgements under different circumstances. While in some cases, audit institutions tent to adopt the approach of decentralized regulation, such as the GAGAS, which consists of financial audit report standards, authentication business report standards and performance audit report standards. The characteristic of such report guidelines is that they focus on the particular regulations on contents of audit reports with the purpose of guiding auditors in how to report problems discovered in audit works or audit opinions formed in different situations. China has never divided the standards of audit reports separately in terms of business, but there are both scattered rules and centralized regulations in terms of form.

As the final carrier for releasing audit results to the public, it is necessary to establish a sound audit report system and improve the audit quality to clearly define the forms and content of audit reports, which will make for the objectivity, impartiality and authority of audit conclusions. From the existing research home and abroad, contents of different forms of audit reports have their own characteristics. For instance, in some cases, more importance is attached to the form, such as the governmental audit report standards of the INTOSAI, which mainly put forward requirements on the entity of the reports instead of specific procedures, and bring the related clauses of regular (financial statement) audit and performance audit into the same system of audit report criteria, which are greatly simplified with more specific provisions and less duplication. Regular (financial statement) audit report is formatted and standardized with predefined audit opinions. Other audit criteria tent to pay more attention to the content of audit reports, for example, with more particular and specific regulations in audit report criteria, the GAGAS covers more detailed regulations on contents of audit reports, so as to guide auditors to report problems discovered or audit opinions formed under various circumstances. Compared with the criteria of the INTOSAI, report standards off the GAGAS lack requirements on elements and forms. No matter in which stage, China's audit report criteria not only have provisions on the content of audit reports, but also have requirements on the procedures of issuing reports, striving to be in line with international practice.

Vicissitude Course of Audit Report Criteria. With the development of auditing practice and the external requirements for more audit information, the forms and contents of audit reports have also changed softly, resulting in significant differences in forms of expression in each stage. In the infancy stage, without specific documents to regulate audit reports, China's audit institutions had to rely on some relevant clauses scattered in Temporal Provisions and Audit Standards.

In the Audit Regulations on Loan Projects of the World Bank issued in 1989, China made detailed regulations on internal audit reports, external audit report, position paper of management, as well as conclusions and results of audit works, with examples of audit reports. Allowing for the wide difference between the infancy stage and the latter ones, only the stages of exploration, development and improvement are covered in the comparative analysis. This book mainly selects changes in 5 aspects, including the scope of the audit report, conditions for issuing the audit report, procedures and requirements on the audit report, main content of the audit report and types of documents of the audit report. Specific changes are shown in Table 6.

Table 6 Changes in Reporting Standards for Audit

Situation Changes		Exploration Stage	Developmental Stage	Improvement Stage
Form	Carriers	Editorial Regulations on Audit Reports of Audit Institutions	Chapter 5, Quality Control of Editorial Regulations on Audit Reports of Audit Institutions	National Auditing Standards
	Provisions	19 articles in total	18 standards in Chapter 5	Article No.119 to No.171 of the Chapter 5, Audit Reports
Content	Category of Audit Reports	Submitting paperwork of audit work and auditing results to dispatched audit institutions.	Submitting paperwork of the implementation of audit work and auditing results to dispatched audit institutions.	Adding the content of "special reports of audit investigation".
	Conditions	Audit reports	Shall submit	In addition to the

	for Issuance of Audit Reports	shall be submitted by auditees receiving advice of audit.	audit reports to audit institutions after finishing the vested audit work.	situations in the first two stages, there is also the situation that "audit institutions may not issue special reports of audit investigation to auditees under special circumstances".
	Main Contents of Audit Reports	The scope, content, method and time of audit works, basic information of auditees, relevant information concerning the implementation of audit, opinions about audit evaluations, punishments and their basis.	Adding the content of 7 aspects, such as commitments on the authenticity and integrity of accounting data provided by auditees, and suggestions on improving the management of financial revenues and expenditures of auditees.	Article No.123 is expanded to 8 aspects. The clause "the commitments on the authenticity and integrity of accounting data provided by auditees" is relocated to audit evidence, and "audit grounds" as well as "the implementation of audit decisions and the adoption of audit recommendations" are newly added.
	Editorial Procedures and Requirements of Audit Reports	Making simple regulations on audit procedures, and putting forward fundamental requirements on auditors, audit leaders, internal review and audit institutions.	The standards stipulate audit procedures and subdivide the responsibility of each stage, the methods set out requirements for each responsibility subject in each stage.	Compared with the previous stage, the requirement "review" is changed to "trial", and the content as well as methods are regulated. In addition, there are also regulations on the audit of economic responsibility and special reports.
	Types of Audit Reports	No regulations.	4 kinds of documents, including opinion letter, audit decision, audit	3 kinds of documents, including audit decision, audit transferred disposal and audit opinion.

			recommendation and transferred disposal.	

Characteristics of Changes in Audit Report Criteria.
Since the establishment of the audit system, China has
established a system of audit reports with Chinese
characteristics in the process of continuous
development and improvement. By sorting out changes
in the audit reports, the following features can be
pointed out:

First, there is an increasing scale of content about
audit reports. Along with the increasingly particular
requirements on audit work, the demand for audit
reports will also incrementally increase, which requires
audit institutions to regulate more on standards of audit
reports to improve the product quality. For instance, in
the exploration stage, there were only regulations on
reading and editing of audit reports, and a new chapter
about the quality of audit reports, which adopted the
way of making standards and methods in parallel, was
added in quality control in the developmental stage. In
the new standards, audit reports are stipulated from the
content, procedures and category, which make the
reports more comprehensive and operable.

Second, there are also distinct era characteristics.
With the improvement of audit works in practice, era
characteristics have gradually been reflected in audit
standards. For example, since the release of the first
announcement of audit results in 2003, the social
influence of audit work has been gradually improving
with the comprehensive proliferation of audit results.

Afterwards, in 2006, the Audit Law after revision brought the content of the announcement of audit results into itself, and in the new standards, the 4th chapter, The Announcement of Audit Results, specifically made regulations on the system of announcement for the first time. In light of the attention paid to the audit rectification and reform of audit institutions at various levels in recent years, the importance of audit rearrangements has also raised incrementally. Criteria from 1996 to 2000 corresponding to main contents of audit reports asserted no claim for rearrangements, while in the new standards, the contents of "the implementation of audit works and the acceptance of audit opinions in the past", the inspection on rectification and reform of audit, and the audit reports issued for inspection results are clearly required.

Characteristics of Changes in China's National Auditing Standards

In light of differences in motivations, institutional changes can be divided into induced changes and mandatory changes. Usually, induced changes of individuals and organizations are advocated, organized, arranged and implemented in the process of pursuing potential interests spontaneously, which are manifested as alterations and supersessions of institutions or creations of new systems. Although there are inevitably shortcomings such as externality and the problem of "free rider", induced changes are characterized by spontaneity, gradualness and consistency of interests. Mandatory changes, whose advantages lie in the coercive forces, the preponderance of national violence and the prompt transition, are usually shown up as orders and laws issued by the government, which emphasize the government dominance.

From the perspective of the vicissitude course of China's national auditing criteria, the government (audit institutions) is leading the way of mandatory changes for the following reasons: First, the Chinese government is equipped with the ability to act as the subject of mandatory changes. Based on the national conditions of China, the government, with enough power of arrangement and appeal, is the mightiest among all relevant stakeholders of national auditing criteria, and other subjects have to obey the audit institutions, which are supported by the government, when utilizing national auditing criteria. From the analysis on the vicissitude course, it can be seen the supreme audit institutions have made relevant regulations and plans, set up special committees and organized core professional members to get engaged in the business before each revision of standards.

Second, mandatory changes have achieved better results. The vicissitude course of China's national auditing criteria is to meet the demand of auditing practice and lower the costs incurred by changes in accordance with the principle of cost-effectiveness, so as to maximize social benefits. Guided by the government by state mandatory planning, the targets can be achieved as soon as possible. From the perspective of the past vicissitude courses, the revisions are be implemented in time with obvious positive effects.

Third, mandatory changes can meet external requirements in a timely manner. Generally speaking, changes in national auditing criteria are aroused by risks and external pressure, which are all solved and settled incrementally by the government, in the process of execution. Therefore, the government has the supreme power in determining all specific details of the changes. With the purpose of pooling the wisdom from all parties and truly solving practical problems, previous revision of standards all witnessed the process of soliciting opinions of all walks of life, but the final decisions were made by the supreme audit institution with no exception.

The choice of the mode of mandatory changes is determined by the power and preference of all interest-related parties, and auditing institutions play a leading role in the vicissitude course for the following reasons: First, changes in auditing standards should first meet the needs of stakeholders, and the demand of audit institutions is the most direct. As shareholders of the most significance, audit institutions can be regarded as carriers of interest appeals of other related subjects.

Second, it is the main function for audit institutions to provide the government with audit information. In view of the development of the current situation and the higher requirements on quality of audit information, audit institutions need to meet the government's needs for information by modifying audit standards.

Third, except for audit institutions, other organizations are unable to bear the burden of changing audit standards. In spite of the increasingly inflating scales of academies, industry associations and research societies, their professional competence in audit work cannot hold a candle to non-government audit organizations, not to say the tremendous gap between the amateurish agencies and international organizations. Therefore, such institutions are not qualified to guide the rectification and modification of audit standards.

In the vicissitude course of China's national audit standards, in addition to the major character of government's mandatory changes, induced changes also act as a supporting role. It can be found that there is a certain degree of inducement in different periods. The bottom-up, grass-rooted practice and exploration have offered plenty of consultancy and suggestions to innovation of audit standards, which have effectively curbed the potential risks caused by the lack of information in the vicissitude course.

Adopting Incremental Changes

Through the analysis on the vicissitude course of China's national audit standards, it can be clearly pointed out that before formulating specific goals and the final step-by-step implementation, audit institutions always drew up the general framework as first. For the rearrangement of audit standards, it is necessary solve the problems according to their priorities and significance. For instance, in the early stage of hierarchical criteria, audit institutions specifically issued the Temporal Provisions as regulations. In the wake of the accumulation of experiences, more problems in practice manifested themselves one after another, and in the meanwhile approaches to solve them also became clear. Finally, a new system of modified standards was formulated served as regulations. By adopting the vicissitude course with gradualness, resistance in the process of reform could be smaller.

Generally speaking, changes in national audit standards advanced step by step. On the whole, from the documentary regulations in the exploration stage, to the 38 criteria, then the hierarchical system of standards, and the final forming of "one-for-all" system, the incremental vicissitude course of audit standards is determined by China's national conditions. From the perspective of specific content of standards, for instance, in the infancy stage clauses of professional ethics were scattered in relevant documents, while in stages of exploration and development the contents were listed as single standards, and finally in the new standards all regulations were refined as 20 words, and so are other contents in the criteria system, which reflects the principle of gradual progress. In terms of cost, gradual changes can effectively avoid radical fluctuations and fearful shocks to all parties of interests, so as to reduce the degree of difficulty in changing old standards, improve the odds of reaching consensus, and efficaciously lower the frictional costs. Also, gradual changes can achieve the regular communication among relevant shareholders and timely comprehend their requirements, which will play a cumulative and subtle role in giving consideration to all parties and alleviate the resistance in the vicissitude course.

Strong Path Dependency

Theoretically, in the vicissitude course of standards, part of shareholders will obtain and strengthen their extra benefits. In other words, once the direction is determined, the changes will be continuously deepened. That is the path dependency. The right direction will ensure the following positive progress, will the wrong direction will cause fundamental mistakes. With the emergency of new system, the rearrangements of interests pattern will produce different outcomes, some will get benefits, and some will not. For those without satisfactory results, there will be more resistance against the new system out of the demand for maintaining their own interests and the influence of original ideologies, social habits and values. The same is true in the vicissitude course of national audit standards. Once the direction is determined, the changes will be continuously deepened in the process with strong path dependency. The path dependency of changes in national audit standards essentially refers to the inertia in the vicissitude course. From the perspective of form, as documents regulating audit works, audit standards are the convention and established practice in international audit activities. China has always taken establishing a perfect set of audit standards as the ultimate target of the vicissitude course, and so they are in the development of many standards. The changes in main factors of the standard system has shown that it is necessary to reference foreign experience in many aspects of the system of standards, such as codes for auditing profession, audit program and audit report. While in terms of the content, each vicissitude basically followed the last framework of criteria, and even if the newly added standards shall be coordinated with other criteria in stylistic rules. For instance, in types of audit evidence and audit methods, regardless of some adjustments, the standards of audit evidence maintained relatively stable. Another example is the Temporal Regulations on Quality Test of Audit Projects of Audit Institutions issued in 2000, which also keeps pace with other criteria in stylistic rules and layout.

Laying Emphasis on Convergence with National Standards

From the perspective of the vicissitude course of national audit standards, the changes are made with the purpose of drawing close and making connection to the international standards. Such efforts are reflected in both form and contents. For instance, in the Field Audit Criteria of the INTOSAI and the Field Standards of Performance Audit of the GAGAS, audit programs are both reflected in audit plans. In China's new audit standards, regulations on audit programs are also covered by audit plans. By taking the audit plans into Field Audit, China achieved the convergence with the international standards. In the meanwhile, China never abandoned its Chinese characteristics by always making differences between audit programs and audit plans in both the frameworks of old standards and new standards. Despite of the audit standards provided by the INTOSAI to member states for reference, the audit standards are basically designed by criteria of countries with higher degree of marketization. For developed countries, the convergence can be a relatively easy process with lower cost, allowing for the fact that some regulations are even transferred to the INTOSAI by them; while for developing countries and backward countries, the immature market mechanism, unsound regulatory system, and the unique cultural background will greatly increase the cost and risk of the convergence.

Chapter Three: How the Audit Works on the Anti-corruption in China

The China's Announcement System of Audit Results

Announcement system of audit results, which has gone through the process from legislation to system planning and then to specific implementation, refers to an institutional arrangement by which national audit institutions announce audit information with audit reports as the core to users of audit results including the public.

The Deepening Announcement System

China's announcement system of audit results has experienced an incrementally deepening process in practice. Since 1996, China has made financial budget reports public through newspapers and other media. Since 1998, the public has begun to partially understand the contents of audit reports, for instance, the audit report in 1998 revealed that the food system had lost ￥214 billion over the past 6 years, and the audit report in 1999 disclosed an extraordinarily serious case of the embezzlement of funds by the Ministry of Water Resources during floods in 1999. In June 1999, entrusted by the State Council, Li Jinhua, the auditor general of the State Audit Office, delivered an audit report on implementation of central budget as well as other financial revenues and expenditure to the Standing Committee of the NPC, making audit results public for the first time. The national State Office also submitted a startling checklist of audit results, which proved that ￥3.1 billion were embezzled. As a result, the event triggered a strong social response among the people and caused an "audit storm".

The State Audit Office started the announcement system of audit results in 2002. Since 2003, in addition to submitting annual audit report to the NPC, the State Audit Office has also disclosed the audit results of special audit projects to the public from time to time. In June 2003, the State Audit Office released the full audit report for the first time in the history. Hailed by the media as the most strongly worded audit report ever, it criticized 4 central government ministries by name and disclosed a raft of major cases. At the very beginning of 2004, CCTV live broadcast the national auditing conference to the nation for the first time, which was also a major audit announcement. On 23rd June, 2004, Li Jinhua rendered a hefty audit list to the standing committee of the NPC, and the blackhole of capital

113

involved 7 central ministries was a huge blow to the whole country. Through auditing the implementation of budgets of 38 central ministers of the last year, the State Audit Office pointed out a series of problems involving ￥9.06 billion, accounting for about 6% of the total audit funds. Moreover, with the promotion of audit informatization, phased progress has been achieved. So far, the State Audit Office have issued 39 Audit Results Announcements in total.

Performance audit has also been explored and implemented in many sectors with encouraging results. In 2002, the State Audit Office arranged ad hoc audit surveys on some airports, including the performance audit on 18 main airports and 38 feeder-line airports. Finally, it was found that 37 of the 38 feeder airports were in the red, losing ￥1.5 billion from 2000 to 2001 in total. Worse still, the passenger throughput was merely one quarter in general of the predicted value of the feasibility study report in that year, and there was one airport that the passenger throughput was less than 3% of the designed capacity, which was a direct need-payoff problem. The Development Plan from 20030 to 2007 issued by the State Audit Office clearly stated that it would strive to make all audit results of regular auditing and specific auditing public, except for those involving state secrets, business secrets and other contents that were not suitable for public disclosure.

Through the continuous improvement of the announcement system of audit results, all relevant audit results were incrementally announced from the internal sectors to the whole society, reflecting the profile of

China's open government affairs. Since the establishment of the State Audit Office, the audit work has pointed the finger at public financial expenditures, fixed-asset investments and state-run enterprises with the development of the market economy. While the audit results have been announced, post-audit accountability has also been the development direction on which audit departments and the public have placed great expectations.

Relevant Legislation and Contents

Article 36 of the Audit Law issued in 1994 stipulated for the first time that audit institutions could report audit results to relevant government departments or make the results public, thus establishing the legal status of the announcement system of audit results. With the deepening of the functions of state audit, the State Audit Office has issued a series of criteria on announcement of audit results, including Regulations on Reports of Audit Institutions and Publishing of Audit Results (abolished), Criteria on Audit Result Announcement of Audit Institutions and Trial Measures on Audit Result Announcement of Audit Institutions, preliminarily making provisions for the subjects, objects, content, scope, procedures and responsibilities of audit work. Among them, audit institutions made clear that: ①the subjects of the announcement are the State Audit Office and local audit institutions at all levels, excluding agency units, audit agencies and resident offices of the State Audit Office; ②for the State Audit Office, the audit notices include audit reports, audit opinions, audit

115

decisions and related conclusive documents, while the announcement of local audit institutions are relatively brief, including only audit opinions and audit decisions; ③the scope of announcements of the State Audit Office includes audit results of the implementation of central budgets and other financial revenues and expenditures, financial situations of government departments and state-run enterprises and institutions, single audit results of financial revenues and expenditures, comprehensive audit results of related industries or special funds, as well as results of economic responsibility audit, but the scope of announcements of local audit institutions is usually determined by local conditions, usually including audit results required to be announced to the public by the government at the corresponding level or audit institutions at the next higher levels, audit results of public concern and other content which is necessary to be announced to the public; ④all announced audit results shall be examined and approved, and all units as well as individuals publishing audit results without approval shall be called to account according to the law.

At present, China's announcement system of audit results consists of 3 laws and regulations: First, Article 9 of the Audit Law issued in 2006 stipulates that local audit institutions at all levels shall be answerable to governments at the corresponding level or audit institutions at the next higher level, and report their audit work. Article 36 stipulates that audit institutions may inform relevant government departments of audit results or make the audit results public to the whole society only under the circumstance of keeping the state secrets and the business secrets of auditees in accordance with laws and regulations made by the State Council.

Second, the Criteria on Audit Result Announcement of Audit Institutions issued in August 2001 clearly regulates the audit results of major audit matters announced by local audit institutions to the public. Article 5 stipulates that "audit institutions shall publish audit results to the public only with the approval of persons in charge of audit institutions, and the announcement of audit results involving major matters shall be approved by the government at the corresponding level". Article 4 provides that audit results may be published through radio, television, internet, press conferences, bulletins, announcements and print media such as newspapers and magazines. Article 7 stipulates that "audit institutions may, in accordance with the procedures of examination and approval, publish the audit results of the following audit matters to thee public: "(1) Audit results at the request of the government at the corresponding level or audit institutions at the higher next level; (2) Audit results concerned by the public; (3) Other audit results that need to be disclosed to the public". Article 9 stipulates that when releasing audit results, audit institutions shall keep state secrets and business secrets of auditees and related units according to the law, and take full account of potential social impact. Article 10 states that press conferences shall be held after submitting to higher authority for approval in accordance with laws. Article 12 provides that relevant personnel shall be investigated for responsibility when publishing audit results without authorization.

Third, the Trial Measures on Audit Result Announcement of Audit Institutions issued in March 2002 was specially designed to standardize the announcement of audit results to the public. Article 6 stipulates that "the announcement shall comply with the following procedures for examination and approval: (1) the announcement related to audit results of the implementation of central budget as well as other financial revenues and expenditures must be approved by the State Council; (2) audit results of major audit projects submitting to the State Council shall be followed by the report rendered at the same time, and the announcement can only be made if the State Council has no different opinions within a certain period of time; (3) audit results of other matters shall be examined and determined by the State Audit Office, agency units, audit agencies and resident offices of the State Audit Office cannot publish audit results without permission". Article 8 provides that the announcement of audit results shall keep state secrets and business secrets of auditees and related units and comply with relevant provisions of the State Council. Audit results involving content not suitable for publication must be deleted or modified. Article 9 stipulates that relevant units and individuals shall be investigated for responsibility according to law if publishing audit results without permission.

Characteristics of China's Announcement System

China's current announcement system of audit results has the following characteristics: First, the government has the final say on whether the audit results should be announced or not. With the scope of announcement of audit results expanding gradually (audit institutions — governments — the People's Congress — the people), and the contents of audit results might be screened layer by layer. It is up to the government whether the audit results of major matters could be announced to the public or not, and the audit results of nonsignificant matters shall be determined by audit institutions themselves, which are also an inalienable part of the government.

Second, the announcement system of audit results is a soft constraint. At present, the legislative basis of the announcement system of audit results is "can be published", or in other words, "may not be published to the public", making the system a soft constraint.

Third, subjects of the announcement system of audit results have to bear a greater risk. From the practical point of view, the government, especially audit institutions, take great ruling risks and individual risks by wielding the power of examination and approval of audit results. On the one hand, the current regulations put forward some requirements on announcing audit results in a passive way, while on the other hand, it is necessary to take full account of possible social impact before stipulating the announcement of audit results in a strong and general way, the content that is not suitable for announcement must be deleted and modified, and those who publish the announcement without the authorization shall be investigated for the responsibility of relevant units and individuals according to law. In addition, no content has been regulated that must be announced, making it hard for the government or audit institutions to act accurately, because on some cases they have to undertake great risks if they choose to hold on.

Fourth, the effect of audit result announcement is not good enough. No matter from the perspective of quantity and content of announcements or forms, time limitations and results, the performance of announcement system of audit results is relatively poor.

How Announcement System Works

The announcement system of audit results is expected to have the performance of satisfying the public demand and institutional targets. The end result of institution lies in the realization of its efficacy, whose important indicator is the "effectiveness", that is, whether the expected targets are achieved or not during and after the running of the institution. Specifically, the effectiveness of the institution refers to the degree of consistency and agreement between the implementation and the expected targets.

The Subjects of Announcement System

The qualification and capacity of subjects of announcement of audit results restrict the performance of audit quality and functions. The effectiveness of announcement of audit results can be evaluated by the quality of the subjects. By drawing lessons from auditing standards at home and overseas, this book believes that the quality of subjects of announcement system of audit results mainly refers to the organization structuring and audit institutions as well as the independence and executive ability of auditors. Independence is the soul and lifeline of audit, without which it is impossible to carry out audit supervision objectively and fairly. An untrue, unfair and incomplete announcement is nothing but an irony to the whole system and the product of government corruption to a certain extent. Executive ability refers to the working competence of auditors to carry out national auditing business, without which audit results can never be announced.

From the perspective of independence, there are some defects in China's audit institutions. Currently speaking, China adopts a system of dual administrative leadership in the state audit: the central audit institution is under the leadership of the State Council, while local audit institutions are directed by local governments at the same level administratively and guided by audit institutions at the next higher level in business. In the current framework of state audit, the audit institution belongs to the government as a department, and the independence is hard to be effectively guaranteed. Yang Shizhan, a professor in the auditing circle, pointed out in the preface to the History of World Auditing: "The government pays for its own business and audit itself. That is issueless, and worse still, sometimes it adds people's mistrust compared with the situation of no

121

audit supervision at all".

From the point of executive ability of auditors, there are also defects in China's audit institutions. The uneven level of working competence of auditors, the single structure of knowledge and the unsuitable overall professional quality cannot fully adapt to the requirements of audit work. At present, audit institutions are in urgent need of inter-disciplinary talents whom are not only familiar with audit business, but understand knowledge of engineering technology, computer technology, law and economic management at the same time.

Therefore, from the perspective of the quality of subjects, the effectiveness of China's announcement system of audit results is somewhat deficient.

The Public Expectations of Announcement System

Audit theory of modern states believes that the main body of the society is the general public, and the power roots in the society, for which the audit must be responsible. Therefore, the relationship of the audit work of modern states per se is a public principal-agent relation. As a public sector, national audit institutions must be able to provide products or services that cannot be efficiently or effectively provided by private sectors, so as to achieve the government's target of meeting the public demand.

All subjects of power are agents of public interests, indicating that they are representing the interests of groups and individuals. Only under the premise of recognized by the government and national audit institutions will they make organizational commitments of "do's and don'ts" within the thresholds of the system. On the contrary, when the group interests of national audit institutions and the government conflict with the system orientation, the impact of the system can be avoided through various methods.

Subjects of power and agents of power are two different interest subjects, and there must be conflicts of a certain degree when powerful persons want to maximize their utility. With their behaviors severely influenced by the demand for individual interests, officials of audit institutions and the government cannot really understand the consistency between the interests of themselves and the public interests sometimes, so they have the tendency to pursue immediate interests. In addition, the information asymmetry between dual agents could lead to cases of victimization, allowing for the fact sometimes agents of power may take advantage of information superiority.

So, whether the announcement system of audit results can meet the demand of the public?

Unfortunately, the answer is hardly optimistic for now. Comparing the audit reports in recent years, it is not difficult to pint out that in spite of more and more audit contents, wider and wider audit scopes as well as longer and longer audit lists, the overall situation of rectification has been less than satisfactory. Because of frequent recidivism and public's "feeling of numbness" toward audit work, the public credibility and image of the government would be directly affected. The reasons lie in two aspects: First, as the designer of the announcement system of audit results, the government—or the agent in de facto—can hardly undermine its own interests for the benefit of the public, so the current situation of sparse information cannot be really ameliorated by the announcement system of audit results. Second, the executor of the system is also the government (national audit institution is a subordinary sector of the government). For the sake of its own interests, it is also difficult for the government to announce when the situation is adverse to itself. Generally speaking, the government designs its own system to monitor itself, and carries out the system in person. Theoretically, for the subject combining legislation, law enforcement with supervision, its effectiveness is somewhat deficient.

Social Utility of National Audit Results

Natural utility and social utility, which respectively represent the naturality and sociality of the effect of fruit of labor, constitute the most basic category of utility. As a public product, the announcement of audit results must have its social utility, which is shown in two aspects: first, it enables all people to abide by the law and discipline through public opinions, creates a harmonious and transparent social climate, promote the social stability, safeguards the state political power, saves the running cost of the state, improves the efficiency of administration, and establishes a good social order; second, it fundamentally restricts the abuse of civil rights through constantly exposing and investigating illegal problems and cases of corruption, curbs corruption of power, maintains financial and economic disciplines, reveals issues of losses and wastages and other economic corruption and improves the service efficiency of fiscal funds, so as to ensure the sound development of the national economy.

So, has China's announcement system of audit results achieved its specific social utility?

Clearly, almost nothing has been achieved. National audit institutions as a whole is an internal auditing sector inside the administrative framework, and its announcement is completely decided by the government. Allowing for the fact that the government cannot publish unfavorable information, the transparent social climate will never be achieved. Concealing the truth may bring temporary social stability, but in the long run it will lead to the mistrust of the public in the government and potential unsustainable results. Due to the lack of subsequent mechanism of accountability, and the announcement must be determined by the government, audit institutions cannot effectively curb the abuse of power. Thus, the problem of "recidivism" is common.

Problems of China's Announcement System in Dealing with the Corruption

Defects in Relevant Laws and Regulations

Article 36 of the Audit Law provides that "audit institutions may inform relevant government departments of the audit results or make the audit results public". The word "may" makes the announcement a discretionary act, weakening the mandatory nature of the legal system. As a matter of fact, due to the lack of clear and rigid provisions on the announcement system of audit results in the Audit Law, the main factor determining whether the audit results shall be announced and the degree of announcement is the government's choice on relevant policies.

The Criteria on Audit Result Announcement of Audit Institutions, the Trial Measures on Audit Result Announcement of Audit Institutions and other normative documents are major legal basis and operational guidance of the announcement system of audit results. However, the documents are just departmental regulations with relatively low legislative levels, their formulation procedures are not strictly regulated and the contents can also be modified optionally. Lack of rigor and stability, the practice of announcement is relatively optional, and the content is not complete.

From the perspective of the current announcement system of audit results, most of the content is general, and the provisions are too simple. Take the Criteria on Audit Result Announcement of Audit Institutions as an example, generally speaking, the lack of range of application, basic principles, legal responsibility, sanction measures, as well as provisions on supervision and remedy measures has caused defects in the legal mechanism. In terms of specific regulations, Article 5 clearly stipulates that "audit institutions shall publish the audit results to the public only with the approval of the principal persons in charge, and the release of content relating to major matters requires the approval of the government". However, in light of the fact that there is no clear provision on the content and evaluation standards of major events, the issue of examination and approval of the authority has been inevitably obscure and inappropriate. In addition, Article 3 provides that "audit results mentioned in the criteria refers to the audit results of major audit matters within the jurisdictional limits announced to the public by audit institutions", and Article 9 stipulates that "before announcing audit results to the public, audit institutions shall keep state secrets and business secrets of auditees according to law, and fully take the potential social impact into account". So, what is exactly the "potential social impact" of "major audit matters"? Fuzzy terms in legal provisions make the content of audit result announcement vague and uncertain, providing an excuse for the government "not to announce" what should be announced.

Defects in Relevant Institutional Arrangements

The effectiveness of a system is not only determined by itself, but depends on its relationship with relevant systems. Once conflicting with others, the system could be less effective even invalid. Currently speaking, the conflict with the national confidential system has made the announcement system of audit results less efficient.

First, the irrational national audit system has made the audit institutions less independent. To a certain extent, China's current audit system hinders the implementation of the announcement system of audit results, mainly because of the lack of independence. As the essential characteristic of audit supervision, "independence" means that audit institutions are independent of auditees in terms of organization, personnel, work and expenditures, and they shall not be intervened by other administrative bodies, social groups and individuals when wielding the power to supervise through auditing, so as to ensure the objectivity, impartiality and authority of audit. Currently speaking, China's state audit adopts the system of dual leadership: the central audit institution is directed by the State Council, and local audit institutions are under the leadership of local governments at the same level as well as audit institutions at the next higher level respectively in administration and in business. In the prevailing state audit framework, the audit institution is substantially a department of the government, and its independence cannot be guaranteed. The "lifeline" of audit is independence, without which audit supervision cannot be carried out objectively and fairly.

Second, the state audit system is in conflict with other laws, especially the Secrecy Law. According to the Provisions on State Secrets and the Specific Scope of Security Classification in Auditing, "audit surveys and audit results relating to major issues of party and state leaders" are top secrets, that is to say, audit results involving senior government officials cannot be announced, and the performance auditing in connection with the working competence and professional integrity of leading cadres will never be made public. In addition, "auditing or audit survey on the situation and results of violations of the law and discipline in provinces, autonomous regions, municipalities directly under the central government and nationwide systems of business (industries)" and "audit surveys and audit results referring to issues of party and state leaders and major issues of leading cadres at the provincial or ministerial level" are at the secret-level. Allowing for the excessively strict secrecy mechanism, the administrative situation of leading cadres in the government can seldom be exposed to the public, and a huge raft of announcements of economic responsibility audit have been "impossible missions". As a result, the authority and public credibility of the announcement system of audit results have been seriously questioned.

In foreign countries, as a principle in the auditing sector, the announcement system contains most of the matters, while "no announcement" is exceptional. By this way, the scope of secrets is reduced as far as possible. However, the legislative practice in recent years has shown that the scope of secrets in China has been expanding incrementally. If audit institutions keep following the current system of determining "state secrets", many important announcements of audit results will neve come true, and under the secrecy mechanism, the public's right to be informed has been greatly restricted. The issues of determining the scope of "unpublishable contents" and connecting it with the confidential system in order to balance the two parties appropriately should be clearly solved in formulating the announcement system of audit results, with no blank area of law left.

Third, China lacks the accountability system of auditing. The accountability system for officials has been established throughout the whole countries, and the responsibility-seeking mechanism against security incidents has been gradually extended to other sectors, but the audit accountability is still a blind point in China. Although revealing problems frequently, audit institutions have almost no real power to hold related units or individuals to account, and in addition to debriefing audit institutions, the Standing Committee of the NPC has no specific procedures or means to solve the problems. Audit institutions are not able to overcome the difficulty of recidivism by reforms of themselves merely, neither the Audit Law, a department law. The primary cause is that the basic responsibility of audit work is to find out problems, while settling problems is related to the mechanism of administrative management, personnel arrangement of leading cadres, discipline inspection and supervision, public security and other aspects, which can never be superseded by audit institutions in China at present. Without the effective coordination with other departments, the "one-sided development" of audit institutions cannot form an integrated mechanism covering auditing accountability, punishment and rectification, and the actual effect of auditing cannot be fully achieved. Therefore, it is not enough to rely solely on the "mining hunting" of audit institutions in the supervision on economic activities of public sectors. In the meanwhile, organization departments and personnel departments must hold those who "bury the mines" to account.

The Institutional Changes Hinder Operating the Effectiveness of the System

From the perspective of institutional economics, the implementation of the announcement system of audit results belongs to institutional change, which takes place under the joint effect of multiple subjects. In that process, different subjects have different influences on institutional changes. There are 3 main subjects participating in changes of the announcement system: the public, the government and audit institutions.

The public is the largest beneficiary group of the announcement system, thus is the most resolute supporter. However, due to the size of the populace, the bargaining cost within the interest group is relatively high, and the problem of free-rider is relatively serious. Therefore, the democratic decision-making of the people is restricted by Arrow's Impossible Theorem. Because of free riding, the public pays too little attention to the announcement of audit results, so it is difficult to fully understand the significance of the system.

Out of their own interests, government sectors, as auditees themselves, is loath to make their problems disclosed. Whether individuals or groups, most of the auditees are not likely to face or understand audit reports directly. Worrying that audit notices may spoil the images of units and reputation of individuals, most auditees are reluctant to make their problems exposed to the public. Some officials, especially the ones with real power, get upset even terrified when speaking about audit notices, and regard audit notices as opponents of social stability. Therefore, announcements of audit results are severely obstructed and intervened.

As auditors, audit institutions themselves are exposed to the public after announcing audit results, and their position are shifted from supervisors to supervisees. On this occasion, unreliable factors such as poor quality of audit work, violations against audit procedures, insufficient evidence and major careless omissions in audit reports will gradually show up. The potential audit risks will surely expose the "skeleton in the cupboard" to the public and even cause legal disputes. Once losing the lawsuits, the image of audit institutions will be further spoiled. In the meanwhile, because of institutional factors, audit institutions lack independence. Therefore, in the absence of strict requirements from laws, regulations and supervising authority, audit institutions are subconsciously loath to announce audit results or audit contents, or in other word, they are reluctant to make complete, true and timely announcements.

Functions of China's State Audit

As a basic concept, audit function occupies an important position in audit theory. Therefore, a complete and accurate understanding of state audit functions is of vital significance for the study of the mode selection of state audit. Generally speaking, function of state audit is the internal function in the social economy. However, in light of the fact that the concept neither reveals its connotation nor point out its extension, it is nothing more than the definition of state audit function. As a consequence, the concept in de facto fails to meet people's needs of understanding the state audit function. However, one thing is for sure—instead of a cast-iron rule, state audit function develops as the objective socioeconomic environment changes. The understanding of the state audit function in this book is based on the revised result of the prevailing theory of "three functions".

Responsibility Supervision

Responsibility supervision is the basic function of both traditional and modern state audit, which fully embodies the intrinsic nature of audit. One thing must be got straight is that supervision is not the only function. The responsibility supervision of state audit mainly refers to supervising and urging whether the economic activities of auditees are carried out on the normal track within a certain scope through investigation; examining whether those who are economically responsible have faithfully fulfill their duties or not; and exposing the violation of laws and disciplines, inspecting losses and wastes, finding out malpractices, identifying management defects and investigating economic responsibilities at the same time. The focus of state audit is to get to the bottom of auditees through examination and verification, and arrive at a conclusion whether the economic activities of the auditees are true, legal and effective or not according to certain standards. From inspection, to evaluation, making decisions and supervising the implementation of the final decision in line with laws, all steps reflect the functions of responsibility supervision.

Responsibility Authentication

Responsibility authentication can be divided into two parts, namely responsibility verification and responsibility assessment. According to Michael, A. , Alexander, K. , & Vasarhelyi, M. A. . (2003), "authentication is a specification of opinion (or statement of judgement), namely the opinion or judgement conveyed by independent, competent and authoritative individuals based on credible evidence as to the degree to which all accounting information of an entity is consistent with established standards". From this point of view, authentication, as a larger category, covers assessment. Therefore, "there is no need to list responsibility assessment as an independent function of state audit".

Responsibility authentication of state audit refers to the inspection and verification of audit institutions and auditors on accounting statement and economic data of auditees, with the purpose of determining whether their financial situation and business performance are true, fair and legal or not. In addition, a written document is required in order to provide the government with accurate information and win the trust of the public. Moreover, it is the task of responsibility authentication to make the facts analyzed and judged according to certain standards in its process, including affirming the achievements, pointing out problems, summarizing the experience, ameliorating the management, and boosting the efficiency of operation. It is worth noting that the socialist audit evaluation in China must not be confined to the assessment on micro-economy, but must deal with the relationship between micro-economy and macro-economy correctly, and carry out microeconomic assessment from the perspective of macroeconomic interests, so as to ensure the rationality and accuracy of the assessment.

In the process of studying audit functions, in addition to the "couple-function theory" insisted in this book, some scholars put forward that state audit also has the functions of service, management and counsel. Allowing for the increasingly complex economic activities, dramatic social progress and enormous scientific development in the current stage, audit functions are bound to evolve themselves instead of standing still. Therefore, new situations and problems shall be seriously taken into account, and emerging ideas cannot just be simply denied, but responsibility supervision is still the basic function of state audit.

Evolution of Functions of China's State Audit

At the beginning of the founding of the People's Republic of China, audit supervision was carried out in the financial activities and supervision. During that few years, surveys on final settlements of financial budgets and the supervision on the budget enforcement were up to financial departments and supervisory sectors, which handled issues of breaching financial disciplines and laws of various units and departments. The situation did not change until 1952.

In addition, the Draft of the Financial System of the PRC proposed that "financial auditing and accounting affairs shall be administered by competent departments of finance of governments at all levels. Within the budget, they have the power of approval and verification of financial expenditures as well as fiscal transfer according to law, and agency departments can discharge their duties of auditing and accounting on behalf of provincial governments". In 1954, the Ministry of Supervision was established under the leadership of the State Council. Its main tasks included economic investigation and supervision on administrative organs, state-run enterprises and institutions at all levels across the whole country. In 1959, the Ministry of Supervision was abolished.

Because of the erroneous understanding of socialist revolution and construction, the Cultural Revolution emphasized the ideas of "taking class struggle as the key link" and "politics is in command", "politics instead of national economy that really counts". Under such circumstances, economic construction was completely left in the basket, and economic responsibility was nothing. China's state audit system was greatly weakened. During that period, with no independent audit institution in operation, the function of audit was absolutely lost. The condition did not improve until 1980, when the Ministry of Finance regulated in the Notice on Several Provisions on

Financial Supervision that "the Ministry of Finance shall establish the Department of Financial Supervision, and corresponding financial supervisory institutions shall be set up in all provinces, autonomous regions and municipalities directly under the central government". Its main task was to conduct financial supervision and examine problems of violating financial discipline. In 1982, the Ministry of Finance abolished the Department of Financial Supervision.

The 3rd Plenary Session of the 11th Central Committee of the CCP in 1978 established the basic direction of China's economic reform. China's traditional planned economy was transformed into a commodity economy with economic plans. In the 1990s, the economic pattern was further transformed into a socialist market economy. With the purpose of meeting the needs of Reform of Opening up as well as the development of socialist market economy, the 5th Plenary Session of the 5th NPC held in 1982 determined to establish the system of audit supervision in China, and added the idea into the constitution, specifying the independent power of supervision of audit institutions at all levels. In the following dozen of years, the Audit law as an independent legal instrument was absent due to the immature conditions for lawmaking. To gradually put audit work on the track of legalization and standardization, the State Council promulgated the Interim Provisions of the State Council on Audit Work and the Audit Regulations of the PRC in 1985 and 1988 respectively to guide the audit work. In 1994, the 9th Session of the Standing Committee of the 8th NPC adopted the Audit Law, which set out comprehensive provisions on the basic system of the state audit, including fundamental principles of audit supervision, obligation of audit institutions and auditors, authority of audit institutions, audit procedures and legal responsibilities. The promulgation of the Audit Law indicated that audit work in China began to ran on the track of legalization. After 12 years of development, the Audit Law was revised in 2006. The new Audit Law provides that "China's audit institutions shall carry out audit supervision on the financial revenue and expenditure as well as the authenticity, validity and performance of financial revenue and expenditure of all departments of the State Council, local governments and all government sectors, state-run financial institutions, enterprises and public institutions, and other necessary auditees". Besides, the revised Audit Law further clarified the supervisory role of the state audit, emphasized the independent status of audit institutions and auditors, and strengthened the reporting obligation of the government to the representative institution of the people—People's Congress at all levels.

From 1983 to 2008, the development of China's state audit can be roughly divided into 4 stages. The first stage (1983-1992) was an active exploratory stage aiming at reorganizing financial disciplines. On that stage, state audit mainly focused on the aspects of authenticity and compliance. In areas of financial budget and state-owned property, the maintenance of value of national assets was ensured by audit of authenticity and compliance. Audit functions were mainly reflected in essential supervisory functions, including certification, evaluation and law enforcement. The second stage (1993-1997) was the stage of steady improvement aiming at ameliorating the asset-liability situation. In that stage, audit institutions not only focused on the authenticity and compliance, but paid more attention to economy, efficiency and effect. In the area of public budget, the importance of audit was reflected in the performance audit of state-owned property with the purpose of management control and output. Through audit, enterprises were encouraged to establish sound models of company operation to ensure the operation quality. While aiming at authenticity and validity, efficiency audit was also carried out. During that period, in addition to certification, evaluation and law enforcement in the first stage, the state audit derived a new function, construction. The third stage (1998-2007) was a stage of integrated development with economic responsibility as the goal. In that stage, the scope of audit work extended to the economic responsibility audit targeted at government officials and managers of state-run enterprises. Other than certification, evaluation, law enforcement and construction, state audit newly added the function of authentication. The fourth stage (2008-present) is a new stage with the goal of maintaining the national security. At present and in the future, the functions of state audit, including certification, evaluation, law enforcement, construction and authentication will be constantly deepened, and a new opinion is put forward that state audit is the immune system of the national economy. In this case, state audit derives new functions such as defence and hint.

Characteristics of China's State Audit

Functions of state audit are adaptive to the public fiduciary responsibilities. Accordingly, the two parties have similar characteristics, but the forms of expression are different. This book expounds evolutional traits the functions of the state audit from two aspects respectively.

In ancient times, functions of the state audit reflected the individual will of monarchs instead of the will of the people. Public fiduciary responsibilities showed the nature of "despotism", and on this basis, functions of state audit also showed characteristics of autocratic times. From the single function — authenticity at the beginning, to the function of evaluation later, the core function of state audit at that time was to supervise over officials in lower echelons on whether they could execute the will of supreme rulers and whether they could discharge their duties of maintaining the rulership of monarchs and the authority of the government. The function of evaluation was to evaluate the executive conditions of junior officials, so as to achieve the target of controlling the minions in mind and behavior. Under the democratic system, the modern public fiduciary duty embodies the democratic thoughts, and as the tool to promote the democracy and the rule of law, the state audit is carried out for the interests of the people fundamentally speaking. Through the audit supervision of audit institutions on behalf of the people, the public fiduciary duties of governmental agencies, enterprises and public institutions essentially represent the public will, which continuously derives new functions and enrich the content of state audit in the development of the society and history, making functions of state audit as a whole an open system.

With the deepening and expansion of the scope of public fiduciary duties, functions of state audit are promoted to develop in depth and breadth, which are mainly manifested in the expansion of content and process. In terms of the content of function of state audit, it refers to the expansion of functional competency on the strength audit supervision. It is known to all that functions of state audit are dynamic. From ancient times till today, in addition to supervision as the basic function, other functional competencies have developed from error recovery in old times to new functions of evaluation, authentication and construction in modern times, and with the development of social economy in the future, state audit will derive more new functions. The deepening of public fiduciary duties also leads to the deepening of functions of state audit. There are significant differences between the same function of state audit in antiquity and that in modern time, and the differences are manifested in the content and process of audit. State audit in old times focused on the authentication of the use and management of property, while the modern audit is developing in depth aiming at the authenticity, compliance, validity and performance of economic activities. To a certain extent, the enhancement of audit technologies and the improvement of working competence of auditors promote the audit quality. In the same way, with the development of democratic politics, the public sets a higher demand on state audit, which is manifested as the deepening of supervision. Moreover, the independence and authority of audit institutions are increasing, which endows audit institutions with greater independent power to better explore the depth of functions of state audit. Similarly, under the circumstances of continuous development of there factors, other functional competencies of modern state audit will be more profound than their counterparts in ancient times and modern history.

Factors Affecting the Fulfillment of State Audit

China's state audit began at almost the same time with that in some other countries with a long history of civilization. However, China's state audit has fallen far behind western developed countries in terms of audit functions so far. For instance, the function of evaluation in the current stage only stays the on specific matters, while the United States, the United Kingdom, France and other countries audit with the purpose of policy evaluation and strategic early warning in the mass, and have achieved excellent fruits. This book believes that there are 7 major factors affecting the fulfillment of the functions of state audit.

State Audit System. With the same public fiduciary duty, the effect of audit functions is different because of various audit systems. As a part of the political structure of the government, the audit system and its formation are closely related to the state operational mechanism. Therefore, the political pattern affects the audit system, which in turn influences audit functions.

The state audit system may limit or amplify the realization of the functions of state audit. Traditional ideas believe that independence is the soul of audit, and the two factors form an indivisible relation. Generally speaking, most scholars divide the independence of audit into the independence in form and the independence in nature. The so-called independence in nature requires that auditors and their clients have no relationship of interests legally, and audit institutions must be strictly impartial in the audit process. Moreover, auditors must maintain their professional judgements not to be swayed when issuing audit opinions as well as their objective attitude and professional suspicion. The independence in form is relative to the third party, namely that auditors must perform as an independent party to the entrusting party. When the state audit system id established, the independence and authority of auditors will be increasingly distinct. The legislative audit in the United States, the juridical audit in France and the administrative audit in China all reflect the authority of audit institutions and independence of audit work in different extent. However, the administrative audit system in China at present is closely related to the political climate. The ruling party and its policy actuator — the government master the real power, and bear the burden of planning and regulating the whole national economy. Relatively speaking, with less power, legislature can hardly influence the use of public resources, and the supervision mechanism on governmental departments is not perfect. The administrative audit system is basically built and organized with the demand for decision-making and management of the supreme administrative institutions as the core. Therefore, the will of senior administrative bodies to a large extent affects the job objectives and tasks of audit institutions, making the independence in form or in nature affected somewhat. To some degree, the functions of audit institutions are limited.

National Economic Development Level. Audit system belongs to the category of superstructure. Dialectical materialism believes that superstructure is the sum of social ideology as well as its corresponding systems and facilities on the basis of a certain economic base. The superstructure is influenced and limited by the economic base; whose status is reflected by the level of productivity. So audit is the product of the development of social productivity in a certain stage, and in the meanwhile, the more developed the productivity is, the more frequent the activities of financial revenues and expenditures are, and the more extensive the scope is involved.

There was no fiduciary duty in primitive society when the productivity was underdeveloped and the human beings had to maintain the lowest living conditions to survive. With the development of productivity, the public ownership and the old relations of production in primitive society could no longer meet the needs of the society. To survive and develop the human society, new ownership and relations of production must be designed to supersede the old ones. The new ownership is the private ownership, and the new production relation is the relationship among people, namely the relationship between masters and slaves with necessary responsibilities. The audit in slave society formed its embryonic framework of state audit. allowing for the limited financial revenues and expenditures, the scope of audit supervision was also restricted, and audit could only exercise the single function of authentication nominally. Entering feudal society, state audit made great strides with the development of productive forces. Above all, the state audit hit its peak in the flourishing age in Tang Dynasty. With the financial revenues and expenditures covering more economic activities, the number of auditees also increased, the new audit functions were derived. In addition to giving priority to authentication, the state audit also had the function of evaluation preliminarily. When China was still in the feudal age, the national economy of European countries advanced by leaps and bounds after the industrial revolution and broke the shackles of feudalism. Therefore, advanced audit systems of modern countries were first established in Europe.

Before the reform and opening up, China adopted the strict planned economic system, which emphasized the fundamental economic system that the state-run economy is the main body of the national economy, and the public sector of the economy predominated China's economic development. Under such circumstances, the people and the government could not be clearly separated, and the complicated relationship between the two parties confused the different concepts of trustors and trustees. As a result, the fiduciary duty lost its significance. After 1983, the continuous deepening of economic restructuring, the opening-door policy and the incremental establishment of market economy have jointly contributed to the dramatic expansion of comprehensive national strength of China. In the meanwhile, the increasing scale of public expenditure promoted the development of audit and the recovery of the legal system, and the fiduciary duty has been increasingly clear. The objectives of audit work have been more and more clear-cut, and the scope of audit have also became more and more extensive. With changes in audit climate, functions of state audit have gradually switched from the supervision on compliance, validity and authenticity to the evaluation on performance, efficiency and effectiveness.

From the development track of audit, it is not difficult to dope out that the more developed the productive forces are, the higher the voice of the society attaching importance to audit will be, the greater the role of audit will play, and the more comprehensive the functions of audit will be. In the course of economic transition, it was found that with more factors of disharmony pointed out in the economic development, the role of state system would be more irreplaceable. It can also be seen from the development of audit of the United States that since it became the largest economic power in the world, the state audit system of the United States has been incrementally ameliorated and has surpassed that of other old capitalist countries, ranking at the top in the world. This also further showed that "audit supervision will be of more significance with the economic development". In addition to determining the importance of audit supervision as well as the chronological order and the soundness of audit systems of various countries, the development of social economy also directly influences the progress and reform of the methods and technologies of state audit.

Governmental Functions. As an instrument of violent domination by one class over another in nature, the state is the product of history as well as the expression of the will and interests of the ruling class. State audit emerged with the birth of states, and its functions are closely related to state functions as tools to achieve the targets.

In slave society and feudal society, ultimate rulers are bestowed with supreme power, and all people within the border are their subjects. The division of administrative areas and the entrusted level-to-level management deterred the rulers from personally supervising over officials on whether they could perform their duties according to the will of the rulers. Therefore, officials in charge of audit supervision were appointed. They took orders from supreme leaders and were dependent upon the leaders' power to supervise officials in lower echelons. At that time, the state functions were political tools of supreme leaders to maintain their despotic power, suppress their subjects and resist against foreign invasions. Under such influence, audit functions were concrete embodiment of state functions correspondingly in social affairs, as a tool for supreme leaders to consolidate their places as despots. Therefore, state audit played a significant role in supervising subordinate officials.

In China's socialist phrase, the government function in the planned economy period was to build an "all-function" government. Since its establishment, state audit institutions had taken orders from the government. Although had little independence, audit institutions had always played a mandatory role in supervision, as one of the tools for the state to exercise the supervision of "all-function" government.

With the deepening of China's economic reform and the rise of government restructuring campaign across the world, the political system that hindered the economic development has also been incrementally reformed. The reform of the socialist market economic system has made remarkable progress. According to the 11th Five-Year Plan and the Decisions on Several Major Issues about Building a Harmonious Socialist Society, there were 2 noticeable points, the first was to emphasize the limitation of the government, which could only make a difference in macro-control, market supervision and social administration; the second was to emphasize the effectiveness of the government, that is, the government must try to innovate the management as well as strengthen the executive force and public credibility. Therefore, the government reform has changed from "power-based" to "responsibility-based" the concepts of limited government and responsible government has been the new governing ideas of the Chinese government, and the requirement of building a service-oriented government has been the basic point of political system reform. Service-oriented government means that the government functions are transformed from "governing the people" to "governing the officials". According to new concepts of reform, the Chinese government is advocating the government transformation and supervision, and the mechanism of supervision and counterbalance has been transformed from economic-construction-based and all-function government to public-service-oriented and modern responsible government. In these changes there emerged new public funds concerning the development of national economy and people's livelihood. The duty of the state audit determines that there is no shrinking the responsibility to supervise on the use of public funds, and the transformation of government functions objectively requires the innovation of functions of the state audit. In the meanwhile of exploring new sectors of state audit, the intrinsic functions of audit will be enriched, and the potential functional competencies will also be unearthed.

Degree of Democratization. The emergence of state audit is not an accident. It has a profound social background on the basis of the demand of the public for the construction of democracy and rule of law. The state audit of both modern states and ancient countries are based on the need of inspecting economic responsibilities. However, there are essential differences in the connotation of economic responsibilities checked, and the main factor leading to such differences is the degree of democratization. The level of democratic development has a direct impact on audit and audit functions.

For ancient states which were usually despotic regimes, the supreme state power, including legislative power, judicial power and executive power, was concentrated in the hand of the ultimate ruler, and the people had no power at all, not to say democracy. On behalf of the monarch, state audit supervised over the economic responsibilities of subordinate officials and were responsible for the monarch. However, the development of state of modern states is caused by the birth and rise of modern democratic politics. Professor Yang Shizhan expounded the relationship between the modern states and democracy that "democracy is the essence of modern audit, and audit is the manifestation of modern democracy; democracy is the purpose of modern audit, and audit is the means of modern democracy. Modern audit is the product of modern democracy, and the audit system must serve the democracy system in turn. The fiduciary duty of modern government is produced by modern democracy, without which there would be no audit of modern state". Throughout the world, there is a phenomenon of convergence on the way to modern state, which is the transformation from autocracy to democracy. Under the principle of democracy, all administrative institutions and officials of the government are entrusted by the people with the management of public funds and resources, and shall be restricted by the strict system of economic responsibility. It is the duty of the audit of modern state to supervise the economic responsibilities of the government on behalf of the people. It can be said that it is precisely because of the emergence of the modern democratic politics that government administrative organs and officials are endowed with new economic responsibilities, on the basis of which the audit of modern state is produced. During the period of democratic enlightenment, the working competence to obtain evidence from the people was limited, so audit functions were mainly reflected in the stage of financial audit, focusing on checking mistakes and correcting errors. With social progress, the degree of democracy of the public improved gradually, bringing the following influences: on the one hand, the scope of supervision expanded as public fiduciary duties covered more affairs, the demand of the public for the right to know about national political and economic activities also increased, and the demand for audit also expanded; on the other hand, the status of audit institutions improved, and the authority of audit institutions was also elevated. As a result, audit functions have been continuously expanded. On the strength of traditional financial audit, economy audit, efficiency audit and effectiveness audit appeared successively, and audit functions have been fully realized.

Legal System. As a mean to ensure the effective performance of the public fiduciary duty, state audit supervises parties involved in the entrusted economic responsibilities, so as to serve as the basis for the principal to terminate or continue the entrusted responsibility. However, audit institutions must be guaranteed by certain laws and regulations when wielding the audit authority granted by clients.

In the ancient society, the authority of state audit institutions was impowered by supreme rulers, who were also mandators of the public fiduciary duty. On most cases, audit institutions were entangled with supervisory departments and financial sectors. Later, the power of state audit was licensed to subsidiary departments of the Ministry of Penalty and the Department of State Affairs. Lack of independence, and allowing that auditees were awarded or punished according merely to the audit results produced by auditors on the basis of other laws because there was no specific audit regulation at all, moreover, under the autocratic system, the authorization of supreme rulers was the majesty, all related factors made for the functions of audit supervision, but the whole audit climate curb the development of state audit fundamentally. The rise of democratic movements has forced the progress of modern state audit. Compared with that in despotic system, the audit of modern state is a bottom-up supervision, namely the restriction and supervision on officials on behalf of the public in the condition of being responsible to voters and taxpayers. Moreover, the democratic power will be more real as the scope of democracy expands, and voters and taxpayers will impose more restrictions on the economic responsibility of the government through audit institutions. However, there is a prerequisite, namely that the degree of democratization is dependent on corresponding laws and regulations as a guarantee. In modern society, audit institutions shall be entrusted by the people to supervise the public power which accepts public funds and material resources. Because of the dispersion of the people, namely the group of trustors, the clientage is considerably weak, and only by forming a government by virtue of the public power released by the people to wield the power of supervision can audit institutions carry out their auditing work. Trustees may prevaricate or not cooperate with the work for a variety of reasons, influencing the exertion of audit functions. Therefore, characteristics of state audit, including planning, enforceability, universality and generality, must be guaranteed by corresponding laws and regulations.

China made fundamental provisions on the establishment and functions of audit institutions in the Constitution amended in 1994. At present, China's audit system takes the Audit Law of the PRC and the Enforcement Regulations of the Audit Law as the basic law and supplementary instructions respectively. In addition, the Basic National Auditing Criteria and 6 specific auditing standards released in the form of order of auditor general serve as the operational guidance. However, lack of bases of handling and punishment, the regulations are mainly designed to address issues at the technology level. Auditing regulations mainly follow the corresponding laws and regulations of various departments, but such laws are not sound enough, which in fact increases the difficulty of auditing work. On the flip side, audit institution will find and handle problems swimmingly and fully perform audit functions with a complete legal system and sound laws.

Audit Techniques. Audit techniques refer to various methods by which state audit institutions and their personnel obtain sufficient and appropriate audit evidence. To a certain extent, the development of audit techniques affects and restricts the performance of audit functions. However, audit techniques are the products of the progress of social economy, which adapt to the economic climate and social background in a certain period and develop with changes social economic conditions. By feat of the achievements of other disciplines, audit techniques may make major breakthrough.

Throughout China's audit history, audit on account books accounted for the vast majority. However, because of audit technological disparity, there were big differences in depth and breadth of audit on account books in different periods. Audit techniques in ancient times were backward, the supervision of state audit was considerably limited. On most cases, the principles of equity and justice could not be fully enshrined, and audit was to a large extent determined by the subjective judgement of auditors, which made audit results less convincing. According to the theory of public fiduciary duty, all events relating to fiduciary duties shall be supervised by audit institutions. At present, China only has a limited number of auditors, but the State Audit Office has put forward the audit guideline of "carrying on comprehensive audit and stressing the key points". In the process of auditing, audit institutions adopt the method of sampling audit, whose degree of rationality has some impact on the audit performance. In this respect, sampling audit can be developed with the aid of statistical results.

Along with the development of information technology and network technology, government agencies, state-run enterprises and financial institutions in China have basically realized the office automation. In this context, to better perform audit functions, the State Audit Office has implemented China's Golden Auditing Project since 2002, with the purpose of closely tracing the system of financial information of the finance, banking industry, tax administration, customs, state-run enterprises and public institutions as well as related electronic data, and incrementally achieving the "3 transformations" in the respect of information systems of effective audit supervision on the authenticity, validity and efficiency of financial revenues and expenditures, namely the transformations from post-audit to the combination of post-audit and concurrent audit, from static audit to the combination of static audit and dynamic audit, from field audit to the combination of field combination and remote audit. The project, on the one hand, promotes the expansion of depth and breadth of audit supervision; on the other hand, increases the accompanied risks accordingly, and requires more advanced audit techniques to lower the audit risks. In the meanwhile, with the continuous expansion of public fiduciary duties, new audit techniques will manifest themselves to boost new audit functions.

Working Competence of Auditors. The implementation of audit works must be dependent on relevant auditors, so the working competence of auditors will surely affect the performance of audit functions. It is known to all that the early audit work was nothing more than the re-examination of accounting information to evaluate whether the information could truth reflect the financial facts that had occurred or not. Moreover, auditors are bound to examine the audit objects with a skeptical attitude during the process of audit supervision. Therefore, the professional ability and necessary prudence represent the working competence of auditors, which could affect the final results of the performance of audit function. As early as in the Spring and Autumn Period, Guan Zhong clear put forward the audit principle of "knowing laws well and auditing economic data", which contained 2 aspects: first, auditors should be familiar with relevant regulations and act according to laws; second, auditors should be clear on conditions of financial revenues and expenditures and carry on audit works accordingly. The principle was not designed specifically for audit, but it was undoubtably the basic standard of auditors to engage in audit supervision at that time. This essentially required the working competence to serve as auditors. Modern auditors must be equipped with professional skills, the ability of legal logical reasoning, macro judgement and other capacities. The service ability of auditors is the key factor determining the quality of audit. In its process of establishing the audit system, with the purpose of improving the working ability of auditors, the State Audit Office asked all audit institutions to organize learning projects to offer auditors with a certain amount of education, because of the severe shortage in qualified auditors. With the expansion of public fiduciary duties, the scope of audit requires not only depth, but also breadth. In addition to pointing out problems, it is more important to guide auditees to solve the problems, so as to realize the expansion of audit functions of management and comprehensive audit.

The Direction of Functions of State Audit

State audit originates from the relationship of public fiduciary duty, and develop with the evolution of public fiduciary duty. That is applicable to the whole development process and the future trend of state audit. Audit of modern state arose because of the gestation of democracy, and the corresponding democratic political movements promoted the public fiduciary duty from implicit to explicit, while the construction of social legal system provided a guarantee for the effective implementation of the public fiduciary duty. It can be seen that the audit of modern states, which is the tool to realize democracy and rule of law, lies in the public fiduciary duty essentially.

At the present stage, China's political system determines that the people are the masters of the country, and as a major part of state administrative organ, national audit institutions shall reflect the socialist democracy, work on behalf of the public will and be responsible to the people. However, the democracy and rule of law contained in the state audit itself are abstract, which can only be reflected by functions and effects of state audit. In a manner of speaking, the nature of state audit determines the scope and direction of functions of and effects of state audit. However, in any period of the evolution, the nature and root of state audit are fixed, and the 7 above-mentioned factors in this book are the only variable ones that affect the performance of audit functions. Disparities of the 7 factors in different periods will affect the specific audit functions within in certain era.

Determining by the public fiduciary duty, the nature, root and functions of state audit all affected by the 7 factors. With time going by, changes in the factors lead to disparities of functions of state audit in depth and breadth. It means that functions of state audit will propel forward as time goes by, but throughout the history of state audit, there were several cases retrograde development, for instance, there were backward situations in China from the Yuan Dynasty to the Qing Dynasty and after the founding of the People's Republic of China. One point should be noted that it is obligatory to explore the evolution direction and analyze the influence of the 7 factors of state audit in the future on the basis of public fiduciary duty. The 7 factors affect different aspects of the state audit and its functions. Among them, the state audit system and governmental functions determine the independence and authority of state institutions, which directly affect the specific audit functions on the one hand, and straightforwardly influence the breadth and depth of audit functions on the other hand. The mode of audit system determines the independent status, scope and authority of state audit. In the current model of audit system, China's audit system belongs to the typical mode of administrative audit. Therefore, governmental functions will to a large extent affect the independence and authority of state audit as well as the depth and breadth of state audit immediately. For instance, compared with those in the service-oriented government, functions of the all-function government will severely curb the independence of the audit system, the scope of audit, as well as the breadth and depth of audit function. Moreover, the other 5 factors, namely the degree of democratization, economic development level, legal system, audit techniques and the working competence of auditors, will jointly influence the breadth and depth of audit functions. First, the degree of democratization reflects the requirement of the performance of trustors' public fiduciary duties, the higher the degree of requirement is, the deeper and wider the audit functions will be. Second, the legal construction will require more with the development of social economy and the increase of audit affairs, and audit functions will also expand. Third, the legal system is the guarantee of audit work, and the guarantee is embodied in the scope and content of the specific audit work. In the condition of market economy, an excellent system of laws and regulations is necessary to deepen and expand functions of state audit. Fourth, audit techniques and the working competence of auditors will affect the performance of audit functions as well as final audit quality. In addition to the 5 factors, the other 2 factors will also influence the depth and breadth of audit function to some extent, so does the legal system. The 7 factors, on the whole, have a cross-influence on functions of state audit. The absence of any of the 7 factors will eventually affect the functions of state audit, but the extent and emphasis will be different.

From the 7 factors, this book tries to explore the evolution directions of the functions of the state audit.

For instance, this book analyzes the status of development when any of the 7 factors develops to the acme. First, China adopts the administrative audit system at present, and the system will last for long in future, but the political system of China determines that ultimate audit system is legislation-based, which reflects the will of and power of the people on the one hand, and embodies the independence and authority if the state audit on the other hand. Second, governmental functions can greatly influence the state audit under the administrative audit system, and similarly, the legislation-based system is no exception. After the reform in the administrative system, China may completely establish a "service-oriented" and "responsible" government. Third, a sound democratic system, rich forms of democracy and diversified democratic channels are conducive to making the people the true masters of the country and improving their own quality. In terms of affairs of social administration, the rights to know, to participate political affairs, to express and to supervise are required. Fourth, according to a series of socialist theories including Deng Xiaoping Theory, Scientific Outlook on Development and the Theory of Building a Harmonious Socialist Society, China's national economy will continue to develop and grow until it meets the material and spiritual needs of the people to the greatest extent. Fifth, the development of information technology, audit theories and other related disciplines will enrich the means of audit techniques, and more complicated audit business can be performed. Seventh, the working competence of auditors will improve as audit technology develops, and auditors will be qualified to perform audit business of higher levels.

When the 7 factors develop to acme, functions of state audit will develop into the following aspects:

First, the inherent functions of state audit will show up to the hilt. As mentioned above, functions of state audit are inherent of audit institutions themselves, which cannot be transferred by subjective wills. The current and previous functions of state audit are just part of the inherent functions, and the internal part of implicit functions cannot be fully brought into play because of restraining influence of the 7 factors. As carriers of the fulfillment of state audit functions, the 7 factors will encourage the full play of the inherent functions of state audit when they reach the acme. For each function, the development to the extreme will fundamentally achieve the audit supervision and make it the tool of social democracy and rule of law.

Second, the content of state audit functions will cover all areas of public fiduciary duty. State audit institutions have complete independence, authority and a sound legal system serving as the guarantee, which can eliminate all blank spots in the state audit. As long as the public fiduciary duty is involved, there must be auditing business. Where audit affairs exist, all inherent functions of state audit must be brought into full play to ensure the effective performance of public fiduciary duty.

Third, state audit supervision is becoming more and more significant in the socialist country, and will be sustainable. The stability and development of the society require supervisory systems of many aspects to play their roles in their respective sectors. As a part of the mechanism of supervision, audit institutions shall audit on not only affairs, but also people, so as to achieve the unity of audit supervision. In addition, the improvement of the 7 factors has promoted the position of audit institutions in the supervisory system. In the meanwhile, allowing for the characteristics of state audit, including publicity, transparency, objectivity and equity, the public will endow the supervision of audit institutions with more confidence, and under such circumstances, supervision can be better realized. Driven by internal and external factors, the audit institution will be the most important part of the social supervision system by exerting its functions. With the development of national economy as well as the continuous improvement of people's material life and spiritual life, the law consciousness of the whole society keeps enhancing, and many unlawful acts will be reduced even disappear. As a result, the status of taxation supervision, discipline supervision and legal supervision will be diminished, but the importance of state audit supervision on economy, efficiency and effectiveness will be stronger and stronger. No matter to what extent the human society develops, the pursuit for the economy and efficiency of human, financial, material and natural resources will never end. It can be inferred that even if the communism is realized and the state dies out, functions of state audit or similar audit functions will still exist.

163

Chapter Four: Environment Analysis and Mode Selection of China's State Audit

Classification of Audit Patterns

The formation of audit patterns all over the world is closely related to the national polities historically. At present, more than 160 countries and regions in the world have established their audit patterns in line with their national conditions. In consideration of the tremendous gap in social system, political institution, development degree, geographical environment, historical factors and composition of nationalities, the nature of audit institutions in these countries varies. Generally speaking, there are mainly two categories of audit patterns:

First, modern state audit can be subdivided into 6 modes. (1) Anglo-Saxon Mode. some countries including the United States and the United Kingdom adopt the mode, which is characterized by the establishment of a unified audit organization. The organization, whether built by the parliament or not, keeps in close touch with the parliament and is accountable to the parliament for audit results. (2) Latin Mode. France, Italy and some other countries adopt the mode. Instead of attaching itself to the parliament or being closely related to th parliament, the audit institution is usually a cooperative organization. (3) German Mode. Applying to Germany and Austria, the mode provides that the audit institution shall carry out its work as a mass organization does, although a unified audit management agency has been established. Whether the audit institution is affiliated with the parliament and whether it is equipped with officials with audit decision-making power are determined by the law. The auditing and consulting work shall be responsible to the parliament and the government. (4) Scandinavian Mode. Although similar to the German mode, the Scandinavia Mode requires audit institutions to cooperate with each other on the strength of performing their respective duties. (5) Latin American Mode. Under such system, audit work is usually directed by a specialized agency, but on some cases, there can be two audit institutions in a country at the same time: one is responsible for audit, another takes charge of juridical supervision. (6) Audit mode of centralized democracy and national economy. The audit pattern was popular in the USSR, Hungary and some other countries. Under normal circumstances, audit work is set up by the government, and the audit institution may be either a ministerial unit or a department or bureau-level unit subordinating to the central bank.

Second, state audit institutions can be divided into 4 parts according to the system of decentralization of state audit institutions. (1) Legislative state audit mode. This mode means that the state audit institution is subordinate to legislative branch. Under constitutional monarchy, the mode is the balance mechanism to ensure the separation of the three powers, namely legislative, judicial and administrative power. The mode was first established and implemented in the United Kingdom and further improved in the United States, so it is also known as the Anglo-American Mode, which has been widely imitated by Commonwealth nations and other countries.

Major characteristics of legislative state audit are as follows: First, the formation and perfection of legislative state audit lie in the democratic constitutionalism based on theories and principles of "separation of the three powers", "check and balance of powers", "popular sovereignty" and "limited government". Countries adopting the mode have relatively perfect legislative systems and procedures to ensure their function display. The mode can be fully developed in the advance of democracy and rule of law, and finally take the constitutional government as its institutional guarantee. Second, the development of democracy profits from its transparency, close connection to the public, and the scientific nature. The legislative state audit mode requires the audit institution to be responsible to the parliament—the represent of the public, and to check and balance the fiduciary responsibilities of the government on behalf of the people or taxpayers. The mechanism fully demonstrates that the audit work directed by the legislative mode is an indispensable method to strengthen the power of the parliament and realize the core of democracy—the mechanism of checks and balances of power. Third, audit institutions are considerably independent in the legislative mode. The legal status, personnel appointment and removal, fund guarantee and exercise of the power of supervision of audit institutions are usually protected by national legislation, making audit institutions quite authoritative in the national economy. Fourth, in terms of audit results, audit institutions are delegated only with the power of investigation instead of disposal. Under such circumstances, the macro-service functions of state audit institutions can be stronger. Audit institutions do not issue audit decisions straightforwardly, but they can still influence the decision-making of the parliament to a certain extent by restricting users of funds through making audit reports public.

(2) Judicial state audit mode. Judicial state audit mode means that the supreme audit institution exists in the form of court of accounts. The mode emphasizes the authority and strengthens the functions of state audit in the form of law, stipulating that auditors have legal standings and judicial capacity. Originating from an ancient system in Europe, the judicial mode, also known as "the second path to the modernization of audit", is also a major choice of modern state audit. Compared with the legislative mode, the judicial mode focuses on authority, and the administrative mode emphasizes counterbalance.

Characteristics of the judicial mode are as follows: First, the authority of audit institutions is strengthened law, so as to highlight the institutional independence and strengthen the function of audit supervision. Second, stability is the most significant nature of the judicial mode. Senior officials of the court of accounts enjoy life appointment, so the stability of audit institutions as well as the consistency of audit policies can be effectively guaranteed. Third, audit institutions in the judicial mode are bestowed with special judicial functions and corresponding powers, by feat of which audit institutions can investigate those responsible through judicial procedures and ensure the propitious progress of audit work.

(3) Independent state audit mode. Independent state audit mode provides that instead of belonging to any state agency, audit institutions are independent from legislative, judicial and administrative branches. The organizational forms of the mode are usually procuratorates of public accounts or courts of auditors. At present, typical countries adopting the mode include Germany, Japan and South Korea. Among them, courts of auditors from Germany and procuratorates of public accounts from Japan are the most representative ones.

Independent state audit mode has the following characteristics: First, audit institutions are independent from the legislative, judicial and administrative branches, so they are free from interference when performing their duties. The working mode of investigating and analyzing according to needs ensures the strong independence of audit institutions. Second, although lacking the power of disposal, audit institutions can still provide legislative, judicial and administrative branches with advice, and refer the issues to relevant bodies, so as to ensure the results of audit supervision.

(4) Administrative State Audit Mode. State audit institutions in the administrative mode are attached to the administrative branch and are responsible to the government. The mode was first established by the USSR and later adopted by some other socialist countries. audit institutions may be directly affiliated with a governmental department or subordinate to an agency of a certain branch. The will of the government can to a large extent influence the scope of work and audit sanctions of audit institutions. making the audit mode a semi-independent or non-independent one. Essentially speaking, it is an important method for the state to strengthen its administration. China's state audit belongs to the mode.

Main characteristics of administrative state audit mode are as follows: First, subordinating to governmental departments, audit institutions usually have the power of disposition, which may provide the enforcement of audit recommendations with favorable conditions. Second, audit institutions can conduct audit supervision over the financial budget as well as revenues and expenditures of all departments and units of the government, by feat of the power conferred by national laws. In the meanwhile, they must be answerable for the government to ensure the normal performance of financial policies and decrees of the government. Third, state audit institutions are strongly time-efficient, but their independent status is not as solid as that of their counterparts in the above-mentioned 3 modes.

China's State Audit Environment

Generally, "the sum of all external factors influencing the emergence, existence and development of audit" is known as audit environment. Therefore, the state audit environment is the premise and foundation of all development phases of state audit and also the starting point of the system of audit theory.

Political Environment. Political environment refers to the degree to which the state authorities affirm the legal status of such independent economic supervision under the social and political system of a certain period. Political environment has a direct impact on audit, which is not only the basis of audit work, but restricts the rise and fall of audit for significant measure.

China's political system reform at the present stage has provided the prosperous economic development with favorable and stable political environment. The government pays great attention to the audit work, and audit institutions have continuously assisted the decision-making of the government by virtue of audit results. In recent years, audit institutions have been widely acclaimed by the government and the public because of their outstanding performance in anti-corruption and dealing with major economic cases. However, China's state audit is subordinate to the administrative branch, and the dual-leadership system, which stipulates that audit institutions at all levels are directed by local governments at the corresponding level and audit institutions at the next higher level at the same time, has objectively affected the functions and authority of state audit, resulting in stronger protectionism and weaker independence.

The problem is particularly acute in local audit, because local audit institutions are enslaved to local governments in aspects of human, financial and material resources. Sometimes, the audit work is inevitable to be a mere formality because of the intervention of local governments. Thus, it can be seen that the local governments' degree of emphasis on audit could significantly affect the status and functions of audit in local political systems. Comparatively speaking, government intervention cannot greatly affect the central audit institutions and their agencies, because their personnel, expenditure and material resources are under the unified management of the State Audit Office. However, the problem solving and error correction also show two different trends due to the importance attached by the chief executive: problems that are concerned and instructed by senior officials will be severely dealt with, and those responsible will also be punished accordingly; issues that are not taken seriously by top officials will be transferred to senior departments of auditees or other relevant units. Out of the consideration of their own interests, some departments may merely solve their problems internally or just neglect the seriousness of the problems and let them go. In order to reverse the situation completely, China's reform in state audit mode is imperative under such circumstances.

"As the superstructure, audit system is one of the basic state political systems and a major part of organizational form of state power". No matter the state audit of western countries or China, it is impossible to overstep the objective constraints of the class nature of state political power. That is to say, the state system and political system chosen by the state determine the status, nature and performance of functions of state audit. At present, the state system and political system of the People's Republic of China are respectively people's democratic dictatorship and the system of people's congress. Therefore, in the construction and development of the state audit mode, the basic tenet that the audit must serve the interests of the socialist system shall be established at first. In addition, the National People's Congress is China's supreme legislature, the State Council is the highest organ of state administration, and the Supreme People's Court as well as the Supreme People's Procuratorate are bestowed with the highest judicial power and procuratorial power. The institutional arrangement, combining the separation with cooperation of power, implies the ideas of democracy and checks and balances of power, just like the patter of the separation of the three powers in western countries. Practice has proved that the design of China's state system and political system is conducive to effectively protect people's power as masters of the country, strengthen people's capacity and awareness to participate in political affairs, and establish the political environment for the development of public audit.

In the new historical era, the Report to the 16th National Congress of the CPC put forward the slogan of developing the socialist democracy and establishing the socialist political civilization. The construction of the socialist democracy is a powerful mean to ameliorate China's political environment, so as to transform government functions and reform the administrative mode, namely the top tasks of China's construction of democracy. Under the planned economic system, the government wields ultimate power. With the establishment of the socialist market economy and the development of socialist democracy, it is required to transform government functions and restrain the power. On the on hand, the market economy is running with the guidance of laws, and the political meaning of market economy is the separation of politics and economy, and the government is not empowered to directly interfere economic affairs; on the other hand, to establish and perfect the socialist democracy and power supervision system, it is necessary to impose clear restrictions on government actions with the assistance of laws and the constitution, so as to control the administrative power to the maximum extent from the source of power. Therefore, the development of socialist democracy and the transformation from unlimited government to limited government create a good political environment for the reform in state audit modes.

Economic Environment. The economic environment of state audit refers to the objective requirements of the social and economic development and its operation mechanism on audit performance in a certain period. Audit is the product of economic development to a certain stage, and the process of audit development and reform is in nature the course in which audit adapt itself to the economic development and evolve with changes in economic factors. Audit always plays a role in a certain economic environment. In different economic climates (various economic systems and management systems), the importance of audit varies in breadth and strength. China's state audit, founded on significant administrative qualities, was born at the end of the era of planned economy. In the political and economic climate at that time, state administrative organs played their due roles.

Since the Reform and Opening-up, China's economic management system has developed by leaps and bounds. In 1982, China put forward the idea of establishing the management system dominated by planned economy and supplemented by market regulations. Breaking the framework of pure planned economy, the concept of market was raised in China for the first time. In 1984, the economic idea of planned commodity economy was put forward, which broke through the theory that market economy and planned economy were opposite, and introduced theoretical basis for further development of market economy in China. The 14th National Congress of the CPC came up with the target of establishing socialist market economy, and the 15th National Congress determined that "public ownership playing a leading role and a diverse of ownership growing side by side" as China's basic economic system. After joining the WTO, the economic system would be destined to be more developed and mature, and various economic components of China would witness more sea changes inevitably. Under the guidance of such economic system, a good deal of non-state-run economic sectors may undergo a phase of rapid development, while the proportion of state-owned economy will experience a slump. For now, the accelerated withdrawal of state capital from small and medium-sized enterprise speaks volumes. After the accession to the WTO, it is unescapable for the state capital to disinvest from some indifferent sectors and industries in order to hold favorable positions in significant economic fields, with the further improvement of the market economic system and expansion of opening to the outside world. Pure state-run enterprises will be fewer and fewer. These changes will lead to transformations in scope, targets and contents of auditees, and in the meanwhile, the state audit is required to make adjustments in such aspects appropriately, so as to concentrate the limited auditing resources on major sectors and industries closely relating to the national economy and people's livelihood and put more energy on the effective monitoring of state-owned economy.

To sum up, with the gradual establishment of the system of socialist market economy, functions of the government and enterprises will be separated completely. The government will no longer directly interfere the management and operation affairs of enterprises, and the priority of work will be shifted into improving the economic environment, then it is necessary to transit the focus of state audit as well. To give full play to the responsibility and the function of supervision, the state audit is possible to get rid itself of the administrative branch of the government and the macroeconomic regulatory framework, and make itself a significant method of re-control, namely a legislative state audit mode. Thus it can be seen that changes in economic environment provides a prerequisite for the reform of state audit mode.

Legal Environment. Whether in political life, economic life or other aspects, a state always needs laws to restrain all domestic affairs in addition to morality. Modern society is a society ruled by laws, and the behavior of any organization and individual must act in line with laws and regulations. Audit institutions and auditors are, of course, no exception, and the state audit must be carried out within the framework of the national legal system.

The legal environment of audit refers to the interference and guidance of national laws on audit work within a certain period, the protection of the interests of auditors in accordance with laws, as well as the authority and scope of state audit, which are all defined by laws. Since the establishment of the State Audit Office by the State Council on 15th September, 1983, local audit institutions have been set up successively, and the audit work has been carried out with the assistance of the constitution. Later, the promulgation of Audit Regulation, the Audit Law and Enforcement Regulations of the Audit Law in succession have incrementally guided the state audit into the track of legislation. Introduced in 1995, the Audit Law in particular clearly sets out basic principles and major items of the audit system in detail, and its provisions elaborate the duties, authority, audit procedures, legal responsibilities and other functions of audit institutions and auditors, and determine the specific job requirement, which both offer audit institutions at all levels with law enforcement basis and make all kinds of administrative law enforcement behaviors clear, including audit works.

Audit behaviors, which are both restrained by laws and regulations and conducive to improve the legal climate, are produced and developed in a certain legal environment as a major means to strengthen the legislation. In the present legal environment, the achievements made by the state audit over the past few decades should be fully recognized, but the defects and shortcoming cannot be just neglected. For instance, with the acceleration and deepening of China's market economy, audit work is usually insufficient in some aspects because of the absence of law, allowing for the awkward situation that some major laws and regulations have not been enacted yet, and a significant number of the established laws are not perfect. The dilemma inevitably requires China to constantly explore new ideas for the development of state audit and seek new solutions to the current problems. In the new historical era, various laws and regulations have been incrementally improved as the economic society evolves. The Report to the 16th National Congress of the CPC formally set the governing strategy of "implementing law-based governance and establishing a socialist country under the rule of law", indicating that China had made a transformation from policy-based governance under the planned economic system to law-based governance under the market economic system. Law-based governance mainly refers to administering stat affairs by feat of the established laws and systems. In the national governance system, the status of laws is higher than that of policies, and policies cannot exceed the boundaries drawn by legal instruments. The institutional design makes up for the deficiency of policy-based governance. The key point of law-based governance is the law-based administration of the government. Whether administrative bodies could manage state affairs by law will decide if China can establish a socialist law-based state on the whole. The core of administration by law is to standardize and restrain the administrative power, namely the transformation from governing the people to governing officials and the power and strengthening the supervision and restriction on administrative power. The Report to the 16th National Congress of the CPC has positioned the state audit as an important tool of power balance, requiring audit institutions to "strengthen the power restriction and supervision". That was the new requirement that the CPC put forward to the state audit in order to deepen the reform of political system and improve the mechanism of power operation and supervision, indicating the major development in China's political democratization and the new breakthrough in the function orientation of state audit in the construction of China's democratic system. therefore, this book believes that the transformation in governance strategy not only provides the operation of China's supervision system of state audit with institutional guarantee, but offers legal basis to the construction of China's legislative state audit mode.

In addition to the three types of audit environments

discussed above, the state audit is, of course, affected by other factors, such as the social cultural background, the managing environment of audit work and the skill environment.

Mode Selection of China's State Audit

Current Situation of Local Governments

In May 1982, China formally joined the International Organization of Supreme Audit Institutions (INTOSAI). In December of the same year, according to the constitution China decided to implement the audit supervision system and establish audit institutions. the constitution stipulated that the State Audit Office shall be established as a subordinate body to the State Council, and take charge of the audit work across the whole country under the leadership of the Premier. In the meanwhile, local government at or above the county level shall be required to establish audit institutions which are responsible for the audit work within the scope of jurisdiction under the leadership of the local government at the corresponding level and audit institutions at the next higher level. With the Promulgation of the Audit Law of the PRC, a relatively effective audit system was established quickly in China, and the audit mode was fixed therewith. With all audit institutions incorporated into the administrative branches, China's state audit mode is a typical administrative mode with the following characteristics:

Institution Setting. There are two kinds of audit institutions in China, the central one and the local ones. The central audit institution, also known as the State

Audit Office, is the audit organ under the direct leadership of the Premier of the State Council. As part of the State Council, the State Audit Office is China's supreme audit institution. It has dual legal status: on the one hand, as a department of the central government, it is dominated by the State Council, and must enforce the administrative regulations, determinations and orders of the State Council and organize and lead the audit work throughout China; on the other hand, the State Audit Office also has its own spectrum of duty, namely it must directly carry out the audit work within its own responsibility range as an independent administrative subject. In order to strengthen the audit supervision over central agencies in key areas, the State Audit Office has established commissioner's office in 16 major cities in succession since the year of 1986. Authorized by the State Council in 1987, the State Audit Office has set up agencies in 41 ministries, and to meet the demand of the institutional reform of the State Council, 25 audit bureaus are in operation in different ministries and departments.

Local audit institutions refer to audit organizations set up by local governments of provinces, autonomous regions, municipalities directly under the central government, cities with districts, autonomous prefectures, counties, autonomous counties, cities without districts and districts directly under the central government. Local audit in China practices a dual leadership system, namely that audit institutions are responsible for their audit work under the leadership of local governments at the corresponding level and audit institutions at the higher next level.

Leadership Pattern. The leadership pattern of audit

institutions is a major part of the state audit system. It refers to the position of audit institutions in the organizational structure of the state, the specific higher authority and the leadership relationship with audit institutions at the next higher and lower level. At present, there are 3 basic characteristics of the leadership pattern of China's state audit: First audit institutions are directly under the leadership of the chief executive of governments at the correspond level. Second, local audit institutions adopt a dual leadership system, namely that they are directed by governments at the corresponding level and audit institutions at the next higher level at the same time. Dual leadership pattern refers to the mode in which there are two superior leading organs at the same time, with the purpose of better unifying and coordinating the institutional work and giving play to the working enthusiasm of both the central and the local institutions. Third, the auditing business of local audit institutions is mainly directed by audit institutions at the next higher level, which facilitates the implementation of audit works. Different from those of the leadership pattern of other organs, the 3 characteristics mentioned above constitute the basis content of the leadership pattern of China's state audit.

Personnel Appointment and Removal. In order to ensure the independence of audit institutions and auditees to wield the power of audit supervision, China has made strict provisions for the personnel appointment and removal of persons in charge of audit institutions and job qualifications of auditors according to the international practice. The procedures of appointment and removal of the Auditor General of the State Audit Office are as follows: the candidate is nominated by the Premier of the State Council and determined by the NPC; and the personnel appointment and removal is up to the standing committee of the NPC during the inter-sessional period; the Deputy Auditor General is appointed or removed by the State Council; the NPC has the power to recall the Auditor General. The procedures of appointment and removal of persons in charge of local audit institutions are as follows: chief leaders are nominated by the chief executive of governments at the corresponding level and appointed and removed by the standing committee of the People's Congress, and the personnel appointment and removal shall be reported to the government at the next higher level; deputy leaders shall be appointed or removed by governments at the corresponding level. In addition, changes of personnel of main leaders of local audit institutions shall seek for opinions from audit institutions at the next higher level at first.

Source of Funds. The guarantee of funds necessary for audit institutions to perform their duties is a basic condition for audit institutions to wield the power of audit supervision independently according to law. In China's legislation, issues of funds of administrative branches are not always clearly stipulated by laws or regulations. However, it is the major task of audit institutions to carry out audit supervision over the financial revenues and expenditures of the government, and there is a direct relationship of supervision between audit institutions and financial departments of governments, which is different from that of other governmental agencies therefore, the Audit Law provides that the funds necessary for audit institutions to perform their duties shall be listed in the financial budget and guaranteed by governments at the corresponding level. To a certain extent, the institutional arrangement is conducive to the improvement of China's audit supervision mechanism.

Characteristics of the Local Governments

From the perspective of its status quo, the audit system of China's local governments has the following characteristics:

Dual Leadership System. The dual leadership system is an obvious characteristic of the audit system of local governments, that is, audit institutions are responsible for the audit work within their own administrative regions under the leadership of chief executives at the corresponding levels and persons in charge of audit institutions at the next higher levels at the same time. The audit business and administrative management of local audit institutions are respectively directed by superior audit institutions and local governments. The central audit institution does not have a "dual" problem, because as the supreme audit institution, the State Audit Office is responsible to the Premier of the State Council, and the relationship of accountability is one-way. The system makes audit institutions of local governments faced with the dual leadership of business management and administrative control respectively from audit institutions from the next higher levels and governments at the corresponding levels, bringing up the chance of generating conflicts. In western countries, there is no subordinate or leader-led relationship, and local audit institutions are only answerable to local parliaments by reporting the work progress, with the purpose of maintaining the one-way relationship of accountability and reporting.

The Power of Handling and Punishment. China's audit institutions of local governments not only exercise independent economic supervision and administrative oversight, report audit reports and relevant audit work, but have the power to correct, compensate (audit treatment) and punish (audit punishment) relevant acts violating state regulations in fiscal and financial revenues and expenditures. This is quite different from that of western countries, in which the institutions of state audit only have the procuratorial power and the reporting power, but do not have the power, or direct power, of handling and punishment, and in some countries, the state audit has no other power but the right to make suggestions on handling and punishment and the power of juridical transfer. Thus, state audit is honored as "the knight with the sword". However, in China, the state audit is equipped with "sword" in hand, and is supposed to have greater deterrent force and higher authority.

Responsibility System of Administrative Chiefs. Persons in charge of audit institutions of China's local governments assume the overall responsibility for the audit work within their own terms of reference and offer dominate opinions on the decision-making of the professional work and administrative management of audit institutions, enjoying decisive weight among the collective leadership of audit institutions. Comparatively speaking, audit institutions in western countries mostly adopt the responsibility system of division of labor, which is relatively independent, and the collegial system (leading members reach consensus through consultation on the decision-making plan) or voting system (make decisions by voting and the principle of minority submitting to majority) is employed to discuss official business and make decisions when it comes to internal decision-making.

Appointment and Removal Procedures. Persons in charge of local audit institutions in China are nominated by the chief executives of the government at the same levels, and appointed and removed by the People's Congress at the same levels, the deputy posts are appointed and removed by the government; the changes in leaders of audit institutions at various levels shall seek for opinions of superior agencies in advance; the teams of offices of the head of audit institutions are equivalent to those of chief executives at the same levels. However, in most western countries, the chief auditor is listed as the officer with special appointment and removal mode, like the chief justice and the chief procurator. In addition to the different procedures of appointment and removal, the term of office of the chief auditor is usually longer than that of other commissioners. Without special reasons, the chief auditor cannot be dismissed from the post at will, and chief auditors are tenured in some countries.

Local Variation and Audit System of Local Governments. Within the framework of the Constitution and the Audit Law, local governments at all levels, especially governments of provinces, municipalities directly under the central government and autonomous regions, have mostly enacted local laws and regulations to make clear provisions on the duty and authority, and the relationship of leadership, subjection and reporting, highlighting local characteristics of social, political, economic and cultural development. Some regulations are involved in certain links of the audit system of local governments, for instance, some provinces set up audit agencies within their own administrative divisions; some regulations touch the relationship of business leadership among audit institutions at provincial, municipal and county level; some rules extend the duty and authority of audit institutions as well as their scopes of audit; and some have made more strict and specific provisions on the guarantee of operating funds of audit institutions. However, the laws and regulations cannot substantially impact the basic structure of the current audit system.

Chapter Five: Government Audit of

State-Owned Enterprises

State-owned enterprise is an important means and tool for the government to intervene and regulate the national economy and to control the economic artery of the country. In a manner of speaking, state-owned enterprises are significant guarantees for the national economic security.

Government Audit and Anti-Corruption

The corruption of state-owned enterprises greatly undermines the fair environment of market competition and obstructs the economic development. Therefore, with the purpose of maintaining the sound and stable development of the national economy and the economic security, it is out of question for the government and the party to take the anti-corruption in state-owned enterprises seriously. Under the theoretical framework of national governance, both its roles in safeguarding national economic security as well as combating corruption and upholding integrity require that the government audit must devote itself to anti-corruption.

Functions of Anti-corruption in Government Audit

Prevention. Government audit plays an important

role in preventing state-owned enterprises from being contaminated by corruption. Offering early warning and preventing corruption in state-owned enterprises, the function of prevention of government audit is mainly reflects in the following two aspects: First, ideological restriction. Audit institutions can make managers of state-owned enterprises aware of their entrusted economic responsibilities in mind by auditing their economic duties and performance as well as reinforcing the audit and supervision on key projects and their major links, so as to exert mental pressure on the managers and deter them from getting involved in corruption, strengthen the supervision on standard management and self-discipline outside enterprises, form an effective internal-external system of audit supervision, and eventually achieve the desired effect of preventing state-owned enterprises from corruption. Second, legal restriction. Throughout the development of audit-relevant laws in modern China, it can be pointed out that the restriction of powers is a basic function entrusted by laws to audit institutions. The essence of audit is the restriction on powers, the supervision and evaluation of government audit on the economic duties of state-owned and state-holding enterprises are in nature the restriction on powers of persons in charge of the companies. The assessment of government audit on state-owned enterprises' performance of macroeconomic policies and the implementation of major policies, with the purpose of ensuring their sound and stable development, requires the government audit to shift from pre-audit to concurrent audit and post audit, so as to prevent corruption through controlling in an effective and efficient manner. Government shall not only evaluate the entrusted economic duties, but are responsible and mandatory to provide institutional and political suggestions for problems pointed out on the process of supervision and evaluation, which requires a mountain of work of pre-audit and concurrent audit.

Disclosure. On the strength of the fiduciary relationship arising from the entrusted economic duties, the supervision of the government audit on state-owned enterprises shall cover the entire financial operation and management. It is known to all that the audit itself is far from the objective, but just a tool to supervise the operation and management of state-owned enterprises. The purpose of government audit is to facilitate enterprises to take corresponding measures to cope with corruption by revealing issues of violations against laws and regulations in the operation and management as well as punishing relevant parties through legal means and economic compensation, so as to prevent the recurrence of similar incidents. The definition of audit objective in the Lima Declaration offers a good illustration of the function of disclosure of the government audit in the struggle against corruption. The Government audit is an important regulator in China, and as long as there is a fiduciary economic relationship, the government audit must supervise over it. By feat of the means of financial supervision, auditors must supervise over the auditees to collect the audit trail of corruption and reveal the problems. For instance, in 2014, the State Audit Office released the result the announcement of the financial revenues and expenditures of 11 state-owned enterprises in the year of 2012, revealing that 2 companies, including the Thermal Energy Co. Ltd at the Chemical Industry Area in Nanjing, Jiangsu Attached to China Resources (Holdings) Co. Ltd, collected 8.54 million Yuan by falsely listing the raw material cost and other problems. The disclosure of corruption has had a great deterrent effect on corruption, making potential corrupt officials dare not engage in corruption at will. By transferring clues of cases of illegal activities, the Chinese government is performing its utmost to reveal, investigate and punish corruption-related cases, promote the construction of a clean and honest administration, and play its role in anti-corruption.

Penalty. Compared with other supervisors, the government audit is free from the impact of other relevant principles thanks to its independent status, thus is can be more objective and punish the corruption subjects accordingly. Audit penalty is the correction and sanction on violations against laws and regulations found by audit institutions. After receiving the notice of audit penalty, auditees are required to turn in the fraudulent gains and hand back the misappropriated assets, or audit institutions may transfer the cases to relevant departments if necessary. Audit institutions of the government have the power to deal with violations against law and discipline according to law, which can dig into the origin of the discovered corruption, cope with corruption at the source, confine the harm brought by corruption within a limited scope, and recover the losses of the state timely. Through auditing, audit institutions have pointed out some problems of breaching of law and the risks that have emerged, and have put forward audit opinions in a targeted way.

Audit institutions of the government have also cooperated with relevant departments to further bring corruption under control. For instance, according to clues of cases of corruption transferred by audit institutions, judicial organs conduct in-depth investigations by virtue of their professional skills to ascertain the facts, file lawsuits against corrupt principal parts, and corrupt principal parts liable for their violations against laws and regulations; based on audit results, discipline inspection departments summarize the status quo, areas an development tendency of corruption, so as to strengthen the construction of a clean and honest administration in high-risk areas; through the announcement of audit results, the public can also participate in the external supervision over SOEs. The disclosure and punishment of corruption are not the ultimate purposes of the government audit, but a sound and perfect mechanism for rusk prevention is the final embodiment of audit efforts.

Correction. Correction of corruption of the government audit refers to that auditors shall wield the power granted by law to stop the corruption of auditees timely in the course of audit, so as to correct the illegal behaviors of that harm the assets of SOEs. As supervisory institutions of public power, audit institutions of the government correct the corruption of SOEs by their independent function of audit supervision. In the course of work, audit institutions can take compulsory measures against the violations of laws and disciplines of auditees, and correct their ongoing corruption. To be explicitly, audit institution has the power to ask for a compulsive cease if it just found violations against law and regulation of auditees, or close the relevant files and information coercively.

Paths of Government Audit in dealing with Anti-Corruption of State-Owned Enterprises

First, prevent the corruption of SOEs by feat of the deterrent government audit. State laws bestow the government audit with independence and provide that auditees must accept the audit investigation of audit institutions unconditionally, promoting the deterrent effect of government audit on corruption principal parts. In simple terms, by severely punishing the corruption, the government audit acts as a psychology deterrent and deters people from corruption. Since the establishment of State Audit Office, cases of corruption pointed out are innumerable, and tens of thousands of cases have been transferred to discipline inspection departments and judicial organs through the government audit. By disclosing the cases of corruption and punishing the corruption principal parts, the government audit awes the public in mind and exerts mental pressure on those who have not been involved in corruption yet. For example, by collating the audit announcement of financial revenues and expenditures of SOEs released in 2014, it was found that the financial management in 2 subsidiaries of China resources was disorganized, and the welfare distribution to the staff is partially illegal. In the fiscal year of 2012 alone, more than 8 million Yuan of the company was taken in batches for employee benefits under the direction of the leaders in charge in the form of fictitious cost. In addition to exposing corruption, the government can also make corruption principal parts clear that all their misconducts are very likely to be under the surveillance of the government by regular government audit, and once got involved in corruption, the violations of law would be pointed out immediately, and relevant responsible bodies would be punished severely. In this way, the government audit can deter potential victims of corruption from committing crimes psychologically. However, there are still many cases of corruption that cannot be disclosed even after the investigation of government audit, and the function of disclosure cannot be brought into available play, which offer corruption principal parts an illusion that the government audit in fact exists in name only, and as a result, they are likely to be more greedy and ambitious, and try to further abuse the power for personal interests. In fact, the public and relevant interest subjects cannot be too hard on the effect of the government audit, and it is because that audit institutions are restrained by the scarcity of audit resources and the lack of assistance of external units. Therefore, it is of significance to strengthen the cooperation with other departments to remedy the defects of audit itself, enhance the deterrence and improve the efficiency of punishing the corruption.

Second, expose the corruption of SOEs by implementing the procedures of the government audit. The demand of the public for SOEs to fulfill their economic fiduciary responsibilities enables audit institutions of the government to discover the expose the corruption through audit procedures including audit of financial revenues and expenditures, performance audit, follow-up audit and audit of economic duties. Auditors shall, according to the law, carry out the corresponding auditing procedures for annual financial revenues and expenditures of SOEs and expose the corruption by feat of the professional means. Auditors shall, for instance, keep the track of the whereabouts of each sum of funds by checking the papers of auditees, collect important clues, discover cases of corruption step by step in the process of implementing special auditing procedures for auditing financial revenues and expenditures of SOEs by virtue of their specialized knowledge an acute professional quality, and in the meanwhile timely expose cases of embezzlement and corruption such as using funds illegally and feathering their own nests with relevant data as evidence. It is also found that in the course of their work, audit institutions can also stop corruption with their statutory power in addition to exposing corruption, such as depriving corruption principal parts of the rights to appropriate or use the funds. Taking financial revenues and expenditures as an example, government audit institutions are empowered to stop auditees from using state-owned funds illegally—such as unauthorized departmental coffers—and ask relevant banks and financial departments to freeze the special funds already allocated.

Third, punish corruption in SOEs by making the results of government audit public. In according to relevant laws and regulations, audit institutions are entitled and obliged to make the audit results and related content exposed to special groups and the public. Audit results mentioned in this paper refer to not only audit results of the government, but opinions of auditors submitted to relevant departments in the course of audit, notices of audit penalty decisions transmitted to auditees and rectification results of problems released to the public. In a manner of speaking, announcements of audit results can reflect the problems of SOEs pointed out by audit institutions in the course of implementing relevant audit procedures in an open and transparent manner, promote the information disclosure system of governmental departments, boost the supervisory management of the public on SOEs, broaden approaches for the public to participate in the management of state affairs, propel the construction of democracy and rule of law in China, and contribute to form a system of effective supervision by public opinions. Therefore, by establishing a sound audit results announcement system, China may build a fair and transparent government image and eliminate the ill effects brought by corruption, and in the meanwhile, audit institutions of the government can also actively react to hot issues of the public, improve the efficiency of rectification of problems, and effectively prevent and dissolve the social risks caused by corruption. Thus, through the announcement of audit results, audit institutions can not only guarantee the people's rights to be informed of problems pointed out by audit supervision, but guide the public to participate in the system of government supervision consciously, arouse the enthusiasm of the people to take part in the management of public affairs, combine the audit supervision with citizen supervision and media scrutiny, and improve the work efficiency of audit institutions on auditees. In addition to the right of audit disposition, opinions of the public can also facilitate the punishment against corruption, so as to form the multi-access mechanism of anti-corruption from state laws to social opinions.

Fourth, correct the corruption of SOEs by strengthening government audit. Not merely finding out and punishing corruption, it is also necessary to correct the corrupt behaviors from the root, which is the rudimentary target of China's audit institutions to curb the corruption in SOEs. As a fundamental function of the government audit, audit correction differs from other functions because of its greater job difficulty, longer work cycle, less obvious short-term effect and the requirement of sustained attention. The accountability system for persons in charge of SOEs has been the inevitable choice. At present, however, the audit accountability system in China is far from perfect, and audit institutions have to cooperate with discipline inspection departments, judicial organs and other relevant governmental departments to further hold leaders of SOEs responsible up to the hilt, and construct an environment in which SOEs are afraid of or reluctant to get involved in corruption. In addition to strengthening the accountability mechanism, of course, audit institutions can also correct the corruption of SOEs by following the implementation of audit recommendations. Firstly, government audit shall not only track changes in prone areas of corruption, but also follow up the progress of problem solving and the related influences, which requires the central audit institution and local ones to interact with each other, follow up the implantation of audit recommendations, keep close attention to the effect of audit opinions, and further promote the successful audit recommendations by national legislation. Secondly, audit institutions shall elaborately analyze the sources of various malversation, and regard the causes of corruption as defects in levels of institution and internal management, so as to point out common problems of corrupt behaviors, propose suggestions starting with enterprises systems, and correct corruption at its source.

Economic Responsibility Audit of Persons in Charge of State-Owned Enterprises

The evaluation of economic responsibility audit of persons in charge of SOEs has expanded dynamically with the reform and development of SOEs. Since the 18th National Congress of the CPC, the Central Committee has made new systematic arrangements for comprehensively deepening the reform of SOEs. The Guiding Ideas on Deepening the Reform of SOEs issued by the Central Committee and its supportive documents have defined 6 key tasks for further reforms, including strengthening and improving the leadership of the Party, separately promoting the reform in SOEs, optimizing the modern enterprise system, perfecting the management system of state-owned property, developing the mixed ownership economy and preventing the loss of state-owned assets. The audit of economic duties of leaders of SOEs should and must focus on the reform plans, and determine the content and indicators of audit evaluation scientifically on the basis of Stipulations in Audit of Economic Responsibilities and the requirements of supervision and management of leading cadres under new situations.

According to the Guiding Ideas on Deepening the Reform of SOEs and its supportive documents as well as laws and regulations including the Ideas on Strengthening Audit, the Implementation Opinions on All Coverage of Audit and the Development Program of State Audit in the 13th Five-Year Plan =, this book divides the audit of economic duties of persons of charge of SOEs into 8 aspects: implementation of decisions and arrangements of the Central Committee, major economic decisions-making, financial revenues and expenditures, internal management, self-dependent innovation, overseas assets management, risk control and the construction of the party conduct and of an honest and clean government.

Implementation of Decisions and Arrangements of the Central Committee

State-owned enterprises, especially those concerning the state security and the lifeblood of the national economy, serve as backbones and pillars of great significance in the performance of the economic operation as well as the reliable force under the direct control of the state to strengthen the macro-control, cope with emergencies and dissolve major economic risks. The special status of SOEs in the economic and social development determines that the primary task of persons in charge of SOEs is to implement the significant political measures of the central government. In terms of the audit content, the economic responsibilities of persons in charge of SIEs in implementing major political measures of the central government include: implementing policies of macroeconomic development of the central government and the reform in SOEs, formulating and carrying out development strategy program of business operation, and completing the assessment of accountability targets.

Implementation. The economic responsibility in this aspect includes the executive conditions of supply-side structural reform with capacity reduction, de-stocking, deleveraging, cost reduction and improving underdeveloped sectors as key tasks, reforms in SOEs, industrial policies, distributive policies of income (including the relation of distribution between the state and enterprises, namely the budgetary policies of the operation of state-owned assets, and the relation of distribution between enterprises and employees, namely pay policies), pricing policies and the "Go Global" Strategy, especially the construction of "One Belt and One Road" Initiative. First, implement the policy of supply-side structural reform. More attention shall be paid to the major development and achievements in promoting and coordinating capacity reduction, de-stocking, deleveraging, cost reduction and improving underdeveloped sectors. Relevant departments shall focus on checking whether the adverse impact on economic development has been countervailed, whether relevant parties have boosted the economic transformation and upgradation through innovation and entrepreneurship; whether the production capacity failing to meet the requirements of national standards on energy consumption and environmental protection has been withdrawn from the market in accordance with laws, whether there are problems of environmental pollution or resource destruction, whether there are newly-added excess capacity of steel, coal and shipbuilding violating against regulations; whether there are serious problems of inventory backlog in real estate enterprises, whether there is excessive debt which results in serious debt risks; and whether there are non-compliant and unreasonable institutional transaction costs and labor costs. Second, implement policies of reforms in SOEs. Audit institutions shall check the rationality of the structure of state-owned capital to promote the concentration of state-owned capital in key industries and areas; check whether enterprises can promote the concentration of state-owned capital in their main businesses by strictly following the investment direction set by their principal works; check the construction of enterprises' technical innovation system, the integration of scientific and technological resources and the investment in research and development, so as to facilitate the major national scientific research and innovation tasks and enhance the ability of enterprises in independent innovation; and check the corporate governance structure as well as the shareholding of non-state capital to promote the reform of shareholding and mixed ownership in enterprises. Attentions shall be paid to whether enterprises have effectively organized, promoted and implemented the new round of reforms in SOEs including the system of benefit packages of persons in charge of enterprise, introducing non-state capital into investment projects and mixed ownership in accordance with guiding ideas and instructions, whether problems left over by history that enterprises have to take over part of the government functions—for instance, enterprises must be responsible for water delivery, power supply, heating and property management in families residential areas—have been solved, and whether the reforms in some collectively owned factories have been carried out in line with requirements. Third, implement industrial policies. Attentions shall be paid to whether enterprises have strictly complied with relevant regulations on industrial structure adjustment, whether investors have participated in restricted projects (villa real estate project, golf courses, etc.) and the eliminated projects (equipment with backward manufacturing techniques and outmoded products); whether the supporting systems, measures and institutional arrangements raised in line with the plan for adjustments and revitalization of key industries meet the policy requirements for adjusting the economic structure and transforming the development pattern; whether relevant parties have vigorously promoted the development of high-end equipment manufacturing and other key industries in line with the decisions of the state to accelerate the development of emerging industries and strategic tasks and priorities set in the Made in China 2025 Initiative; whether the projects for revitalizing key industries and upgrading the strength of technologies arranged by the state are plagued by problems such as the shortage of investment funds, absence of development plans, and projects that have been completed and put into operation have not achieved the expected goals; whether there are any problems such as blind expansion of production capacity, excess production capacity caused by premature construction and repeated construction, low operation efficiency and squander of state-owned assets and funds. In addition, audit institutions shall also focus on enterprises of electricity, coal, telecommunications, petrochemistry, military industry and finance, implement the specific industry policies, and check whether there are problems of implementation deviation or poor execution as well as new problems and conditions in the course of policy implementation, so as to offer advice and suggestions for further perfecting the macro-industrial policies. Fourth, implement the distributive policy of income. Audit institutions shall place emphasis on revealing problems such as deficient gain sharing mechanism of state-owned assets, same work with different pay (especially staff allocated by the service dispatch system), unsound scientific innovation-driven and incentive mechanisms, and occupying or using public resources for free or at low costs by unlawful means, so as to promote the fair market competition and equitable use of essential productive factors of economic entities under different forms of partnership according to law; check whether the compensation level and position-related consumption of managerial staff are in compliance with requirements, whether the increase in remuneration exceeds the growth level of the social and economic development and the economic benefits of enterprises, and whether there are situations such as extra income in addition to salary as well as investment and shareholding; and problems such as illegal income, invisible income and the chaotic distribution of income, so as to boost the standardization of income distribution. Fifth, implement the pricing policy. Audit institutions shall focus on whether the government intervenes in prices that should have been set by the market, whether central enterprises have followed the government fixed prices of public utilities, public welfare services and links of natural monopoly of network facilities, whether relevant enterprises have strictly implemented the pricing policies set by departments of prices of the government, whether enterprises have made the prices up or down all by themselves, and whether there are preferential prices without state approval. Sixth, implement the "Go Global" Strategy. Close attention shall be paid to how enterprises have participated in the construction visions of the "Go Global" Strategy and the "One Belt and One Road" Initiative, whether the enterprises have actively explored the international market and got involved in the infrastructure construction and industrial investment of countries along the belt and road, whether there are problems of poor implementation and bad effect of policies, especially problems such as haphazard investment, cutthroat competition, overseas projects that fail to meet the requirements of strategic targets of the state, and those may cause heavy losses and negative global effects; in the courses of the operation of overseas capital and the cooperation with foreign enterprises, whether there are cases of unsuccessful technology introduction, acquisition of important state assets by foreign enterprises, or occupation of the domestic market by foreign agents. Seventh, implement the policies for energy conservation and environmental protection. Audit institutions shall keep an eye on whether the unit energy consumption, the index of chemical oxygen demand (COD), and the discharge of major pollutants such as sulfur dioxide can meet requirements of plans and assignment book concerned, whether there are problems of environmental pollution caused by discharge of pollutants illegally, and whether business activities are in accordance with the regulatory and binding requirements in terms of resource utilization and environment protection of the state.

Initiating the Development Programs. The formulation and implementation of development programs of enterprises in economic responsibility audit aim to guide them to recognize the status quo and development tendency, fully mobilize favorable factors and effectively mitigate business risks on the strength of following the macro policy orientation of the state. The main content consists of two parts: first, whether the development program formulated conforms to the national policy-oriented work. To point out underlying problems, development programs of enterprises shall be considered in comparison to the ones made for industrial development by related government organs, and check whether they tally with the national requirements. Obligatory targets mentioned in industry development plans shall, in particular, be paid close attention to. Moreover, audit institutions shall also attach importance to activities of directing staff in their terms of office, and check whether there is absence of clear business and development strategy, whether there are mishaps of haphazard development, competitive inferiority and lack of development opportunities or driving force because of malpractice, whether the development strategies are designed deviating from the reality or the main business, whether there are problems of overexpansion regardless of the business needs, whether there is waste of resources led by frequent changes of development strategies, and whether the sustainable and healthy development has been achieved. In the meanwhile, the economic responsibility audit of persons in charge of SOEs should be carried out from the perspective of audit investigation, and audit institutions shall watch closely whether the similar contents in development programs of different enterprises will cause latent risks which may threat the major guiding principles and policies of the state on the whole. Second, whether the implementation of development programs conform to the national policy orientation. Audit institution shall focus on whether there are problems of "deviation" or "deformation", and check whether there are cases of violation against state policies.

Completing Targets of Assessment of Liabilities. The targets of establishing the assessment of liabilities are of great significance to encourage enterprises to actively adapt to the new normal of China's economy as well as the general tendency of reformation and development, rearrange the economic structure, transform the mode of economic development, accelerate the economic readjustment for higher quality and efficiency, carry out social responsibilities and make the Chinese economy stronger, better and greater on the whole. At present, the targets of assessment of liabilities signed between related departments supervising over state-owned assets and leaders of SOEs, including assessment targets of business performance, energy conservation and emission reduction, and safety production, should be taken seriously as important items of economic responsibility audit. First, the completion of the assessment of business performance. Audit in this aspect focuses on whether enterprises have accomplished the targets of assessment of business performance agreed in liability statements signed with regulatory departments. According to the Interim Measures for the Assessment of the Business Performance of Responsible Persons of Central Enterprises and other acts, indicators for performance appraisal of persons in charge of SOEs include: basic financial indicators such as total profit, economic value added (EVA), hedging and proliferating ratios of state-owned assets and average growth rate of prime operating revenue, classified financial indicators such as the ratio of total cost to main business revenue and the velocity of liquid assets, as well as other industrial indicators. The Supplementary Provisions on the Performance Assessment of Responsible Persons of Central Enterprises release the classified economic indicators of enterprises of industry, aviation, water transport, electricity, commerce and trade, as well as research and design, such as generating capacity, electricity sales, proven reserves of petroleum, petroleum production, etc. Second, the completion of targets of energy conservation and emission reduction. Audit in this regard focuses on whether enterprises have achieved the energy-and-emission-related targets within their duties. For instance, audit institutions shall pay attention to whether major targets of energy conservation and emission reduction such as the comprehensive energy consumption per ¥10,000 (ruling price), chemical oxygen demand (COD), sulfur dioxide emission and coal consumption for energy generation can reach the standard according to the liability statements signed between persons in charge of enterprises and regulatory department. Third, the completion of safety production. Audit in this connection focuses on whether enterprises have fulfilled the indicators of safety production issued by state-owned supervision organs, and audit institutions shall pay attention to whether indicators of safety production such as mortality of production accident can reach the standard in the light of the liability statements.

In terms of audit evaluation indicators, the implementation of a specific policy and decision arrangement during the tenure of the leaders of auditees is considered as a significant criterion. Indicators classified by nature include:

(1) economic indicators, including basic financial indicators such as total profit, economic value added (EVA), hedging and proliferating ratios of state-owned states and average growth rate of prime operating revenue, classified financial indicators such as the ratio of total cost to main business revenue and the velocity of liquid assets, and industrial indicators such as generating capacity, electricity sales, proven reserves of petroleum and petroleum production;

(2) business indicators, which are specifically tailored to industries where enterprises are located and the current level of operation and management;

(3) policy indicators, including targets of energy conservation and emission reduction, such as the comprehensive energy consumption per ¥10,000 (ruling price), chemical oxygen demand (COD), sulfur dioxide emission and coal consumption for energy generation; safety production indicators, such as the mortality of production accident; as well as indicators of policies on shutting down outdated production facilities, such as the elimination times for traditional industries with high energy consumption and high emission, such as

steel, electrolytic aluminum, calcium carbide, ferroalloy, coke, automobile manufacture, cement, coal, electricity and textile; and other indicators for performance check such as the proportion of major investments in line with industrial policies and the finishing rate of the system of tenure accountability.

Major Economic Decision-Making

Major economic decision-making of the enterprise refers to the significant decision which matters to the current operating management and will impact the future development made by the leading staff during the term of office, mainly including outbound investments, engineering constructions, capital operation, assets disposal, supplies (service) purchasing and loans on security of great importance. The audit evaluation of major economic decision-making of enterprises aims emphatically to exposing the problems in the process of decision-making and pointing out possible losses, promoting enterprises to establish and perfect the systems and procedures of all economic decisions-making, boosting the decision-making in a democratic, scientific and lawful way, averaging up the management and decision-making, encouraging enterprises to toe the line of financial regulations, and maintain the security of state-owned assets.

In regard to audit content, audit institutions shall reflect the formulation and implementation of major economic decisions-making and procedures as well as their effect in a fair, objective, practical and realistic way.

Establishing the System. First, formulate the systems and procedures for major economic decisions-making. For audit institutions, it is necessary to master all systems and procedures related to the management of major decisions made by the leaders of the auditees during their tenure, including the scope of application, the entry-into-force time and the revocation date, and fully understand the newly formulated and revised systems and procedures related to decision-making as well as the main content. Second, whether the systems of major economic decision-making are sound. Audit institutions shall focus on whether the systems can cover the mechanism of decision-making, implementation, supervision, assessment and accountability, and whether important links such as "public participation, expert argumentation, risk assessment, legitimacy review and collective discussion and decision-making" have been clearly defined.

Contents and Procedures of Major Economic Decision-Making. First, major outbound investment, including establishing new companies with various assets in addition to existing enterprises, and long-term equity investment by taking shares and jointly operating. In such cases, audit institutions shall emphasize on whether there are feasibility study reports, whether the final decisions are made after multivariant comparative optimization and scientific demonstration, whether the investment is democratically determined, examined and approved in line with regulations, whether there are cases of heavy losses to enterprises caused by arbitrariness or violation against relevant laws led by leading cadres, whether the investment projects are implemented in accordance with major principles, decisions and arrangements, as well as the state industrial policies, whether the development programs are carried out with the main business as the core, whether there are redundant construction projects, whether the structure of investment on the whole is reasonable, and whether the investment projects are strictly managed. Second, major construction projects, which refer to business activities in which an enterprise upgrades its equipment or improves its techniques, and investment for the construction of new sites for production and operation, with the purpose of maintaining or expanding its business scale. Audit institutions shall mainly inspect whether there are compliant documents about project approval and feasibility study reports, whether there are official documents issued by agencies in charge of land and environmental protection, whether the construction projects are implemented in line with fundamental policies, decision arrangements and industrial policies of the state, whether the projects are carries out focusing on main businesses, whether the investment structure is reasonable, whether there are problems of repeated construction, extravagance and waste as well as illegal construction of buildings, etc., whether appropriate bidding procedures are adopted in accordance with the regulations, whether there are problems of bidding collusion and manipulations of bidding results, whether the project decisions are made through collective research and democratic decision-making process, and whether there are major economic losses to enterprises caused by simplified decision-making procedures, arbitrariness and abuse of power of leading cadres. Third, major capital operation, which refers to all types of mergers and reorganizations and other trading activities of stock rights, share options and other financial derivative instruments with the purpose of short-term holding. In this field, audit institutions shall mainly inspect whether there are feasibility study reports, whether the decisions are made through comparative optimization and scientific verification, whether the trading activities have been reported to relevant agencies for approval and confirmation as required, whether the objects have been evaluated, audited, inquired for credit status and issued with legal documents by relevant intermediary agencies, whether relevant units have fulfilled their necessary procedures of announcements and the obligation to disclose required information, whether enterprises have paid necessary attention to the property rights and access qualification if the recipient when it comes to the purchase of equity of non-state-owned enterprises, whether the decisions are made through collective research and democratic decision-making process, whether there are economic losses caused by arbitrariness and violation against regulations of leading cadres, whether the fundamental policies and decision arrangements are implemented strictly, whether the current program conforms to the development strategy of the enterprise and whether the targets have been achieved, whether there are losses to state-owned assets and revenues led by improper capital operation. For the stock, futures, options and other financial derivative instruments, audit institutions shall focus on whether the procedures for internal control are sound, whether there are sturdy and complete operation plans and procedures, whether a corresponding committee for risk control has been set up, whether the feasibility study is sufficient, whether an efficient method for risk control is established, whether a proper loss limit is set, whether the staff are qualified to meet the business needs or have the prescribed qualifications, whether the incompatible posts are completely separated, whether the procedures of decision-making are in compliance with regulations and carried out strictly in line with requirements, whether there are rule-operation for speculative purposes, whether relevant risks are effectively controlled, whether necessary regulatory measures have been taken for the investment funds, whether relevant funds are safe, whether there are kerb transactions, whether the situation of profit and loss is true, and whether the post-investment assessment has been carried out regularly. Fourth, major assets disposal, which refers to activities of disposing and cleaning up the equipment, equity and other assets owned by the enterprises. Audit institutions in this field shall mainly inspect whether the disposal of assets has gone through collective research and democratic decision-making, whether there are huge economic losses to enterprises caused by arbitrariness and abuse of power of leading cadres, whether the disposals of property have been examined or approved by relevant departments, whether assets of enterprises are sold or donated without permission, whether there are cases of embezzling public assets for personal benefits, whether the assets are assessed by social intermediary agencies in accordance with regulations, whether there are problems of false write-off and transfer of assets, etc. Fifth, procurement of staple commodities (service), which refers to the purchase of bulk raw materials, power, equipment and important labor services. In this field, audit institutions shall focus on whether items of bulk purchase have been in annual purchase plans or confirmed by budget approvals, whether the decisions are made through collective research and democratic decision-making, whether there are huge economic losses to enterprises because of arbitrariness and abuse of power of leading cadres, whether appropriate bidding procedures are adopted in line with regulations, whether the bidding procedures are in line with regulations, whether there are problems of bidding collusion and manipulations of bidding results, whether credit investigation has been conducted, whether the suppliers are appointed against the rules, whether there are extra costs caused by purchasing links artificially added, and whether there are quality problems and loss or waste in procurement. Sixth, major loans on security. On this issue, audit institutions shall mainly inspect whether major guarantees and outbound loans are in accordance with the decision-making process, whether the decisions are made through collective discussion, whether the credit status of both the secured party and the fund users has been investigated, whether businesses such as guarantee, mortgage and pledge are made in line with provisions, whether counter-guarantee agreements have been signed, whether economic guarantees to other units are made without authorization, whether stakeholders have lent funds to private enterprises without permission, whether the lent-out funds are effectively monitored, whether necessary measures can be taken timely in case of possible losses, and whether there are problems of economic loss caused by joint liability or difficult recovery of the principal and interest of the lent funds.

Implementing Major Economic Decisions. First, whether major economic decisions are carried out timely and strictly. On this issue, audit institutions mainly check whether the launch time and the implementation time span of each link are in line with expectations, whether the implementation process is consistent with the content of decisions, and whether the implementation is adjusted without approval. Second, whether the implementation of major economic policies is effectively supervised. Audit institutions shall focus on whether leading personnel have implemented effective supervision over major decisions-making, solved the problems appeared in the process of implementation timely and accurately, adjusted the major decisions-making in a timely manner according to the new problems and conditions, taken corrective measures to cope with the problems in the process of implementation, and implemented the mechanism and system of accountability. Third, whether the major economic decisions have achieved the expected targets. Audit institutions shall focus on whether there are problems of low executive capacity, poor implementation and failure to achieve the expected targets, whether major economic issues have realized the anticipative economic, social and environmental benefits, and whether there are problems of low decision-making efficiency, waste of funds, losses of state-owned assets and damage for ecological environment caused by implementation deviations.

In terms of audit evaluation indicators, since major economic decisions cover a wide range of contents, including both the procedural contents and effect contents, the evaluation of major economic decisions of enterprises shall adhere to the principle of combining quantitative and qualitative methods. There are 4 major evaluation indicators:

(1) proportion of illegal decisions, which can clearly reflect the compliance of decisions.

(2) proportion of the amount of money related to illegal decisions, which can reflect the compliance of decisions from another perspective.

(3) effect of major economic decisions. For audit institutions, qualitative description is adopted to reflect the various effects of major economic decisions on enterprises.

(4) risk and loss ratio of decisions. The loss and risk of decision-making cab ne reflected by calculating the proportion of decision errors or risks involved in the total amount of the major decision-making items examined by the audit.

Financial Revenues and Expenditures

As the basic content of economic responsibility audit of SOEs, audit of financial revenues and expenditures aims to evaluate and inspect the accounting information of enterprises and the financial activities it reflects, other economic information and the authenticity, legality and efficiency of the economic activities. In terms of audit content, it is one of the paramount contents of the economic responsibility audit of the persons in charge of SOEs to supervise over the assets, liabilities, profits and losses and related economic activities with the financial accounting statements as the general catalogue and business as well as capital flows as the guidance.

Assets. Assets audit is mainly to determine whether

216

the assets recorded in balance sheets are real, whether all information on assets should be recorded is archived, whether the assets on file are owned or controlled by auditees, and whether provision of impairment loss of assets is reasonable and accurate. Among them, the audit of the authenticity and legality of assets is a link of great significance to supervise the maintenance and appreciation of state-owned assets, as well as an important premise and basis for the audit of liabilities and profits and losses. Enterprises assets mainly include fixed assets, long-term equity investment, inventory as well as other items. First, fixed assets. Audit institutions on this issue mainly focus on whether the internal control systems of fixed assets of auditees are sound and effective, whether the items of fixed assets listed in balance sheets are real, whether the use of such items is restricted, whether the assets are owned by auditees, whether the fixed assets are priced and the capital expenditures and revenues expenditures are divided correctly, whether the current fixed assets business is recorded in the account timely and correctly and shown truthfully in balance sheets, whether the depreciation methods of fixed assets are compliant and consistent, whether the period of depreciation and salvage value estimation are reasonable, whether the calculation of depreciation is right, whether the liquidation records of fixed assets are true and complete, whether the ending balance is correct, and whether the financial statements can truthfully disclose the related information. Second, long-term equity investment. Audit institutions shall focus on two aspect: first, whether the confirmation basis of the classification and methods of long-term equity is sufficient. The effectiveness of long-term equity investment and accounting method can be judged through the classification of control, joint control and significant influence. Second, whether the accounting treatment of equity accounting is correct. For long-term equity investment obtained by enterprises via cash payment, audit institutions mainly check whether the investment is correctly measured by cost, and whether there are cash dividends or profits which have been declared by investors but have not been paid yet in the payment. For long-term equity investment obtained by issuing equity securities, audit institutions shall mainly inspect whether the measure of the cost of investment is accurate, whether the enterprise investors determine the investment costs according to the value agreed by the parties in the contract agreement when investing in the long-term equity investment of the enterprise with the investment held in the third party, and whether the agreed value is unfair. Third, inventory audit. audit institutions shall keep an eye on whether the inventories are real, have been recorded, owned or controlled by auditees and recorded in balance sheets with appropriate amounts. Fourth, accounts receivable. Audit institutions shall mainly check whether relevant financial indicators related to accounts receivables, such as the ratio of cumulative amounts of accounts receivable to prime operating income, the turnover rate as well as days of turnover of accounts receivable, are reasonable or not, and whether auditees have inflated the accounts receivable.

Liabilities. Liability audit mainly aims to determine

whether liabilities recorded in balance sheets exist, whether all liabilities are recorded, whether auditees regard the recorded liabilities as current obligations instead of ones in the future, whether the liabilities are formed legally and rationally, whether the debt-to-assets ratio is too high for enterprises, and whether the enterprises are plagued by awkward situation of insolvency. According to the classification of contents, debts can be divided into circulating debts, including short-term loans, accounts receivable, deposits received, other payables, payroll payable, tax payable, profits payable, other payables, accrued expenses, etc., and long-term debts, including long-term loans, bonds payable and long-term payables, etc. Among them, 3 aspects shall be specifically focused on: first, accounts payable. It is audit institutions' duty to judge whether the composition of the balance of current accounts payable, number of days of purchase on credit, long-term buying on credit, ratio of accounts payable to current goods in stock, ratio of accounts payable to circulating liabilities, increase or decrease of accounts payables and other changes are reasonable or not. Audit institutions shall also judge whether there are liabilities out of the account by paying attention to off-book data, whether there are accounts payable which have not entered into the account in time, as well as the authenticity of accounts payable, etc. Second, long-term loans. On this issue, audit institutions mainly focus on the internal control system, authenticity and compliance of long-term loans, the use of funds in line with the investment projects, the accounting of interests on long-term borrowings, and the solvency of enterprises.

Third, long-term accounts payable. Audit institutions on this issue shall mainly inspect whether the internal control system and its implementation measures are sound and effective, whether the long-term accounts payable are real, whether other revenues are falsely established and concealed, whether it is appropriate to transfer the short-term payables into long-term ones, whether the long-terms payables listed in financial statements are real, and whether enterprises have falsified the asset-liability ratio by falsely listing figures on the statements.

Owners' Equity. The audit of owners' equity chiefly aims to check whether the owner's equity recorded in the balance sheets really exists, whether all owners' equities have been out on record, whether the increase or decrease of owners' equity comply with the provisions of laws, regulations, contracts and articles of incorporation, whether the appropriate amount of owners' equity has been recorded in financial statements, whether the distribution of profits conforms to provisions of the Company Law, and whether the accrual, handover and use of budget funds of state-owned capital are in keeping with regulations. First, paid-in capital. Audit institutions at this point shall inspect whether the invested capital is real, whether investors have delivered the investment at the time and in the way stipulated in the contract, agreement and articles of association, whether auditees and their subsidiaries, joint ventures and associated enterprises are holding shares in violation against regulations, and examine the reasons for the increase and decrease of paid-in capital (share capital). Second, capital reserve. Audit institutions shall mainly check whether businesses such as capital stock premium, paid-in capital transferred from capital reserve, stock repurchase, etc. are authorized by internal and external laws, and whether the capital reserve has been properly presented in financial statements in line with provisions of Accounting Standards for Business Enterprises (ASBE). Third, surplus reserve. In this field, audit institutions primarily check whether the accrual of legal surplus reserve and arbitrary surplus reserve are in compliance in terms of the order, base and proportion, whether the shrink of surplus reserve is in compliance, whether the accounting treatment has made right choices in accordance with resolutions of the board of directors and the general meeting of stakeholders, and whether the surplus reserve has been properly presented in financial statements in line with the ASBE. Fourth, undistributed profits. Audit institutions on this issue mainly check whether the profit distribution is legal, whether the accounting treatment of changes in undistributed profits is correct, and whether the undistributed profits have been properly presented in financial statements in accordance with the ASBE. Fifth, the budget of state-owned capital. Audit institutions shall principally check whether the users have employed the project funds according to the prescribed purposes, paid attention to the progress, further promoted the efficiency of the use of funds, and standardized the management of funds, and whether the owners' equity are transferred to the state in time as required.

Profit and Loss. The audit of profit and loss chiefly

aims to check whether the revenue of recognition of the enterprise is correct, whether the cost accounting is real, and whether there are artificial adjustment of profits and losses. In addition, the inspections shall be focused on whether enterprises have adjusted the profits and losses by concealing or falsely increasing the product output or sales volume, retained the revenues for their own use, set up concealed accounts for fictitious costs, given out bonus to the staff violating against regulations, and embezzled or divided the public funds, and whether there are problems such as whitewashing performance and adjusting profits for the completion of evaluation indicators. First, main business income. Audit institutions on this issue shall mainly judge whether the indicators, including sales proceeds and operational cash flows, sales proceeds and production capacity, accounts receivable and rate of increase of sales revenue, the ratio of reserve for bad-debt to accounts receivable, gross profit rate of assets and the staple of the current period, and turnover rates of accounts receivable as well as inventories, are reasonable or not, whether the recognition criteria and methods of the prime operating revenue conform to the relevant provisions of the ASBE, whether the confirmation methods of the revenues of long-term contracts are compliant and reasonable, whether there are physical flows in the distributing business, whether enterprises have gone through approval procedures of sales on account and consignment by paying attention to the bill of sales corresponding to sales entries in subsidiary accounts of the prime operating revenue, whether enterprises have affiliated parties, and whether there are transfers of profits. Second, main business cost. Audit institutions shall inspect whether the main business costs in the profit statement have incurred and are related to auditees, whether all main business costs have been recorded, whether the amount and other data related to the main business costs have been recorded properly in the correct accounting period, and whether the necessary data has been properly presented in the financial statements in line with the ASBE. Third, administrative expense. On this issue, audit institutions shall check whether the administrative expenses in the financial statements have incurred and are related to auditees, whether all administrative expenses have been put on record, whether the amount and other data related to administrative expenses have been recorded properly in the correct accounting period, and whether the necessary data has been properly presented in the financial statements in line with the ASBE.

In terms of audit evaluation indicators, the evaluation criteria of financial revenue and expenditure mainly includes authenticity and legitimacy, as well as efficiency.

(1) Authenticity and legitimacy. First, whether there are major violations against laws and regulations or not, which is the basic qualitative evaluation indicator. Second, the compliance rate of financial revenues and expenditures, which can reflect the real and legal situation of financial revenues and expenditures quantitatively. The calculation formula is: compliance rate of financial revenues and expenditures = the number of cases of illegal financial revenues and expenditures confirmed by the audit / the number of cases spot checked by the audit * 100%.

(2) Efficiency, which mainly includes profit ratio of sales, rate of return on total assets, rate of return on capital, rate of maintenance and appreciation of capital, debt-to-assets ratio, quick ratio, turnover rate of accounts receivable, turnover rate of inventories, as well as the growth rate of revenue of profit of main business.

Internal Management

Internal management is of great significance for leading cadres of SOEs to fulfill their economic responsibilities, perform their fiduciary duties, and administrate their enterprises. In terms of audit content, audit evaluation mainly focuses on 4 aspects, including corporate governance structure, management level of the enterprise, total risk management and compensation management.

Corporate Governance Structure. Corporate governance structure of SOEs is designed mainly to resolve the division of responsibilities, rights and interests among all stakeholders composing the enterprises, and to achieve the mutual checks and balances through a battery of system regulations. The narrow sense of corporate governance structure mainly refers to the relationships among the general meeting of stakeholders, the board of directors, the board of supervisors and the executive management. There are chiefly 5 aspects concerned in the economic responsibility audit of SOEs. First, organizational structure. Audit institutions shall check whether enterprises have established the organizational structure according to the Company Law and other laws as well as articles of association, formulated the working system and rules of procedures of "three boards and one management", established sound mechanisms for the operation pf governance, which can effectively motivate and restrict the staff, and brought the party committee into the corporate governance structure of SOEs as required by the Central Committee. Second, the board of directors. Audit institutions shall be careful on whether the board of directors has set up special committee in line with relevant laws and regulations and clarified the responsibilities, rights, obligations and accountability systems of each special committee, whether the enterprises have been equipped with enough independent directors who can make independent judgements as well as check and supervise the business circumstances and connected transactions of the enterprises, whether the board can strengthen the routine supervision of independent directors as independence, whether the board is clear about the working instructions as well as the scope of responsibilities, rights and interests of each executives, whether a strict accountability mechanism has been set up and implemented in actual businesses, and whether employee directors have been endowed with the institutional guarantee to effectively perform their duties, with the purpose of safeguarding the democratic rights of the staff and promoting the harmonious development of the enterprise. Third, the board of supervisors. On this issue, audit institutions shall keep an eye on whether the board of supervisors, as an internal supervisory organization in corporate governance, has set up the mechanism for supervision, risk prevention and responsibility investigation, fulfilled the function of supervision over the board of directors and the executive management, and put forward suggestions or inquiries on problems discovered, whether the board has supervised over the operating management of the enterprises, such as operating decisions, risk management and internal control, and guided the work of auditing departments inside the enterprises, and whether the board of directors and the executive management have corrected the major problems pointed out in the process of decision-making and operation management. Fourth, the executive management. Audit institutions shall mainly check whether the executive management, as the major organizer of the operation and management of the enterprises, performs its duties in a diligent and responsible manner, complies with laws, administrative regulations and articles of association, and reports the signing and implementing of major contracts, the use of funds, as well as profit and loss of the enterprises to the boards of directors and supervisors timely, whether the executive management can put the national interests first incase of the conflict between interests of their own and the state-owned assets, effectively protect the legitimate interests of investors of the state-owned assets, and promote the efficient development and operation of the enterprises. Fifth, the general meeting of stakeholders. In this aspect, audit institutions shall mainly check whether the convening of the meeting is in compliance with the provisions, whether the major personnel appointment and removal as well as significant operating decisions are approved by the meeting, whether the procedures of decision-making can meet the requirements and effectively safeguard the interests of all stakeholders.

Management Level of the Enterprises. From the perspective of the status quo of development, SOEs in China are still obsessed with the problem of too many management levels, which may easily cause defects such as overstaffing in organizations, out-of-control supervision and administration, lower decision-making efficiency, higher management costs, and negative impact on competitiveness. In addition, it is also one of the important reasons for the loss to the state-owned assets. The State-owned Assets Supervision and Administration Commission (SASAC) of the State Council issued the guiding ideas on promoting central enterprises to sort out and integrate their affiliated companies and reduce the levels of management. In 2016, the SASAC once again encouraged the central enterprises to simplify the management and cut down the numbers of juridical entities. In the economic responsibility audit of leaders of SOEs, there are mainly two aspects that should be noted: first, reduce the management levels. Audit institutions shall inspect whether the enterprises have implemented the requirements of the SASAC to reduce the management levels to 3 or 4, and whether there are problems of low management efficiency and frequent violations against regulations caused by too many levels or overlong chains of management. Second, strengthen the resource integration. Audit institutions shall mainly check whether enterprises have fulfilled the requirements of the SASAC to cut down the number of legal entities to the expected ratio, whether unprofitable firms and zombie enterprises have been shut down, merged or transferred according to corresponding regulations, whether the relations of property, labor and administrative subordination of restructured enterprises have been duly handled, whether the enterprises after reorganization of sub-business can truly be independent market subjects, whether the reform of the main body business is closely combined to the restructure of sub-business and the separation of main and auxiliary businesses, and whether the transformation of operating mechanism of main body enterprises is organically combined with the creation of conditions for the reorganization of the sub-businesses.

Total Risk Management. The total risk management of SOEs aims to control the risk within the acceptable range to ensure the true and credible internal or external information communication, especially between the enterprises and stakeholders, the compliance to relevant laws and regulations, the effectiveness of administrative management and the contingency plans on major risk treatment, with the purpose of averting heavy economic losses. In this aspect, the economic responsibility of persons in charge of SOEs shall mainly focus on two things: first, the construction of risk management system. On this issue, audit institutions shall mainly inspect whether the enterprises have established a comprehensive risk management system including the function system covering risk management strategy, measures concerning risk financing and the organization of risk management, the information system and the internal control system, whether the risk is controlled within the affordable range that is compatible with the overarching objective, whether the enterprises are faced with major risk or marred by unsustainable and unstable development because the main business is unremarkable, the profit made by the main business accounts for a low proportion of the total, and the profit mainly comes from the contribution of non-principal businesses characterized by strong market cyclicality and fierce market fluctuations, especially the industries emphatically regulated by the state, and whether the enterprises are in the face of shoals in high-risk areas of safety production, major capital operation, investment and acquisition, trade of financial derivatives, etc. Second, the establishment of s sound internal control system. On this issue, audit institutions shall check the implementation and effect of the internal control system, whether the system runs through the whole process of decision-making, implementation and supervision, and whether there are cases of poor or slack implementation in the aspects of financial management, investment and financing, strategic planning, sales, environmental protection and other internal systems.

Compensation Management. With the purpose of encouraging the compensation management to play its proper role, namely taking legitimacy, efficiency and equity into account in structural design and routine management, bringing the greatest value to the enterprise with proper payroll cost, boosting distribution justice, process justice and opportunity justice, and ensuring that the system of benefit packages are in line with the regulations of state laws, regional administrative regulations and ordinances of policies, the economic responsibility audit of persons in charge of SOEs shall mainly focus on 3 aspect: first, salary administration of enterprises. On this issue, audit institutions shall mainly inspect whether the compensation gap in SOEs among different industries is too large, reflecting the problems of imbalance among industries, disequilibrium of internal distribution of salaries and excessively high renumeration in monopolized industries, and analyze what caused the more liberal wages of the staff in monopolized industries, the unreasonable and unsound system of distribution, trade monopoly, or non-standard income distribution? Second, compensation management system implemented by enterprises. Audit institutions shall check whether SOEs have established and perfected the internal distribution mechanism according to provisions of the system, and whether there are problems such as poor implementation, extra expenditures for wages in addition to the total wage bill, misuse of the active balance of wage, paying bonuses to the staff and buying shopping cards by withholding the revenues and making false reports to collecting money, disbursing expenditures for wages from employee services and benefits in the mane of distributing welfare, giving out bonus out of scope, disbursing and supplementing endowment insurance (annuity) beyond standard, implementing the occupational pension system illegally, turning in the housing provident funds exceeding the standards, failing to pay the due social insurance and housing provident funds of the employees, and illegally determining the base of total wage bill as the accrual basis. Third, the salary administration of persons in charge of enterprises. On this issue, audit institutions mainly check whether the compensation solutions of persons in charge are examined, approved and put on records according to the administration authority, whether the salaries of persons in charge of central enterprises can reach the standards made by the Central Committee, whether the leaders of SOEs can get other payment in addition to the pay package, whether there are cases that leaders of SOEs set the salary standards for themselves, ask for high salaries beyond standard, take extra salary by holding several posts simultaneously, and obtaining surplus incomes in disguised form, whether enterprises have born the costs of insurance, taxes and other fees that should have been paid by individual for their leaders, whether the system of position-related consumption of persons in charge is open and transparent, and whether the mechanism of stock option incentive for the management is sound.

In terms of audit evaluation indicators, this part plays a role as qualitative analysis, and the quantitative indicators are just for reference. The main evaluation indicators include:

(1) The compliance rate of decision-making of "Three Majors and One Large" (major decisions, major cadres' appointment and approval, major project arrangement, use of large amount of funds), which reflects the whether the corporate governance structure can normally perform its duty. The calculating formula is as follows: the compliance rate = number of events in compliance / number of all events * 100%.

(2) The soundness rate of the internal control system, which reflects the health of the system. The calculating formula is as follow: the soundness rate = number of perfect internal control systems / number of internal control systems of enterprises * 100%.

(3) The number of management levels of enterprises, which reflects the effectiveness of simplified management.

(4) The implementation rate of the internal control system, which reflects the implementation effect of the internal control system. The calculating formula is as follows: the implementation rate = number of effective implementations in the internal control system / number of major internal control systems spot checked.

(5) The ratio of vertical compression in the enterprise, which reflects the compensation gap within the enterprise. The calculating formula is as follows: the ratio of vertical compression = the highest salary / the lowest salary * 100%.

Self-Dependent Innovation

Currently speaking, China's national economy is undergoing the critical period of the superposition of three economic stages, namely the stages of shifts of economic growth bracket, throes of economic structural adjustment and digestion of policies issued earlier. Plagued by a raft of overlapped structural conflicts, China's economy is under the increasingly larger downward pressure. To cope with the new normal, the fundamental path of reform and development for SOEs is to transfer the traditional factor-driven growth to the new growth mode relying on innovation, realize the organic unification of institutional innovation, technological innovation and management innovation. Allowing for its promotion of significance in the economic responsibility audit of persons in charge of SOEs, it is necessary to audit self-dependent innovation as an independent aspect. For enterprises, self-dependent innovation covers institutional innovation, technological innovation and management innovation, and it is the duty of the audit to grasp the overall situation of the self-dependent innovation of the enterprises, disclose and reflect the prominent problems, distinguish the responsibilities in decision-making, implementation, management and other stages, accurately define the economic responsibilities of leading cadres, promote the continuous improvement of the self-dependent innovation capacities of the enterprises, encourage the amelioration of the innovation-driven mechanisms, effectively guard against risks, and constantly boost the core competitiveness. In the aspect of audit content, this part majorly covers the scientificity, effect and risk control in the process of decision-making.

Scientificity of Self-Dependent Innovation. First, self-dependent policy of the state. On this issue, audit institutions shall pay attention to whether enterprises have earnestly implemented the policies and requirements on constructing an innovative-oriented country, whether long-term plans for self-dependent innovation have been made according to the characteristics of the enterprises themselves, and whether there are problems of poor implementation of state policies, absence of scientific plans on self-dependent innovation and impractical self-dependent innovative strategies. Second, strategic plans on self-dependent innovation made by the enterprise. Audit institutions shall inspect whether enterprises have formulated strategic plans and concrete implementation programs in line with their actual situation, and whether the strategies and programs and operable and have been scientifically verified. In addition, audit institutions shall also keep an eye on the implementation and effects of the plans on the sustainable development of enterprise, including the self-dependent innovation, product development, investment projects at home and abroad, capital management and market exploitation.

Effect of Self-Dependent Innovation. First, the authenticity of business of self-dependent innovation. Audit institutions shall check documentary evidence of the enterprise, including relevant documents of promoting and implementing self-dependent innovation business as well as independent intellectual property rights, analyze the general situation of the self-dependent innovation of enterprises, evaluate the capacity and mechanism of self-dependent innovation, assess the overall level in the field of self-dependent innovation by comparing the relevant data and standards of the same industries at home and overseas, and judge whether there are problems of unreasonable system and poor implementation and whether the current system is conducive to the development of innovative business by checking the self-dependent mechanism of enterprises. Second, the profitability of self-dependent innovation. On this issue, audit institutions shall examine the implementation effect, technological research and development, as well as capital investment and its management of the strategies of self-dependent innovation and market exploitation, inspect the profitability of innovative products and their impact on the overall business performance, check whether the profitability structure of the enterprise is reasonable, whether the enterprise is plagued with the problems of unstable and unsustainable growth, blind expansion of the scale of production in the area of innovation, and idleness, waste as well as poor quality of assets. By checking the investment and use of self-dependent innovation and the relevant scientific research and development, audit institutions can verify the authenticity of profits achieved by innovative projects. Moreover, it is also important to check whether the innovative business has achieved the expect effect and whether the economic and social benefits have been realized by calculating financial indicators of the enterprises such as the profit margin of innovative products and businesses as well as the economic value added, and comparing the feasibility study reports with the expected targets.

Risk-Control of Self-Dependent Innovation. In this area, audit institutions shall mainly focus on potential dangers of innovation businesses of the enterprises in the aspect of policy, law, economy and finance. It is necessary for audit institutions to check whether there are underlying economic losses to the enterprise due to problems of failure of technology introduction or development, dispute over patents of innovative issues, assurance of support, lawsuits pending, and debt that cannot be repaid on schedule incurred by the enterprise in financing independent innovation, whether the internal and external environment of the enterprise is suitable for self-dependent innovation, whether the enterprise has established concrete measures for risk factors in the initial assessment, whether the enterprise is faced with major financial risks caused by projects of self-dependent innovation, whether corresponding measures of risk control and prevention have been laid down, and whether there are economic losses to state-owned assets led by inadequacy of risk assessment and ineffectiveness of risk prevention.

In terms of audit evaluation indicators, this part mainly selects the innovation achievements of enterprises, the input-output ratio of R&D, the output ratio of new product, etc.

(1) Growth rate of independent intellectual property rights

The growth rate of independent intellectual property rights = the increase of independent intellectual property rights / the total number of independent intellectual property rights before the terms of office of the current leading cadres * 100%.

(2) Rate of technology autonomy

The rate of technology autonomy = number of independent intellectual property rights / (number of technology introduction + number of independent intellectual property rights) * 100%.

(3) Input-output ratio of self-dependent innovative technologies

The input-output ratio of self-dependent innovative technologies = operation revenue of a single self-dependent innovation project / total amount invested.

(4) The number of industrialized technological achievements and the level of efficiency

Quantitative description

(5) Input-output ratio of scientific R&D

The input-output ratio of scientific R&D = total scientific research input / total expenditure of the enterprise * 100%.

(6) Growth rate of investment to scientific R&D

The growth rate of investment to scientific R&D of the enterprise = (scientific R&D investment in this year – scientific R&D investment in the previous year) / scientific R&D investment in the previous year * 100%.

(7) Rate of development of new products

The rate of development of new products = the number of new products developed / the number of all products of the enterprises * 100%.

(8) Rate of scientifically and technologically innovative products

The rate of scientifically and technologically innovative products = types (output value) of scientifically and technologically innovative products / type (output value) of all products * 100%.

Overseas Assets Management

With the deepening of the "One Belt and One Road" strategy and the growing outbound investment of SOEs, the overseas assets management has already been major latent risk of the operating management of SOEs, and the state audit has attached increasing importance to the audit work on this issue. As a significant and prominent practical aspect of the economic responsibility of persons in charge of SOEs, the study of overseas assets management shall be treated as an independent aspect. State-owned assets overseas are under the unified management of the state and the supervision of governments at all levels. The Ministry of Finance has formulated a series of unified administrative rules and regulations, and departments of finance (state-owned assets management) at all levels are responsible for the supervision over overseas state-owned assets within the jurisdiction. Government sectors such as the NDRC, the Ministry of Commerce, the SASAC and the China Banking Regulatory Commission (CRBC) shall respectively administer the overseas investment projects of enterprises, subsidiary enterprises set up overseas and the management of overseas assets, and central enterprises are responsible for supervising the state-owned assets of enterprises abroad.

In terms of audit content, major targets of the audit of overseas assets management include: first, encourage persons in charge of SOEs to strictly perform their duties in line with the laws by assessing the implementation of major policies, the deployment of the "Going Global" strategy in management of overseas assets, and the abidance by the laws at home and overseas. Second, promote the management and operation of overseas investment and prevent the risks of outbound investment and overseas operations by evaluating the major economic decision-making on overseas projects of persons in charge of SOEs as well as the establishment, improvement and implementation of the internal control system. Third, prevent the loss and maintain the security of overseas state-owned assets by evaluating the business performance and risk control of overseas assets of persons in charge of SOEs.

Business Strategy of Overseas Investment. First, the rationality of overseas development programs. Audit institutions shall check whether the political measures of the enterprise accord with the "Going Global" and "One Belt and One Road" strategies of the state, whether the decisions made by the enterprise are in line with the industrial policies of overseas investment, the distribution of the state-owned economy, and the direction of structural adjustments, whether there are problems of failure to form corresponding mechanisms for overall coordination, blind investment and even throat-cutting competition, and whether the systems and regulations of overseas assets management made by the enterprise are consistent with relevant state laws. Second, the operation of overseas investment. On this issue, audit institutions shall mainly check whether the status quo of overseas investment and operation accommodates the development programs and international operation capacity of the enterprise, whether policy measures related to overseas investment and operation have been effectively implemented, whether progress in relevant projects have been made, whether the expected targets have been achieved on schedule, whether programs and projects of overseas investment are determined, submitted for approval and put on record according to the established procedures, whether the overseas investment projects of non-main business have gone through sufficient feasibility studies and risk assessment, and have been submitted to competent departments for approval.

Abidance by Laws at Home and Overseas. First, abide by domestic laws and regulations. On this issue, audit institutions shall check whether the businesses abroad of the enterprise including overseas investment, establishment of overseas companies and operation of overseas assets have fulfilled the procedures of examination, filing and registration formulated by the NDRC, the Ministry of Finance and the SASAC, and whether the overseas business related to China-funded commercial banks, insurance companies and securities firms has been licensed and approved by financial regulators. Second, abide by laws of other countries. on this issue, audit institutions shall check whether overseas businesses of the enterprise including outbound investment, project undertaking and capital operation comply with laws and regulations of other countries on investment, industry and environmental protection, whether relevant business activities are carried out in line with international conventions and business rules, and whether there are violations against laws such as offering kickbacks to government officials and non-standard payment of commissions.

Major Overseas Economic Decisions. First, the management system of major overseas economic decisions. Audit institutions shall mainly inspect whether the management system of major overseas economic decisions is sound and up to the mustard of relevant laws and regulations, supervision requirements of the superior, internal control of the enterprise and risk management. Second, the compliance of major overseas economic decisions. In this area, audit institutions shall mainly inspect the overall situation of major overseas economic decisions made during the tenure of persons in charge of the enterprise, including the number of decisions and the amount of money involved, and check whether the items of decision-making conform to relevant laws and regulations,, major economic policies of the state and the requirements of the enterprise's own system, whether there are problems of illegal decision-making and unauthorized approval, whether the decisions are made after sufficient feasibility study, whether the systems of expert consultation, conference discussion and group decision-making are applied, whether there are "reverse procedures" of making decisions before collective discussion because of leaders' intervention into decision-making, and whether there are benefit transfer or abuse of power for personal interests by paying commissions or brokage fees to some certain enterprises, offshore companies and some specific related parties. Third, the effectiveness of major overseas economic decisions. At this point, audit institutions shall check whether the implementation of decision-making items is timely, whether there are problems of readjusting the contents of decisions without authorization and new decision-making, and whether there are heavy economic wastes and losses caused by insufficient investigation of relevant environmental factors, inadequate argument on the prospects of the project, lack of experience in overseas investment, absence of technologies and talents and blind investment.

Internal Control System of Overseas Enterprises. First, corporate governance structure of overseas enterprises. On this issue, audit institutions shall inspect whether overseas enterprises have established corporate governance structures with equal rights and responsibilities, coordinated cooperation and effective mechanism for checks and balances among the board of directors, the board of supervisors and the management in line with laws and regulations of other countries, whether the evaluation methods of directors and the board of directors have been established with the purpose of carrying out periodic assessment on directors, and whether the directors responsible for major decision-making mistakes have been decruited or dismissed and held accountable in due course. Second, internal control system of overseas enterprises. On this issue, audit institutions shall mainly inspect and evaluate whether overseas enterprises have established and improved their systems of financial and assets management, risk management and control, financial budget and final account control, internal audit supervision, examination and evaluation and responsibility investigation, whether the foregoing systems have been strictly implemented, and whether the relevant systems violate laws, regulations and policies, focus on the newly added or changed important overseas businesses and management issues presided by persons in charge of auditees as well as the operation risks, and point out whether the systems of internal control and management have been established without delay, whether the systems are in consistent with laws and regulations and can meet the requirements of overseas business and relevant management, and whether there are institutional defects or loopholes, etc. Third, performance of management and supervision over overseas affiliated enterprises. In the area, audit institutions shall mainly inspect whether there are gross violations against laws and regulations or major operating loss led by the bad performance of persons in charge of auditees on management, whether subordinate enterprises are out of control because of too many levels or overlong chains of management, and whether the job performance of persons in charge on management and supervision over subordinate enterprises is decent. Moreover, to inspect the establishment and improvement, institution setting, work development and work efficiency of the internal system of audit supervision is also important for audit institutions.

Risk Management and Control of Overseas State-Owned Assets Operation. First, the management system of overseas state-owned assets. On this issue, audit institutions shall check whether the management system of overseas state-owned system is sound and consistent with relevant laws and regulations as well as the supervision requirements of the superior, whether the establishment of overseas enterprises has gone through the formalities for the registration of property rights of overseas state-owned assets in line with regulations, whether the enterprises which have to entrust others to hold shares on their behalf to obey the laws of states of registry have made relevant decisions, submitted for approval and handle procedure for preserving the property rights of state-owned assets, whether the enterprises set up for special purposes have been reported for approval, and whether the ones which are not necessary any longer are cancelled timely. Second, the management of overseas investment projects. On this issue, audit institutions shall mainly check whether the projects of overseas investment, significant M&A and asset transference have performed the corresponding procedures of decision-making, submission for approval and assets appraisal, whether there are cases of "overrating and overbuying" such as falsely listing assets, falsely raising costs and overestimating the production capacity, and cases of "underrating and underbuying" such as forcing down prices, hiding assets and concealing the profits, which both cause heavy losses to state-owned assets. Third, the overseas fund management. On this issue, audit institutions mainly inspect whether the overseas funds are managed uniformly, whether the use and dispatch of overseas funds are in line with the corresponding duty and authority, whether the management system of large-sum overseas funds is sound, whether the capital operation in the temporary account is subject to strict examination, approval, supervision and inspection, whether all revenues and profits made by overseas enterprises are remitted back to China in due course, and whether there are problems such as embezzling public funds, setting up private coffers under the rose, and paying commissions, consult fees and agency fees without basis or in a large amount of cash.

Audit evaluation indicators on this issue mainly concern major economic decision-making and the system, abidance to laws and regulations at home and overseas, business performance of overseas assets and risk management and control.

(1) Decision-Making Ratio of Violations against Laws and Regulations of Overseas Enterprise

Calculate the proportion of non-compliant items, so as to reflect the overall performance of decision-making.

(2) Proportion of Amount of Money Relating to Illegal Decision-Making Overseas

Calculate the proportion of funds involved in illegal projects, so as to reflect the losses and risk brought by illegal decision-making.

(3) Loss or Hazard Rate of Overseas Economic Decision-Making

Calculate the proportion of funds involved in decision-making misplay or risks, in order to reflect the economic loss caused by decision failure and risk.

(4) Compliance Rate of Financial Revenues and Expenditures of Overseas Enterprises

This reflects how overseas enterprises follow the rules in terms of financial management. The calculation formula is: compliance rate of financial revenues and expenditures = the number of illegal items of financial revenues and expenditures confirmed by audit institutions / items spot-checked by audit institutions * 100%.

(5) Efficiency of Overseas Assets Management

Many quantitative indicators are involved in this regard, including profit ratio of sales, rate of return on total assets, return on capital employed, hedging and proliferating ratio, asset-liability ratio, quick ratio, turnover rate of accounts receivable, inventory turnover ratio, and revenue growth and profit growth of main businesses. The above-mentioned indictors are all general ones, which require no more detailed description here.

Risk Control

Different from the traditional way of preventing latent hazards, risk control is designed to better cope with the uncertainty and keep it within an acceptable range. Risk control is a significant guarantee for the development of SOEs in modern market economy, and the concept of risk control is embodied in all aspects of the economic responsibilities of persons in charge of SPEs in China. This book believes that the audit of risk control mainly check whether the enterprise has established the risk control system including risk management strategy, risk financing measures, functional system of risk control, information system of risk management and internal control system, whether the risk is kept within the range that is compatible with the overall objective and can be accepted under the given conditions, whether the further development of the enterprise is in the face of major risks or marred by unsustainable and unstable development because the main business is unremarkable, the profit made by the main business accounts for a low proportion of the total, and the profit mainly comes from the contribution of non-principal businesses characterized by strong market cyclicality and fierce market fluctuations, especially the industries emphatically regulated by the state, and whether there are prominent problems in the areas of safety production, major capital operation, investment and acquisition, transaction of derivative, etc.

Construction of Risk Control System. First, the organizational system of risk control. Audit institution shall check whether the responsibilities of department and lead agencies of risk control, internal audit, legal affairs and other issues are clearly defined, whether the three lines of defence for risk control, namely the first one consists of operating departments, the second one consists of the department of risk control and the commission of risk control subordinating to the board of directors, and the third consists of internal audit and the audit committee of the board of directors, have been set up, and whether the general meeting of shareholders, the board of directors, the board of supervisors and managers are effectively balanced. Second, the authorization and the accountability system of positions of risk control. On this issue, audit institutions shall check whether the enterprise has explicitly stipulated the objects, conditions, scope and amount of authorization of each post of risk control, whether persons in charge have made risky determinations ultra vires, whether the responsibility system for risk control and management and the mechanism for the duties, reward and punishment of relevant departments, units, posts and personnel are sound, whether the rights and responsibilities are unified, whether the power restriction system of posts of major risk control is wholesome, and whether the incompatible responsibilities are effectively separated. Third, risk management processes, information channels and information systems. On this issue, audit institutions shall check whether the information communication channels for risk control are sound, whether the reporting relationships, responsibility lines and time limit requirements of risk control matters are clear, whether the approval system for risk control is sound, whether items to be approved, stipulations of examination and approval and division of responsibilities are straightforward, whether the information technology is effectively applied to risk control, and whether the information system, which covers basic procedures of risk management and all links f the internal control, has been established. Fourth, the system for internal inspection and evaluation of function departments of risk control. On this issue, audit institutions shall inspect whether the assessment system is sound, whether the execution of risk control is brought into account, whether the mechanisms for legal risk circumvention and major risk early warning are thorough, whether major risks can be continuously monitored, whether the warning information can be released in due course, and whether the emergency plans are formulated and corrected in a timely manner.

Implementation of Risk Control System. First, collect preliminary information. In this area, audit institutions mainly check whether internal and external risk information on financial affairs, market, operation and laws can be collected continuously in a broad range, and whether the responsibility of collecting the preliminary information is assigned to all relevant departments and business units. Second, assess the risks in time. Audit institutions shall check whether the preliminary information on risk management has been effectively and timely evaluated, and whether business management and other important operation flows have been effectively evaluated. The assessment mentioned here mainly includes the identification, analysis and evaluation of risks. Third, develop strategies of risk control. Audit institutions shall check whether the risk preference and risk tolerance are determined uniformly in line with different business characteristics, whether relevant agencies can correctly understand and grasp the balance between risks and benefits, whether the priority for risk control has been determined to ensure that the risk and benefits are balanced, whether the footwork for risk control can be regularly analyzed and constantly improved, and whether the strategies of risk control are effective. Fourth, develop solutions. On this issue, audit institutions shall check whether the risk control solutions are established by category according to risk control strategies, whether the solutions are equipped with clear objectives, proper organization and leadership, relevant processes, methods and means, resource allocation, etc., whether the solutions are in full compliance with the requirements and in balance with the business strategies and operational efficiency, and whether the key links are especially under control. Fifth, improve the supervision over risk control. At this point, audit institutions mainly supervise the implementation of preliminary information collection, risk assessment, risk control strategies, key control as well as solutions, encourage the timely improvement of the systems by verifying the effectiveness through pressure test, and check whether relevant units have focused on risks, affairs, decisions, management and business processes of great significance.

Control of Events of Major Risks. Events of major risks refers to issues that may cause heavy economic losses to enterprises and state-owned assets, serious production accidents, large risk exposures and wholesome floating loss, and other events that affect the social stability, induce fearful environmental pollution, and undermine the economic and financial security of the state. In principle, events of major risks should be audited term by term, and the audit work on this issue shall deeply analyze such events like determining the loss and liability and cluing violations against laws such as illegal benefit transfer. First, clarify responsibilities. Audit institutions shall determine the relevant economic decisions and operational issues which cause major events, as well as the violations against laws, regulations and disciplines and other misplays in the process of investigation, decision-making, operation and examination and approval, and in the meanwhile determine the liabilities to be borne by persons in charge, and check whether there are violations against laws and internal management regulations by key personnel, especially main responsible persons, in events of major risks, whether procedures without democratic decision-making have been directly nailed down, approved or implemented, whether there are cases of dereliction of duty, poor job performance and misconduct, whether the projects are determined, approved and implemented coercively regardless of disagreement of the majority, whether matters such as conference topics, decisions and the specific execution are subject to the intervention of others, whether there are cases that the decision-making level meddles the management or the management outmatches the decision-making level, whether the events of "Three Majors and One Large" have gone through the necessary procedures for elaborating and demonstrating, and have fully sought for opinions from all parties, and whether there are problems of inadequate conference preparations, incidental motions, main persons in charge setting the tone in advance, and insufficient discussion. Second, assess the loss. On this issue, audit institutions shall, one the one hand, quantitatively assess the specific amount involved in heavy economic loss to the enterprise and state-owned assets, major risk exposures and wholesale floating loss caused by events of major risks, on the other hand, qualitatively assess the fallout that cannot be quantitatively descripted, such as social instability, environmental pollution and damage to the economic and financial security of the state. Third reveal clues. Audit institutions shall inspect whether there are clues of major violations against laws and regulations such as transfer of benefits, abuse of power, power-rent-seeking and peculation of state-owned assets, and try to reveal the deep reasons, point loopholes in management, better prevent and punish corruption, and promote construction of the Party conduct and of an honest and clean government.

In terms of audit evaluation indicators for risk control, this book argues that main indicators related to relevant systems, risk occurrence, loss and other factors should be taken into account.

(1) Health Rate of Risk Management System

This indicator mainly reflects how sound and effective the risk management system is during the target period of audit. the calculation formula is: the health rate of risk control system = the number of risk control systems established or improved during the target period of audit / the number of control systems of the enterprise * 100%.

(2) Implementation Rate of Risk Control System

This indicator is mainly employed to test the effectiveness of the risk control system of the enterprise. The calculation formula is: the implementation rate of risk control system = the number of effective implementation of the risk control system during the target period of audit / the number of important internal control systems spot-checked by audit institutions * 100%.

(3) Incidence Rate of Events of Major Risks

Mainly targeting at events of major risks involved in the decision-making and approval of persons in charge, this indicator measures the occurrence of major risks in an enterprise. The calculation formula is: the incidence rate of events of major risks = the number of events of major risks involved with the decision and approval made by persons in charge during th target period of audit / the number of items related to decision and approval made by persons in charge * 100%.

(4) Loss Rate of Events of Major Risks

This indicator is mainly used to measure the loss caused by events of major risks. The calculation formula is: the loss rate of events of major risks = the amount of loss to the enterprise caused by major risks during the target period of audit / the total assets of the enterprise during the target period * 100%.

(5) Incidence Rate of Violations Involving Major

Risks

This indicator is applied to measure the violation against laws, regulations and disciplines related to the decisions and approval made by persons in charge. The calculation formula is: the incidence rate of violations involving major risks = the number of illegal events of major risks involved with the decision and approval made by persons in charge during the target period of audit / the number of events of major risks related to the decision and approval made by persons in charge * 100%.

(6) Loss Rate of Violations Involving Major Risks

This indicator is usually used to measure the loss caused by violations against disciplines, laws and regulations involving the decisions made by persons in charge. The calculation formula is: the loss rate of violations involving major risks = the amount of loss caused by major risks involving illegal decision-making (approval) of persons in charge during the target period / the amount of loss caused by major risks involving illegal decision-making (approval) of persons in charge during the target period * 100%.

Additionally, it is also important to bring conventional indicators, including profitability, quality of assets, debt risks and business growth, into account to evaluate the risk control and management of the enterprise.

Construction of the Party Conduct and of an Honest and Clean Government

Economic responsibility audit is not only economic supervision, but the supervision over leading cadres. The compound attribute determines that the audit responsibility audit shall pay high attention to the honesty of leaders before the economic activities of the enterprise. In terms of audit content, there are mainly two aspects that matters: first, fulfill the entity responsibility of the construction of the Party conduct and of an honest and clean government, second, individual abidance by the regulations on honest conduct.

Fulfill the Entity Responsibility. On this issue, audit institutions shall mainly check whether the persons in charge of the audited SOEs have implemented the arrangement and requirements of the Central Committee of the CPC, the State Council and the departments of supervision over state-owned assets on the construction of a clean government and an uncorrupted party, whether work plans on the construction have been drawn up according to the actual conditions, whether the requirements and specific measures have been declared, whether the disintegration of responsibility on the construction of a clean government and an uncorrupted party has been carried out, whether the responsibility and task allocation of leading bodies and leading cadres have been explicitly stipulated, and whether persons in charge can arrange the major work, look into important problems, coordinate key links as well as supervise and handle significant cases in person within the authority. Second, strengthen the system of party conduct and clean government. Audit institutions shall inspect whether the audited persons in charge have established and improved systems and regulations for the construction of an uncorrupted party and a clean government during the terms of office, whether there is a system for check and evaluation of the responsibility system of the construction, whether there are feasible and effective measures of claiming responsibilities, whether relevant departments have attempted to strengthen the work of accountability, improve the disintegration of responsibility, check and supervision and back investigation, whether the systems have been carried out in an effective manner, and whether all responsibilities of the construction have been honestly fulfilled. Third, enforce the discipline of strict accountability. Audit institutions shall check whether there are general behaviors or mass disturbance which violating the integrity regulations of the central government in the audited enterprises, whether there are adverse social influences led by the poor treatment of the misconducts which have been banned by explicit orders because of the unsatisfactory of the work performance, whether there are problems of unsettled accountability and or unfulfilled decisions on accountability, whether subordinate companies have been urged to solve the problems under supervision, and whether the concealing and overstocking of violations against laws and regulations and the feeble supervision over leading bodies have resulted in serious cases of malfeasance.

Individual Abidance. First, abide by regulations on honest conduct. Attentions of audit institutions shall be paid to whether persons in charge have made the use of public power and position for improper interests, whether there are problems of abusing the public power for private gains, embezzling public property, engaging in profit-making business activities without permission, borrowing or embezzling investment assets of the enterprise in the long term, and drawing water to their own mills through inter-bank business and connected transaction, whether persons in charge under audit supervision have intervened the invitation for bid, submission of tender, supplies purchasing, the service of intermediary organs, examination, approval and transfer of land, disposal of major assets, approval of various capital loans and other economic activities by feat of the convenience of position and personal influence, whether leading cadres have illegally built luxurious buildings for work and other purposes, been equipped with office occupancies and vehicles exceeding the standards, and illegally held various celebrations, whether responsible persons have strictly enforced the regulations on position benefits and expenditures, whether relevant expenditures have been listed in the budget management, whether the incomes of persons in charge can meet the specifications, whether there are violations against regulations such as illegal investment and admission or extra salaries for multiple-job holding, and whether persons in charge have taken shares by investing without permission or got dividends illegally, retained the remuneration relationship in subordinate enterprises without approval, illegally received the extra salaries from other positions, and directly or indirectly allocated the remuneration at their options violating the authority of salary administration. Second, verify violations against regulations on honest conduct. Within their jurisdiction, audit institutions shall verify the problems in the aspect of honest conduct assigned by departments of supervision and personnel division or reported by the public. On this issue, the verification shall be strictly

255

delimited with the ones of the departments of inspection and personnel division, and audit institutions shall carry it out grimly in line with the responsibility of audit supervision, and the relevant circumstances and clues shall be handed over to related departments in a timely manner.

Involving major issues of principle, regulations on performing the entity responsibility of the construction of the party conduct and of an honest and clean government and abiding by regulations on clean conduct jointly make up the untouchable bottom line of discipline of persons in charge of SOEs. Therefore, instead of evaluating quantitatively, qualitative evaluation would be a better choice. On this issue, it is wiser to enumerate the violations against disciplines via qualitative demonstration. As an auxiliary to illustrate the degree of performance of the entity responsibility, the indicator of satisfactory evaluation on the construction of the party conduct and of an honest and clean government determined by the leading group, mid-level leaders and staff representatives in the assessment on year-end summary can be regarded as the verification of the overall situation. Here involves an indicator, the work satisfactory of the construction. The calculation formula is: the work satisfactory of the construction = the number of people who are satisfied with the construction / voter turnout.

Performance Audit of State-Owned Enterprises

Development of Performance Audit of State-Owned Enterprises

Performance audit was known as economic benefit audit in 1983, when China's audit institutions were first established. Since then, the research on performance audit, which points out that China's audit shall develop along the lines of benefit, has developed steadily. In 1985, the State Council issued the Temporary Provisions on Audit Work, which clearly states that the economic benefit audit of SOEs and other units is necessary. With the deepening of the reform of SOEs, rules and regulations on performance audit has been incrementally improved. In November 1988, the State Council amended provisions in the Institutionalization of Audit of the PRC. As a consequence, the scope of audit was extended from SOEs to all enterprises with state-owned assets, and audit targets were also transformed from the authenticity and legitimacy of business operation to the economic benefit of certain significance. At that stage, the audit of SOEs achieved remarkable development. With investigating and treating economic corruption as a key point, units and SOEs of great significance were audited, a periodic and unscheduled system of audit of SOEs was formed, and work regulations such as the economic responsibility audit of legal bodies of the enterprise after leaving office and responsibility audit of contract operation of business entities. In addition to financial audit, it was also necessary for audit institutions to further carry out the research from the perspectives of internal control and economic effectiveness of the enterprise, with the purpose of supervising over the key measures of the preserve and appreciation of state-owned assets and encouraging the audit to develop along the line of the authenticity of financial standing, liabilities and profit and loss. However, at that stage, the audit of authenticity and legitimacy dominated the work of audit institutions, and performance audit was merely carried out. In 1995, the National People's Congress passed the Audit Law, and pointed out that audit institutions at all levels shall take the preservation and appreciation of the state-owned assets and resources as the key point to audit the condition of assets, liabilities and profit and loss of enterprise, units and departments of great significance in order to adapt to the reform of SOEs and the establishment of modern enterprise system, and allowing for the problems in SOEs found out by relevant agencies during the course of audit, the government was empowered to exercise macroeconomic regulation and control through audit reports. With the establishment and operation of modern enterprise system, audit supervision has been carried out to cope with the current situation of diversification. The State Audit Office issued the Regulations on Economic Responsibility Audit during the Tenure of Persons in Charge of SOEs and State Holding Enterprises, which proposed the audit mode with the economic audit as the core and combining the audit of economic responsibility and financial revenues and expenditures, improved the thinking of audit, adopted the multilevel, key-point-high-lightened and normative measures, encouraged the audit of SOEs to adjust to the new development direction of "figuring out the assets, revealing the hidden dangers, and promoting the development", and contributed to the new audit pattern of "giving consideration to special audit, revenue and expenditure audit and economic responsibility audit in the meanwhile".

The Current Situation of Performance Audit of State-Owned Enterprises

In recent years, China has carried out the audit activities in a cumulatively positive gesture all over the country, and the number of projects of performance audit has also increased greatly. However, the performance audit in China is still unbalanced regionally, which is caused by the different development status and starting time of various provinces and cities. This is mainly reflected in two aspects: first, compared with that in underdeveloped western areas in China, the development in eastern areas has presented a swift tendency. For instance, performance audit has been gradually carried out in well-developed cities such as Beijing, Shanghai, Guangzhou and Shenzhen, and the increasing number of projects of performance audit clearly demonstrates that the performance audit has also been incrementally strengthened. However, in Yunnan, Guizhou, Shaanxi, Shanxi, Ningxia, Gansu and other less developed provinces in the west, trapped by the blunted sense of performance audit, the work started relatively late, and not many cases of audit practice have been recorded, the development is much slower than the western regions. Worse still, there have been no project of performance audit in some remote regions. Second, for departments and units in the same province and municipality directly under the central government, the administrative level can also affect the development tendency of performance audit. At present, audit institutions have covered a growing number of items of performance audit, mainly including banking and finance, infrastructure construction, resources and environment protection, social security, medical treatment, education, public health and other aspects. Through the performance audit of SOEs, audit institutions are able to possess the information about the management and capital flows of the enterprises, inspect the rationality of the use of funds and leakproofness of funds management, further analyze the cause of problems, and promote the further amelioration of the enterprise management system, and bring forward rectification opinions according to the problems and objective circumstances of the enterprise by pointing out and revealing problems. Moreover, performance audit can also offer the policy formulation with objective, fair and perfect first-hand information. In light of the increasingly extensive scope of work, performance audit will surely play a role of more importance in terms of boosting the state governance and social progress.

According to the audit projects arranged by the State Audit Office and the audit findings in 2014, it is known to all that the State Audit Office has involved in the audit of financial revenues and expenditures and the audit of asset gains and losses of SOEs.

In the past year, the State Audit Office has incrementally strengthened its audit of SOEs, but performance audit is still generally carried out in the middle of the audit of financial revenues and expenditures and the economic responsibility audit of persons in charge. That is to say, performance audit can only play an auxiliary part in the audit of integrated projects, which pays attention to performance audit and the traditional audit of financial revenues and expenditures as well as the normativity of the management and use of funds.

So far, only a few units have carried out projects of profitability performance audit focusing on whether there have been violations against laws and regulations, whether the business strategy of SOEs is in line with the fundamental policies and industrial policies of the state and local governments or can meet the requirements of economic restructuring. In addition, the implementation of internal management (management performance evaluation) and the management efficiency compared with industrial indicators shall also be included in consideration, and some of the projects also evaluate the resource utilization and environmental protection.

Measures employed by the State Audit Office to issue performance audit are as follows: first, procedural analysis, namely carrying out corresponding analysis through procedures such as planning, execution, inspection and supervision of audit projects; second, the analysis through the information management system on data and evidence of auditees; third, result analysis, namely finishing the performance audit reports of auditees; fourth, case study, namely the case inspection and evaluation with a comprehensive understanding of some complicated issues as the basis; fifth, questionnaire survey, namely the deep analysis and evaluation on the strength of the information collected by questionnaires for auditees; sixth, quantitative analysis, namely to verify the possibility of the occurrence of errors through sampling and other statistical methods.

Chapter Six: Audit of

Administrative Institutions

Instead of economic benefits, what matters most to administrative institutions is the ability to fill the bill of social functions and provide better social services. Different from enterprises, administrative institutions mainly aim to offer social services within the operating range rather than make profits. Since 1986, the audit supervision over administrative institutions has incrementally stepped on the track of regularization and institutionalization. Promoting the audit of administrative institutions towards the direction of consolidation, deepening, improvement and perfection, the system of periodical audit has played a significant role since its establishment. In 1986, audit institutions across the country audited about 15,000 administrative institutions, and the amount of money involved in violations against laws reached ￥1.54 billion.

Development of Audit of Administrative

Institutions

In 1985, the State Audit Office summarized the experience of the system of periodical audit established by the Audit Bureau of Xiangfan, Hubei, and other areas were required to implemented the system step by step. Since then, many audit institutions have put periodical audit of financial revenues and expenditures of administrative institutions into practice. In 1987, the State Audit Office issued the Notice on the Implementation of the System of Periodical Audit of Administrative Institutions, requiring that regions where has carried out periodical audit extensively shall implemented it for all first-class budget units, regions where all first-class budget units have been under periodical audit supervision shall devote greater efforts into internal audit, and incrementally extend the periodical audit to second-class and third-class budget units, regions where have already partially developed the periodical audit shall promote the common practice, and regions without periodical audit shall determine experimental units and boost the extension of periodical audit as soon as possible. Issued with the Notice, the System of Periodical Audit of Administrative Institutions (Trial) stipulated that for all administrative institutions whose expenditures were verified, approved and subsidized by financial departments and their off-budget entities, all financial revenues and expenditures inside or outside the budgets were covered by periodical audit, except for expenditures for secrecy-involved issues of departments of public security, state security, foreign affairs and national defence. According to specific conditions of audit institutions and auditees, audit supervision can be classified into monthly, quarterly, semi-annual and annual ones. Auditees shall, in line with the requirements of audit institutions, regularly submit financial and accounting reports and other relevant materials, and audit institutions shall, when necessary, conduct on-site audit, in order to consult relevant materials and know the rope of relevant circumstances. Since then, the system of periodical audit of financial revenues and expenditures of administrative institutions on a national scale has gradually been set up.

In 1989, the State Audit Office issued Order No. 4, which formally put the System of Periodical Audit of Administrative Institutions into effect, and administrative institutions engaged in periodical audit were required to carry out the system by reference. In accordance with the act, audit institutions shall implement periodical audit of the authenticity, legitimacy and efficiency of all special funds such as administrative expenses, operating expenses, disbursements of fundamental construction, and other financial revenues and expenditures inside or outside the budgets of administrative institutions and other relevant economic activities. The audit content mainly include: whether the accounting agencies and accounting staff have performed statutory duties and implemented the accounting system of the state, whether persons in charge of auditees have fabricated final accounts, embezzled or diverted special funds, transferred budget funds outside the budget, or set up "private coffers" without permission, whether there have been violations against laws such as embezzlement and theft, offering and accepting bribes, fraudulent buying and selling or abuse of power for personal interests, whether there have been dissipation of state-owned assets such as treating guests, offering gifts or touring at public expense, whether there have been cases such as tax evasion, currency arbitrage, arbitrary charge, indiscriminate collection of funds, illegal requisitioning donations, unjustified fines, or concealment and retention of funds that shall be turned over to the state finance, whether there have been cases of procurement of specially controlled products, attracting funds into unplanned investment projects of fixed assets, and allocation, transfer and sell of common property and materials without authorization, whether there have been problems of overstaff, expansion of the scope of expenditure, fallacious spending standards and sending belongings arbitrarily, whether the internal control system, especially the financial accounting system is specific and effective, and whether the auditees have achieved the optimal economic and social benefits in terms of the collection, distribution, use and management of funds.

With the joint efforts of audit institutions at all levels, the system of periodical audit has made remarkable progress. Thanks to the periodical audit of administrative institutions for consecutive years, violations against laws and regulations in such units have been obviously restrained, and the level of financial management has been raised to a new stage. To a certain extent, a system of virtuous cycle consisting of external audit supervision and self-discipline inside auditees has been preliminarily formed. The implementation of the audit of administrative institutions has made the following contributions: first, relevant regulations of the Audit Law have been implemented in a scientific and effective manner. In 2006, China promulgated the Audit Law, which played a role in regulating audit activities. Under such circumstances, administrative institutions shall take the standardization of audit as the key point of the routine work to ensure that they can manage the financial operation effectively and avoid embezzlement and corruption under the new situation, so as to promote the economic and social benefits of financial funds of the state. In a nutshell, guaranteeing the standardization of audit of administrative institutions can availably strengthen the execution ability of the Audit Law, thereby assure the scientificity and accuracy of the audit work. Second, meet the needs of economic restructuring. With the development of national economy and science, China's economic restructuring accelerated, and consequently administrative institutions are also asked to improve their adaptive capacity. In order to fit the changes in economic restructuring, administrative institutions need further improvement and innovation as well as the adaptive capacity to cope with the new situation, so as to strengthen their ability to defuse risks and solve problems. Third, improve the authenticity of audit results. The accuracy of audit results has always been a crux in China's audit activities. The distortion of accounting data and other information has resulted in certain deviations in the authenticity of audit results and to some degree the chaos of the market economy, which severely impacts the development of China's national economy. Therefore, the audit of administrative institutions under new circumstances requires stronger supervision over audit activities, so as to efficaciously improve the authenticity of audit results, strengthen the management and execution of relevant policies, circumvent the misdeclaration and misstatement as far as possible, and assure the steady development of the social economic development.

Audit of Central Administrative Institutions

Since 1986, the State Audit Office has carried out a lot of audit of financial revenues and expenditures and universally implemented the system of periodical audit, with the purpose of judging whether the financial revenues and expenditures are true and in line with financial regulations, whether the internal control system is well-organized and effective, and whether there are violations against disciplines such as squander or jobbery. In the meanwhile, the State Audit Office also strengthened the audit of administrative institutions which had the right of fund allocation, extra-budgetary revenues, confiscated revenues or have been frequently assailed by violations against disciplines, which has got good effects in facilitating the government to observe laws and disciplines.

In 1986, the State Audit Office conducted trial audit of the administrative funds of the Ministry of Textile Industry and the Ministry of Metallurgical Industry successively. After summing up the experience, audit institutions incrementally extended the audit coverage and started the audit of administrative funds of some ministries and commissions subordinate to the State Council. Between July 1987 and July 1988, the State Audit Office audited 31 units in total, and found that most of them were involved in violations against regulations of the financial and economic system, some of which were considerably serious. For some units, the final accounts of administrative funds were not true: there were still balances on their books, but in fact they had already overspent; some rich and powerful departments embezzled and misappropriated large sums of special funds: among the 31 auditees, 27 of them misappropriated up to ￥106 million; some measures of budget management were unreasonable: budgets of financial expenditures failed to take price fluctuations into account, resulting in that some expenditures standards were not in line with the reality. The State Audit Office delivered the audit results to the State Council in the form of memoir, and put forward 4 suggestions including "opening up the front door and blocking the back door". Later, the State Audit Office proposed to improve the management measures of funds of government offices and administrative institutions, and put forward concrete suggestions such as further making clear the expenditure scope of administrative appropriations and undertaking expenditures, checking the quotas of necessary operating expenses of administrative institutions, and preventing relevant units from embezzling operating expenses for other uses.

In 1988, the State Audit Office carried out periodical audit on 32 central ministries and commissions and bureaus directly subordinate to the central government, and the financial revenues and expenditures amounting to ￥3.825 billion were audited. As a results, ￥102 million were found out involved with violations against disciplines. After continuous audit of central units, in 1990, the State Audit Office analyzed the audit results of 36 central departments comprehensively, and the consequences showed that compared with the initial stage in 1988, the amount involved with violations against disciplines in such units had shrunk by 70%, and among them, the amount involved in embezzling special funds, retaining financial revenues, above-standard expenditures and illegal procurement of specially controlled commodities had slumped by 75%-90%, and the proportion of units that completely or basically complied with financial and economic laws and regulations had increased from less than 10% to nearly 60%.

From 1987 to 1988, the State Audit Office, together with the Government Offices Administration of the State Council, conducted inspections on the disbursement of money and goods by departments subordinate to the State Council, national headquarters and specialized banks for 4 times in total (twice a year), and pointed out that many units had the problems of issuing money and goods to the staff arbitrarily on all sorts of pretexts. The State Audit Office submitted a report to the State Council, and the General Office of the State Council endorsed it, emphasizing that "no more celebrations of the Spring Festival and other festivals at public expense will occur in the future", or the punishment would be aggravated. Through several rounds of inspections, the phenomenon of sending out money and goods arbitrarily had been brought under control to a certain extent, and some violations against rules had been rectified, which played a positive role in promoting the clean governance.

In conjunction with the reorganization of enterprises, in 1989, the State Audit Office investigated the enterprises launched by the Institute of Zoology and the Institute of Computing Technology subordinate to Chinese Academy of Sciences. Through the investigation of the registered capital, business scope and financial revenues and expenditures of the 20 subsidiary enterprises, audit institutions understood the positive effects of enterprises raised by scientific institutes on the transformation of scientific research achievements into productivity, but also pointed that there were problems such as excessive number of companies, disorder of financial management and maldistribution of incomes.

With the purpose of ensuring that the audit on administrative units at the central level can both concentrate on crucial points and maintain complete coverage, the State Audit Office improved the audit methods in 1991, stipulating that units under auditing shall be classified into 2 categories: key units and general units. Key units refer to the ones with huge amount of funds, frequent financial and economic activities, poor management and major problems as well as units determined in accordance with operational needs. Those other than key units are general units. For key units, audit institutions shall conduct comprehensive or focuses audit of financial revenues and expenditures, and make audit conclusions and decisions on the problems of violations against disciplines discovered. For general units, audit institutions shall give priority to the inspection of accounting statements and account books, if there is no major problem, audit institutions only voice the audit opinions, and no punishment should be imposed, if major problems are discovered, it is necessary to conduct in-depth audit to ascertain the facts and cope with the loopholes. For the tendentious and emerging problems in auditees, audit institutions shall check up on the facts, put forward suggestions and feedback to relevant parties in time via audit investigation. Auditees listed in the roll of key units issued at the beginning of each year shall be bring into the annual audit program. In 1991, a total of 27 administrative institutions at the central level were adopted as key units.

To cope with the problems such as unfair social distribution as well as poor welfare and treatment of civil servants, in 1991, the State Audit Office carried out audit investigation on incomes of employees of 12 administrative institutions subordinate to the State Council, administrative cooperations, specialized banks and other different units, and the results showed that the incomes of leading cadres of administrative institutions were obviously lower than those of enterprises, bank and other units, and the personal income gap was widening incrementally. the disparity of incomes led to the instability and outflow of personnel in governmental agencies. Consorting with audit institutions of some provinces, autonomous regions and cities, the State Audit Office also carried out audit investigations into the revenues and expenditures of administrative funds of some government departments. The investigation reflected that seriously divorcing from reality, the administrative budgets were considerably low, and the fully responsible management had led to the embezzlement of funds by the back door. As a result, administrative expenses were totally out of control, and the neglected problems such as false final accounts of administrative budgets were made obvious. Finally, the State Audit Office delivered special reports to local governments and the Financial and Economic Committee of the NPC respectively. In the same year, the State Audit Office inspected the revenues of some of the hotels and guesthouses subordinate to government agencies, and found out that the cost of banquets and gifts in conference expense in the first few months in 1991 was 7 times more than that during the same period in 1990. Many units had high standards for banquets, for instance, around 500 people attended a feast on one occasion. In addition, exchanging gifts has already been common. When the information was reflected upward, the superior attached great importance to such situations. In 1992, the State Audit Office once again conducted the audit investigation into the funds and their management and use of 37 administrative institutions subordinate to the State Council, and the problems found were as follows: first, budgetary shortfalls were big, in the year of 1991, 10 of the 37 institutions disbursed 50% more than the budget; second, there was a tremendous imbalance in expenditure among different units, with a 1.8-hold difference between the units with the highest and the lowest expenditures among the 37 auditees; third, there extravagance and waste were prevalent. To cope with the problems, the State Audit Office, in its report to the

State Council, put forward suggestions to strictly strengthen the budget management and control spending. In 1994, the State Audit Office inspected the Ministry of Foreign Affairs and the State Economy and Trade Commission, and the amount of money involved in cases of malpractices reached ￥340 million, of which ￥29.09 were turned over to the treasury, and ￥110 million of the embezzled special funds were recovered. In the same year, the State Audit Office and the Ministry of Civil Affairs formed a joint investigation team to conduct an audit investigation on Top China, a periodical press affiliated to the National Commission on Aging in China, and found out violations against laws and regulations such as concealed accounts, appropriating the budget without authorization and procuring housing and vehicles in the name of individuals. After the audit reports were reported the State Council, the leaders demanded serious investigation and severe punishment. As a result, the commission made a close survey and imposed some internal disciplinary sanctions, persons in charge of Top China assumed responsibility for some problems found out, established and improved rules and regulations, and strengthened the financial management.

Audit by Industry and Development

Audit of Hospitals

In 1991, the State Audit Office and the audit institutions of 11 provinces and autonomous conduct audit on 464 hospitals, including 8 central hospitals and 456 local hospitals, and the amount involved in violations against disciplines summed up to ￥86.23 million. The major problems pointed out included the establishment of private coffers, arbitrary charges, big prescription, the sell of non-medical supplies, and that the incomes of sparetime medical service and normal incomes blurred into ach other. The State Statical Bureau attached great significance to the audit results, and handed the reports to all local statistical agencies, which greatly promoted the improved management and use of the statistical operating expenses. In addition, in 1991, audit institutions also audited TV stations and the final accounts of the Organizing Committee of the 11th Asian Games in Beijing, and audited the pension insurance funds and unemployment insurance funds managed by labor departments of 1820 cities, districts and counties from 27 provinces, autonomous regions and municipalities directly under the central government in 1992.

Audit of Administrative Organs for Law Enforcement

Audit institutions have strengthened the audit supervision over administrative organs for law enforcement such as departments of public security and industry and commerce. In 1986, audit institutions of 21 provincial-level administrative regions audited 959 law enforcement agencies at or above the county level as well as another 6497 at the grassroots level. Among the ￥ 291 million confiscated revenues audited, ￥ 91 million were involved in violations against disciplines, accounting for 31.5% of the total. It was finally pointed out that the phenomena of arbitrary charge, unjustified fines, retention or unauthorized outlays of public funds and arrearages generally existed. On such issues, the State Audit Office delivered a report to the State Council. In 1990, some provincial and municipal audit institutions audited the revenues from confiscation of police, procuratorates, courts, industry and commerce departments and price control authorities, and in 1991 audit institutions at all levels once again audited the confiscated revenues of the public security department. The foregoing audit activities revealed that there were still problems such as arbitrary charge, unjustified fines, retention or unauthorized use of public funds, poor management and unsound systems in the confiscation system of the police.

Reflecting the superiority of the socialist system, civil affairs fund provides strong backing to preferential treatment and placement, disaster relief and social welfare. The appropriate management and use of the fund are of great significance to ensuring the social stability and promoting the construction of socialist material civilization and cultural and ethical progress as well as the healthy development of the reform. Since 1987, audit institutions across the country have carried out the audit on the funds of civil affairs, with the focus on the relief funds distributed by civil affairs departments at all levels. According to the statistical data of 20 provincial-level regions, about ￥2 billion of 1037 departments or bureaus of civil affairs at or above county level and 3846 subordinate units has been audited, and a total of ￥104 million were found involved in violations against disciplines. The major problems were as follows: first, the embezzlement and appropriation of natural disaster relief and social welfare funds were outstanding, and a total of ￥59.21 million were embezzled; Second, ￥23.93 million were misappropriated via fraudulent transfer; third, ￥20.67 million were involved in cases such as setting up private coffers, offering money and goods arbitrarily, abuse of power for personal use, and favored their friend or relatives; fourth, 74 people were suspected of being involved in embezzling public funds of ￥216,000, and 24 of them were handed over to juridical organs;

fifth, some funds for self-help production projects were used improperly, and the economic performance was relatively poor.

Audit of Special Funds

In the audit of administrative institutions, audit institutions have audited all funds managed and employed by such units in the form of industry audit and special audit, which has achieved remarkable fruits.

Current Situation of Audit of Special Funds

Special funds have their own management regulations and methods: first, the funds are stored in special accounts and checked in special accounts in operation; second, finance-related, namely that all special funds shall be appropriated by units at the same or a higher level; third, universality, namely that special financial funds cover a wide range of areas, involving all walks of life, financial departments at all levels all have their own special funds, and the government can also adjust the types and amount of the funds according to the actual situation.

Characteristics. In order to implement a specific state policy during a certain period, the government tends to adopts a special fiscal means — specifically setting up a special financial fund to promote and support the development of a cause, that is, a special fund. With the incremental establishment and improvement of public finance in China, the scale and the proportion of special funds also expand gradually, so it is strongly necessary to put the operation and management of special funds under audit supervision.

The audit of special funds is the key area of financial audit. the operation of special financial audit can be divided into establishment of special projects, allocation of financial fund, transfer of special funds, employment of special funds, management of special funds and the evaluation on the follow-up of use of funds. Therefore, the content and emphasis of audit of special funds can be determined by the targeted audit. For instance, whether the establishment of special funds has fully implemented the corresponding economic policies, whether special funds can meet the conditions for project approval, whether the projects are set up arbitrarily without considering the feasibility, whether the application materials of application units are real, whether the declaration procedures are in line with provisions of laws and regulations, and whether there are problems of project fabrication and multiple declarations of the same materials.

Covering a wide range of allowance and many government departments, special financial funds always involve in large amounts of money and decentralized projects. Therefore, auditors cannot perform audit supervision over the special funds merely by traditional audit methods. In addition, auditees have usually been informationized with the informatization of the audited units in the climate of big data, and the audit method by feat of electronic data has been increasingly necessary for the audit of special financial funds. Along with the continuous development of informatization, it is urgent to carry out the audit exploration on the strength of big data, with the purpose of better perform the function of audit supervision.

Common Tools. Steps of data analysis of audit of special funds can be summarized as: first, analyze the needs of audit of special funds at the current stage, design plans on projects which are in accordance with audit objectives and can be realized with the help of assistive technologies and tools provided by computer science, and establish a data analysis model on the basis of combining audit objectives and the collected audit information, then select the data required by the audit of special funds from basic data, and finally conduct specific data mining to point suspect data and draw analytical conclusions according to the analysis model of electronic data. In projects of data analysis of audit of special funds, auditors are empowered to determine the plans on audit data analysis according to the collected data, the optional analysis models, the computer-aided audit tools they are good at, the programming language they are proficient in and other specific conditions. For the record, the selection of audit tools is the focus of determining the plan on data analysis.

Audit tools can mainly be divided into tables, databases, audit software and other statistical analysis software. Tabular tools for data analysis refer to some commonly used software of spreadsheet, such as Excel, WPS Tables and so on. Database technology, especially SQL query function, has a very powerful function of data statistics and analysis, which can satisfy the data analysis of auditors from multiple perspectives and levels, and has been paid more and more attentions. Currently speaking, commonly used databases mainly include SQL Server, Oracle, Access, Fox Pro and so on. Audit software covers professional software and programs developed in accordance with the of audit analysis, and frequently used audit software at present includes the implementation system of field audit, Golden Sword Audit Software, Zhongyue Audit Software, Yongyou Audit Software, IDEA, ACL, ECPA and so on. Developed for meeting various statistical requirements and on the strength of mathematical statistics theory, statistical analysis software is specially used to statistical survey and data analysis. The usual ones include SPSS (PASW), STATA, EViews, SAS, etc.

Several Major Audit of Special Funds

Audit of Special Healthcare Funds. In 2004, the Ministry of Health of the PRC issued the Interim Measures for Management of the Special Funds for Local Health Protection Subsidized by the Central Government, and the article 2 stipulates that "for the sake of hoisting the emergency capacity of public health, health services in rural areas and to cope with sudden public health events, establishing and improving the system of information network of public health, disease control and prevention, medical treatment and health supervision, and strengthening the prevention and control of major diseases, the central finance has established special healthcare funds to mainly support the house betterment and improvement of health agencies in economically underdeveloped regions in central and western China, procurement of medical facilities and free medicines, wage subsidies for personnel working for major disease control and prevention and staff training". The scope of special subsidies for healthcare in rural areas included: disease control and prevention, maternal and chile hygiene, health supervision, health education and other necessary public health work and medical services. Apart from the characteristics of special financial funds, special healthcare funds are also characterized by vast amount, many projects, wide involved aspects and strong benefits of people's livelihood, which are of significant meaning in deepening the medical reform and ensuring the sound development of heath undertakings.

Audit objects of special healthcare funds mainly include the audit of the implementation of project budgets and supporting funds for basic healthcare funds, maternal and child hygiene and major disease control and prevention, the implementation of preallocation system, and the legitimacy of the use of funds.

Special healthcare funds are closely related to the audit of other special funds. Their common points are mainly reflected in: first, the unicity of audit objects. As special financial funds are project funds established and financial supported by the government, there shall be inevitably strong fiscal natures, therefore audit institutions at all levels are usually the organizers and enforcers of the audit supervision over special financial funds (special healthcare funds included). Second, the audit objects are usually specifically targeted, the audit of special funds usually aims at the revenues and expenditures merely, and other financial activities are excluded from consideration. Third, the legality of the judgement standards. At present, the major value standard of the traditional audit of special financial funds is "conforming to legal provisions", and does not make requests for the benefits and efficiency of the use of funds.

As a special one, the special healthcare fund differs from other funds mainly in the following aspects: first, it offers a wide range of benefits to the rural population and directly involves individuals. Compared with other special funds, the special healthcare fund mainly aims at the capacity of public health and major disease prevention and control in the countryside, diffusely involving th establishment and assistance of health institutions and medical system in central and western China, especially in rural areas. Specific projects, such as delivery subsidy, vaccination subsidy and the New Rural Cooperative Medical Care System and many other projects have directly benefited the individuals. Allowing for the fact that the funds have been subdivided into specific individuals, the workload and job difficulty have been tremendously increased. Second, audit objects are more complex. As the core content of the audit of special financial funds, the allocation and use of special healthcare funds is on most cases determined by health and family planning commissions at all levels, which would distribute the funds to relevant departments at lower levels according to the superior documents. Therefore, the audit mainly aims at units at all levels in the healthcare system, including hospitals, CDCs, maternal and child care service centers, health departments, township health centers, public health inspection offices as well as village clinics. In light of the situation that such units all have their own characteristics and noticeable key points, the job difficulty would out of question be doubled and redoubled by the complexity of the audit objects.

The main content of the audit of special healthcare funds are as follows: first, whether the special funds for public health subsidized by the central government and the supporting funds offered by local governments have been allocated fully and timely according to provisions of relevant policies; second, whether the investment of special healthcare funds is reasonable, whether the use and allocation of the funds are legal and compliant, and whether there are problems of embezzlement, occupation, transfer, retention and waste; third, whether the financial management and internal control system of the execution units and recipients of special healthcare funds are sound and effectively implemented, whether the financial accounting is in line with the standards, whether the statements and vouchers are authentic, well-prepared, compliant and complete, and whether auxiliary accounts of financial revenues and expenditures of special funds have been established; fourth, inspect the application, approval, budget and implementation of construction projects involved in special healthcare funds, and checks out whether the examination and approval are in accordance with the spirit of relevant documents, whether the project is executed exceeding the planned area, standard and budget, and whether there are arbitrarily determined unscheduled projects; fifth, inspect the effectiveness, efficiency and economic benefits of the use of special healthcare funds.

Audit of Special Agriculture-Related Funds. Currently speaking, audit institutions and auditors are responsible for the audit of special agriculture-related funds. Audit objects of agriculture-related funds mainly include departments of finance as well as reform and development at all levels responsible for allocation, appropriation, management and use of agriculture-related funds, relevant competent organizations such as such as departments of land and resources, transportation, housing and urban-rural development as well as water resources, project construction units such as construction management offices at the subdistrict level, project implementation companies, and beneficial owner of the project. The audit content is to check the raising, management, use and benefits of the funds as well as the planning, management and operation of the invested projects, and the audit objective is to confirm the implementation of policies, the management and use of funds invested by departments of all levels, as well as the operation of relevant construction projects in regard to the development of issues relating to agriculture, rural areas and rural people. By revealing problems in the above-mentioned aspects, and then putting forward suggestions on promoting the implementation of policies of agriculture, ensuring the security and efficiency of the use of funds and the high quality of construction projects. Audit Organization modes mainly include audit conducted by the State Audit Office and relevant department, direct audit guided by local audit institutions at higher or corresponding levels, joint audit implemented by audit institutions at higher and lower levels, and off-site cross audit conducted by different audit institutions.

So far, the State Audit Office has carried out the audit of special agriculture-related funds for nearly 20 years. Audit institutions at all levels have investigated and treated problems in the allocation, appropriation, use and management of the agriculture-related funds invested in poverty alleviation, education and medical service as well as the construction projects associated with the construction of infrastructure and water conservancy facilities in rural areas, which has achieved great progress, embodying that the audit work has received increasing attention from the Party Central Committee and the State.

Judging from the scope, there are more and more audit projects about special agriculture-related funds, and audit activities are covering a wider range. Only in the announcement of results released by the State Audit Office, the audit scope of special financial funds related to agriculture and the development in rural areas shall cover the special subsidies from the central government, special expenditures from provinces, municipalities and counties, joint financial input from central and local governments, special funds for improving the compulsory education in rural areas, special funds for new rural cooperative medical system for easier and cheaper medical treatment, special subsidies of poverty relief for ameliorating the living conditions of the rural poor, expenditures of construction projects which offering employment rather than outright grant, allocated funds for the construction of infrastructure which raises the agricultural productivity and improves the living conditions of farmers, and all other kinds of funds for the construction of facilities such as irrigation and water conservancy, for the purpose of grain increase. Allowing for the fact that more special agriculture-related funds have been brought into the audit scope, the audit supervision is playing an indispensable role in dealing with the issues relating to agriculture, rural areas and rural people as soon as possible.

From the perspective of audit objects, the audit of special agriculture-related funds has been effectively combined with that of policy implementation and economic responsibility. The various kinds of special funds have respect to many departments of the party and the government, such as rural affairs commissions, financial departments as well as development and reform departments at all levels which are responsible for the use and management of the funds, departments of housing and urban-rural construction, water resources, land resources and education at all levels which are involved in construction projects with the investment of special agriculture-related funds, and local departments which specifically lead the project construction, including Poverty Relief Office at the county level as well as relevant construction organizations and benefited parties. Compared with the audit of other general items, the audit of a certain agriculture-related fund usually covers many departments, in 2017, for instance, the audit of special funds for agriculture-related water conservancy involved commissions of rural affairs and departments of water resources, education, medical treatment and public health, urban construction, planning, and social security at the county level. In the actual process of audit, auditors not only audited the allocation, appropriation, use and management of the special funds for water conservancy, and then pointed out some major problems, but fully investigated and understood whether persons in charge of relevant departments had thoroughly implemented the relevant policies and conscientiously fulfilled the job requirements, and, in addition, revealed the problems of illegal project management, cheating, embezzlement, low levels of resources utilization, slow progress and failure to give full play to the expected benefits. Effectively combining with other types of audit, the audit of special agriculture-related funds has comprehensively disclosed problems related to the use of special funds for agricultural purpose, the implementation of relevant policies and the performance of duties of personnel, thus improving the audit quality.

Judging from the problems pointed out, the audit of special agriculture-related found has made remarkable achievements. The main problems can be classified into 3 categories: first, relevant departments cannot absolutely implement the policies of special agriculture-related funds. For example, the audit of special funds for agriculture, forestry and water resources carried out in 2016 showed that there were problems such as tardy policy implementation and poor integration of funds, leading to the failure to solve the current problems jointly. Second, there were prevalent problems in the use of funds, such as cheating, embezzlement, decentralized management and waste. All of the 10 items listed in the table were all plagued by the foregoing problems more or less. Third, there are problems of insufficient investment, inadequate management, nonstandard construction and low resource utilization rate due to inconsistency in reality. For example, in 2009, the audit of special agriculture-related funds in 10 provincial-level administrative regions found that the investment in agricultural infrastructure construction was not completely in place, and the audit of special funds for agriculture, forestry and water resources found that a raft of funds was wasted because some construction projects did not conform to the reality. Generally speaking, in light of the situation that all kinds of problems have been effectively exposed, and caused of such problems have also been deeply analyzed, the audit work has made satisfactory results.

According to the rectification of defects discovered in audit activities, the problems pointed out have received high attention from relevant departments and local governments, indicating that audit institutions have taken maximum advantage of its function of audit supervision. First, correlative agriculture-related policies have been put into place, and the regulatory framework has been further ameliorated; second, part of the embezzled agriculture-related funds has been recovered in time, and the decentralized capital has been invigorated; finally, working disciplines have been more strictly enforced, promoting relevant departments to strengthen the self-management. For example, after the audit of special funds for the New Rural

Cooperative Medical Care System in 2011, which recovered ￥ 25.901 million in total, relevant departments issued normative documents, and the systems for pharmaceutical procurement and hospital reimbursement were also improved. The foregoing rectifications show that audit is playing an increasingly significant supervisory role in strengthening the management of special agriculture-related funds, ameliorating the construction of systems and promoting the relevant personnel to perform their duties.

Summing up the above, the audit of special agriculture-related funds conducted by the State Audit Office has been cumulatively strengthened and deepened, and the audit work has been significantly effective in general. Aiming at various types of funds, the audit has effectively revealed the problems in the implementation of agriculture-related policies, the use and management of funds, the construction of agriculture-related construction projects as well as the performance of duties of relevant personnel. On this basis, with the purpose of solving the problems as soon as possible, more targeted suggestions have been put forward through analyzing the causes of problems from the perspective of institution and mechanism. In the meanwhile, audit institutions also carried out continuous supervision over the rectification of problems, and release the results in due course, which further enhanced the public supervision over the audit matters and the audit work itself, resulting in better audit quality, richer audit results and higher audit values. To a certain extent, the audit of special agriculture-related funds has made tremendous contribution to solving the problems relating to agriculture, rural areas and rural people, achieving a comprehensive well-off society, and building China into a modern socialist Country.

Audit of Special Employment Funds. The audit of special employment funds belongs to both the audit of people's livelihood and the audit of special financial funds. Audit in this aspect means the inspection carried out by audit institutions and specialized agencies on the raising, use and management of the funds as well as the implementation of employment policies. Audit institutions shall pay enough attention to the compliance and legality in terms of the collection and use of employment funds, while the management is mainly concerned with performance in aspects of economy, efficiency, effectiveness, and fairness as well as the objective and fair evaluation and assessment in all respects, and moreover, the implementation of employment policies shall also be paid attention to. By carrying out the audit of special employment funds, relevant departments can have an overall grasp of the specific use, service efficiency and the response of the expected targets of the special employment funds. However, audit should not only focus on the authenticity and legitimacy of the use of funds as well as the funds themselves, but the fund achievements and the social efficiency. Through the audit investigation, the problems and cruxes in the use and management of special employment funds can be pointed out, so as to provide the government with basis for improving the service efficiency of the funds, issuing policies, and ameliorating relevant systems and mechanisms as well as management methods.

From the State Audit Office and its special agencies to local audit institutions at all levels, more attention has been paid to the audit of special employment funds in recent years. However, compared with the arrangement of audit projects as a whole, the project arrangement of special employment funds is still not enough, which cannot match the importance of the use of special employment funds. In addition, many problems have been pointed out in the management and use of the funds as well as the formulation of policies through the current audit activities. According to the information from websites of the State Audit Office, provincial audit departments and local audit bureaus, many regions in China have carried out the audit of special employment funds since 2008. In the past 10 years, the audit of special employment funds was usually carried out incidentally in the process of the audit of financial revenues and expenditures or other extended audit, and the audit of this issue as an independent item was rare. However, for the past few years, many governments at different levels have started to actively launched the special audit of employment funds, taking audit in this respect as an independent item, and issuing independent audit reports. So far, the audit of special employment funds has not been a major audit item in the government audit yet.

By analyzing the audit reports on the official website of the State Audit Office, it can be pointed out that, compared with the integrated audit activities across the country, the audit of special employment funds is mostly conducted by audit institutions at the provincial and municipal level. Since 2017, the number of audit activities of special employment funds has increased visibly, and some provincial-level administrative regions which had never conducted the audit of this issue before also listed it in their audit plans in 2019.

In the initial stage of the audit of special

employment funds, audit institutions used to adopt the methods of discussion and review frequently, namely at first made an appointment with persons in charge and ask for relevant information, and then made spot tests focusing on suspicious items, conducted detailed surveys on data, documents, archives and other materials submitted by employers, and made extended investigation on contents outside the auditees. On this issue, audit institutions mainly inspected whether there were cheating and misappropriation of funds, fraud and other illegal acts by checking the fund flows. In 2007, for instance, the Audit Bureau of Haiyan, Zhejiang, conducted the audit of the fund use for re-employment training 2005-2006. By cooperating with the Discipline Inspection Commission, auditors collected the relevant annual business data in short order, and ferreted out a major case in which relevant personnel colluded with each other to swindle the funds for training. In 2008, the Wuhan Special Agency of the State Audit Office conducted an extended audit on the labor and social security department of a county. After finding something abnormal, auditors further collected information from primary data including standing books, vouchers and contracts. After repeated talks and reviews of materials, it was finally ascertained that relevant personnel had jointly defrauded the special training funds up to ￥4 million.

In recent years, in addition to the compliance of the use of funds, the audit of special employment funds has paid more attention to the implementation of employment policies and the fund performance of employment departments. For developing the audit on this issue better, audit institutions from place to place have also put forward many innovative and excellent measures. For instance, the audit institutions of Jing' an and Zhabei in Shanghai keep a watchful eye on the structure of expenditures of funds, while the audit institution in Shiyan, Hubei province, pays close attention to the management of the employment information system during the audit of special employment funds. Broadly speaking, however, audit on such aspects has been largely ignored. Moreover, some audit institutions also entrust accounting firms to audit the special employment funds through public bidding.

The audit of special employment funds in China has the following characteristics: First, the project scale is relatively small. Compared with the audit projects such as the audit of poverty relief funds and healthcare funds, the audit of special employment funds pales by comparison in size, though its significance is self-evident. When it comes to the personnel arrangement, only relatively few auditors and short time schedules can be assigned to the audit on that aspect. However, allowing for the different requirements and conditions of all the people enjoying the subsidies, the large number of stakeholders and the long timespan, the audit of special employment funds has a wide range of target audience, resulting in large workload and onerous tasks. How to finish the audit tasks with high quality and high efficiency be feat of limited audit resources is the focus of the audit of special employment funds. Second, the audit content is extensive and much attention has been paid to the fund performance. In light of the fact that massive stakeholders and many departments are involved with the subsidies of the special funds, the amount of data related to employment is colossal. Therefore, for the audit of special employment funds, the audit on the information system of employment data is also necessary. Audit institutions shall, at the same time, audit the compliance and legality of different links such

291

as the raising, use and management of the employment funds, and spare no efforts to achieve the target of promoting employment on the strength that the ultimate goal of appropriating the employment funds is the implementation of employment policies. What matters most to the audit of special employment funds is the evaluation on the effectiveness and fairness of the use of funds. In addition, auditors are required to evaluate the establishment and implementation of the system of special employment funds as well as the mechanism of publicity, and the scientificity, rationality and implementation of the employment policies. For example, the audit of vocational training subsidy shall focus not only the authenticity and compliance of the use of funds, but the effect of training, namely whether the trainees can find jobs as they wished after the training and whether the design of vocational training is in line with the local situations. Third, regional divergences and the influence of policies really matters to the audit. Besides the Employment Promotion Act of the PRC and the Measures for the Administration of Employment Subsidy Funds issued by the central committee, the audit of special employment funds mainly takes the actual situations, employment policies and management measures of employment funds as references. In view of the regional divergence in policies, subsidy projects developed in various regions also differ, which requires sufficient preparation according to the status quo and characteristics of employment, employment policies, and enforcement regulations of management measures of employment funds. Also, it is overt that relevant policies can strongly impact special funds and are closely related to the interests of a mass of job seekers and unemployed groups in China. For the audit of special employment funds, it is significant to improve the operability and accuracy of policies and implementation rules, and potentiate the supervision and control of funds. The management of special employment funds must be performance-oriented and result-oriented.

Audit of Special Educational Funds. As the material conditions to ensure the development of education in China, educational funds occupy an important position in the state financial expenditure. Funds for education have been increasing year by year since the Reform and Opening up. After the audit of educational funds in 1985, audit institutions at all levels continued the audit on this issue in the next year in accordance with the unified arrangements of the State Audit Office. In 1986, over 2,200 competent administrative departments for education at or above the county level, more than 8,000 schools all over the country and educational funds summing up to ￥7.35 billion were audited, and ￥424 million were fund involved with violations against financial disciplines, accounting for 5.76% of the total. The main problems found included: misappropriation and embezzlement of educational funds, arbitrary charges and indiscriminate distribution of money and goods, serious extravagance and waste, poor management and illegal busines in some school-run enterprises, making false final accounts and transfers of funds. 80% of educational departments at or above the county-level and over 10,000 schools were audited during the that 2 years, achieving remarkable results. In 1990, audit institutions audited the educational funds of 130 institutions of higher learning, according to the statistics of 90 of which, ￥130 million were found violating the disciplines. Moreover, audit institutions also pointed out problems such as embezzlement, false making and transfer of educational funds and that the incomes from social services were not included in the financial management of the school. As a consequence, ¥3.05 million were turned over to the treasury, and another ¥ 58.48 million were newly added to the educational funds. After that, educational funds were audited every year, all stakeholders violating financial disciplines have all been seriously dealt with after audit activities, and suggestions on strengthening the financial management of colleges and universities were put forward, which attracted the attention from the State Education Commission and relevant institutions of education.

Audit of Special Scientific Research Funds. The audit on the use and management of funds for scientific research started in 1989, when the State Audit Office conducted the audit on this issue together with 11 provincial-level administrative regions including Hunan and Jiangxi. As a result, over ¥49 million were found involved with violations against financial disciplines, accounting for 5.6% of the total. The main problems were as follows: embezzlement of scientific research funds for building houses, procuring vehicles and doing business, low fund recovery rate led by the poor management of compensated use of funds, loss caused by improper selection of scientific research projects, etc. Under the mew situation of deepening the implementation of innovation-driven development strategy, the government's investment to scientific research has shown an escalating trend. Since 2012, the average annual growth rate of research input has been 11.4%, and in the year of 2015, China spent a total of ¥1.4 trillion on the scientific research and development. Over the past few years, the state and local governments have successively issued a series of regulations on reinforcing the management of funds for scientific research, and the guidelines have incrementally been evolved from "combining strict management with precaution" to "combining proper management with service, and streamlining administrative procedures". In September 2011, the Ministry of Finance and the Ministry of Science and Technology put forward the measures for optimizing the appropriation expenditure in the Notice on the Adjustment of Some Provisions on the Administration of Special Funds for Scientific Research of the National Science and Technology Plan and Public Welfare Industries (the Ministry of Finance, the Ministry of Education, [2011] No. 434), such as moderately adjusting the appropriation budgets, clarifying the corresponding procedures and authority, and gradually introducing the incentive mechanism to define the performance of researchers as indirect expenses. However, the government failed to explicitly stipulate how to standardize the use of performance expenditures in scientific research projects and whether the expenditures could be brought into the performance plate of the performance-based salary reform of public institutions launched at the same time, and the subsequent incentive expenditure policies have not been implemented yet. In practice, financial departments and audit institutions both believe that the incentive distributed in the scientific research fund is also a part of the performance plate of public institutions, and it has basically not been implemented in colleges and universities. As misuses of funds for scientific research have been constantly exposed, the Ministry of Education issued the Notice on further Implementing the Management Policies and Strengthening Scientific Research Funds for College and Universities (the Ministry of Education, the Ministry of Finance, [2011] No. 12), to supervise over the funds for scientific research in a more strict and regulatory manner, indicating that the state was determined to run a tight ship on this issue. The budget requirements became more specific and rigid, and the content of spending was further restricted within clear purposes. For example, in order to prevent the abuse of power for personal gain, it is specially stipulated that only relevant staff without incomes from wage and salary can obtain service fees, and the intellectual and labor value invested by scientific research personnel is strictly controlled. By analyzing the results of special inspection on the management of scientific research funds in colleges and universities, many factors such as inactive implementation of macro-policies, unsound management system, insufficient supervision, weak financial consciousness and lax execution of internal systems of universities have jointly contributed to the current plights. In order to smoothly complete the projects, scientific research personnel must accomplish the spending plans in line with the compulsory budget, which constrains scientific activities. As a result, chaotic phenomena such as "slack spending", "crash spending" and "random spending" emerge in endlessly. For structural over-expenditures beyond the reimbursement scope of regular scientific research funds, in some cases, stakeholders attempted to claim refunds through other invoices in an "ant move" way or falsely claim labor fees by fabricating fake staff lists, and the illegal use of scientific research funds also occurred from time to time. Some researchers have been sanctioned because of their infringements against laws and regulations, wanton reimbursement of scientific research funds, academic corruption and other problems emerged thick as hail. As a consequence, scientific research personnel in colleges and universities became the cynosure of ant-corruption. In July 2016, the General Office of the CPC Central Committee and the General Office of the State Council issued the Several Opinions of Further Improving Policies of Management of Scientific Research Funds of the State Revenue, indicating that administrative departments shall "predigest budgeting and delegate the authority of budget virement", "increase the share of overhead expenses and reinforce performance incentive", "declare the expense range of labor fees and take off the limit of proportion", "improve the treating methods of retention of carried forward funds and balance", and "manage the transverse funds in an independent and normative way". This was the design made for the management of funds of top-level research projects, and also the reform as well as innovation of the use and management of scientific research funds combining policy loosening, standardized management and supervision and accountability, which optimized the appropriation budget, management process and administration privilege. Since the 19th National Congress of the CPC, China has attached more significance to the management of scientific research funds of colleges and universities. For instance, in 2018, the State Council issued the Notice on Measures of Optimizing Scientific Research Management and Improving Scientific Research Performance, and in 2019, the Leading Party Group of the Ministry of Education promulgated the Notice on the Implementation of Relevant Documents of Endowing Scientific Research with Greater Autonomous Rights.

Chapter Seven: Audit of Investment in Fixed Assets

Contents of Audit of Investments in Fixed Assets

For the time being, main content of audit of investment in fixed assets in China runs through the whole project construction and operating cycle, and audit content varies in different periods.

Audit Content of Project Management at Early Stage

Project Decision-making. Audit in this aspect mainly investigates whether investment projects can meet the demand of economic development, people's livelihood and regional economic planning, and whether there are problems of abandoned construction work, low efficiency, waste of investment and poor construction quality because of inadequate research or hasty decision-making and decision failure caused by leaders' pursuit of political performance and face-saving projects. By auditing procedures of decision-making and discussing the scientific and normative nature of the projects, the validity of construction procedures of investment projects can be ensured. Such audit activities are usually carried out by browsing and investigating the research reports of investment projects, meeting minutes of decision-making meetings and documents at early stage, such as proposals for the project and feasibility study reports, so as to revel the problems in the early stage of decision-making of investment projects.

Project Construction Procedures. Audit in this aspect mainly focuses on whether proposals for the project, feasibility research reports, preliminary design and initial budget estimates have been replied by the national or local Development and Reform Commission and administrative departments of construction, whether there are false information in assessment reports of energy and environment, and whether the construction plans conform to the requirements of the overall urban planning. In addition, attentions shall also be paid to whether construction permits are obtained before starting the projects, whether the projects are launched blindly without necessary requirements, and whether the projects are started before the survey and design service. A complete set of legal construction procedures of investment projects can to a large extent ensure the smooth implementation of construction projects and their quality, security, cost and schedule. However, in spite of the importance, some investors and construction units still go their own ways and fail to carry out the engineering construction in accordance with legal procedures, which will inevitably cause loss in the national economy.

2. Audit the Funds of Project Construction

Fund Raising. Audit in this regard mainly checks whether the fund is raised in line with laws or through normal channels, whether there are loans or mortgage business related to false contract, and whether there are embezzlements of funds from other special funds or capital with written replies from supervising authority. The main purpose of audit of fund raising is to make sure the validity of sources of funds and the reliability when disposing the money, for fear that the funds may be frozen suddenly.

Fund Appropriation. Audit in this respect mainly checks whether the special funds are allocated in time in line with the schedule, whether there are problems such as intercepting and retaining project funds under false pretenses, and whether the quality and the progress of work are impacted because of unpunctual payment of funds. To ensure the abundant funds for construction is the prerequisite for timely completion of investment projects. Project delay will not contribute to squeezing the construction cost, but will on the contrary cause cost inflation and affect the final economic benefits due to rising material prices and changes in the economic environment.

Use of Construction Funds. Audit in this respect checks whether an account for special fund has been set up, whether the fund is used rationally according to construction plans, whether cost accounting is clear and accurate, whether expenditures are in line with requirements of project construction, whether the cost of construction comes out from the special account, whether there are problems of embezzlement, whether the signing of contract and the allocation of funds are strictly in accordance with the bidding agreement, and whether the financial statement is made according to the progress of works. The safe and compliant use of funds during the period of construction can effectively guarantee the construction progress and prevent the construction from suspension or being unfinished because of shortage of funds.

Audit Content of Project Construction

Management

Project Internal Control System. Audit in this aspect mainly checks whether an internal control system is established and strictly performed, whether the project decision-making is made according to articles of association, whether the construction project management team is made up of competent and conscientious staff, and whether there are supervisory and restraining mechanism for personnel in key position.

Project Bidding. Audit in this aspect mainly checks the bidding management of investing enterprises, namely whether the Bidding Law and the Control Regulations of Regional Construction Market are strictly implemented, so as to earnestly strengthen the investigation, design, supervision and procurement of equipment and materials. In addition, it is also part of the duty to investigate whether there are too many thresholds in bidding documents of investors or problems of cooperation with bidding, whether the bid is opened publicly in the place specified by th government, whether there are scandals of together-conspired bidding, contracting bidding or bull campaign by feat of false qualification. Tendering and bidding in the process of project construction is a corruption prone area in construction projects. Statistical data shows that almost 40% of corruption in construction projects occurs in the process of tendering and bidding, which is a weak point of the current supervisory system and the key link that shall be paid attention to in the investment audit.

Project Contracting. Audit in this respect checks whether there are problems of parceling out the contract to several parts or subtracting illegally, whether tenderers are qualified to take over the projects, whether there are issues of undertaking projects bypassing the due level. Moreover, it requires extensive investigation on whether managers of the investor have broken rules for their own profits, forced up prices illegally or practiced jobbery. The state bans the subcontracting in the project construction by explicit order, but driven interests, subcontracting is considerably common in the actual construction. In the meanwhile, it is found in the audit that subcontracting is not easy to define exactly, and the evidence collection is even more difficult, which is a prominent difficult problem in the current investment audit.

Performance of Service Institutions. Audit in this aspect mainly checks whether the engineering consultants have set the bidding prices in line with the contract and missed no item, whether the project funds have been strictly audited in project settlement, whether the quality of detective work could meet the requirements, whether there are cost inflation and other problems led by inaccurate investigation, whether the design papers are provided in time, and whether the design changes are reasonable. As a third-party quality-control unit, supervisor is of self-evident importance. In the process of audit, it is necessary to focus on checking whether the supervisory system is sound, whether the supervisory personnel can fulfill the terms of the contract and be devoted to their duties, whether the records of vital nodes and concealed work are supervised by supervisory personnel.

Contract Management. Audit in this aspect mainly checks whether elements of contract signing are complete, whether the content of contracts violate laws and regulations, whether the interests of investors are materially infringed, whether the contracts are registered in relevant departments for reference, whether there are problems of duplicate contract, whether there are additionally signed supplementary contracts which are in violation of the substantive positions of the contract documents, whether the project settlement and claim are adjusted and calculated in strict accordance with the terms of the contract, whether the management of contracts of investors are well-organized, and whether there are problems of investment losses, lagging progress and poor construction quality caused by ill contract management.

Schedule and Quality. Audit in this respect mainly checks whether the investment project has carried out effective field construction control, whether the quality control system has been strictly implemented, whether measures such as active inspection and random check have been taken to control the construction quality, whether the project construction schedule is in accordance with the plan, and further analysis is required if there is any deviation, whether the quality of construction conforms to national standards, whether the actual situation accords with contract requirements, and whether there are problems of cheating on workmanship and materials and manufacture in a rough way.

Audit Content of Engineering Cost Management

The Budgetary Estimates of Construction Projects. Audit in this aspect checks whether the investment projects exceed the scope of budget estimates for what reason, whether the construction projects are approved in the condition of being beyond the budget, and whether the procedures are complete. If the expenditure exceeds the budget estimates, audit in this aspect mainly checks whether the budget of the construction project has been adjusted and whether the adjustments are legal. After investigating the reasons for changes in preliminary design, whether the changes of designing scheme have been fully discussed and demonstrated and conform to the decision-making procedures, and whether the changes can be conducive to the construction of the project and saving the investment.

Management of Project Cost. Audit in this aspect mainly checks whether the costs of institutions of engineering consulting service are reasonable, whether the project price settlement has been strictly reviewed, whether there are problems such as overestimation of prices and work quantity, whether the payment of project funds is approved in accordance with the prescribed procedures. In addition, audit in this respect needs to focus on changes in verification and price calculation, checks whether the prices are set strictly according to contracts, whether the design sizes up the requirements, and analyzes the standardization of the cost control procedures and the effectiveness of cost management.

Audit Content of Post-Construction Management

After the project construction is finished and put into service, the interest post-evaluation of the investment project shall be carried out. Through the comparative analysis of the research reports of the operating efficiency after completion and estimated efficiency before completion, the actual benefits of the investment could be objectively evaluated. The evaluation shall not only focus on the economic efficiency of the projects, but the social and ecological benefits brought by the investment. For some investment projects with poor efficiency, more attention shall be paid to whether the inadequacies can be confronted directly, and effective measures should be taken improve the efficiency according to their own conditions.

Auditing Methods for Investments in Fixed Assets

Audit methods refer to means and approaches employed by auditors to collect audit data, process audit information, analyze audit issues and collect audit evidence in the specific audit process. In the narrow sense, audit methods refer to all technical means that auditors take to obtain sufficient and effective audit evidence, and in a broad sense, audit methods also cover all techniques, means and approaches used in the whole process of audit in addition to technical methods used to collect audit evidence. Auditors' employment of appropriate and reasonable audit methods is an important guarantee to improve the audit quality of investment projects, but the audit process may be restrained by law, cost and time limit, so the investment audit of fixed assets shall make the most of the limited cost and time on the premise of complying with state laws. Therefore, employing audit methods suited to characteristics of investment projects is of great significance to making efficient audit programs.

Currently speaking, audit methods of construction projects of fixed assets in China mainly include hypothesis verification, experience-based judgement, observation, investigation, sample check, information query, clue collection, questioning, field review, data query, tracking down capital movements, analytical review and follow-up auditing. The auditing methods commonly used in the process of audit are as follows:

Hypothesis Verification

Hypothesis verification requires auditors to be problem-oriented and implement audit business with suspicious minds. The method is a prerequisite for audit of fixed assets investment, namely that only on the basis of irregularities in fixed assets investment projects can audit be carried out and problems be pointed out, so as to avoid the subsequent huge economic losses. In the course of audit, auditors shall make pointed references to introduce potential problems of construction irregularities, and take the problems as the focus to further collect related audit evidence so as to demonstrate the hypothetical problems. The main steps are as follows: first, point out vulnerable spots and possible doubtful points in project management according to the files submitted by auditees, then analyze the degree of influence of the doubtful points on the investment projects and collect audit evidence around the problems, and at last judge whether the audit doubts exist or not through the evidence and information.

Clue Collection

"A fortress breached from within", as an old saying goes. Within a short period of time of the course of audit, auditors cannot always clearly know the rope of the decision-making, construction and use of funds of investment projects, and it is, of course difficult to find out the illegal criminal activities under the cloak of legality. Participants and users of construction projects of fixed asset investment are insiders under normal circumstances, and it is auditors' duty to make these insiders clue providers. In the process of fixed asset investment, it is destined that the interest of one part will be infringed with the purpose of benefitting another part, and those who suffered economic losses are objectively likely to report the people with vested interests. For auditors, pointing out violations in massive construction data is nothing short of looking for a needle in a bundle of hay, and it is out of question that extensively mobilizing the masses to report violations of laws and disciplines is an audit method which yields twice the results with half the effort. The main steps are as follows: first, audit institutions announce the reporting measures on the audit site, then further collect audit-related clues through internal reports and analyze the authenticity of the clues combined with the reality of the projects, and finally further get to the bottom of the problems according to the analysis of these clues.

Experience-based Judgement

Auditors usually incrementally accumulate audit experience in the long-term audit course and the whole career, but the experience can be multifarious because of differences in professional learning ability, knowledge system, length of service and specific audit projects of auditors. Even for audit of the same project, different audit views can be formed because f different personal viewpoints, positions and perspectives. Therefore, audit experience varies with each individual. However, audit experience can still be learned and inherited. Excellent auditors may generalize and summarize their experience accumulated in years of audit work and impart the experience as well as good practice to the new generation of auditing staff. On the strength of research and learning audit experience and combining with practical work, the new blood may cultivate the professional sensitiveness and audit intuition by learning, analyzing and summarizing each audit project and audit cases. For instance, experienced auditors can judge the authenticity of a deposit slip by the shape of the seal instead of going to the bank in person, which saves the manpower and time.

Tracking down Capital Movements

Fixed assets investment always involves a huge sum of money, and the most common audit method is to audit according to fund flows. Funds for special construction and loans are particularly suitable to be investigated by tracking down all links of capital movements, so as to find out whether there are problems of intercepting and misappropriating the money, and whether the money is used legally and effectively on demand. In the actual course of audit, auditors can usually point out the problems of waste and embezzlement of funds in construction projects, which prevent the investment from achieving its originally planned targets and harm the interests of the state and investors. By taking all links and the whole course of capital movements under auditors' control, the methods can surely achieve satisfactory results. However, the method also has its own significant shortcoming: tracking the final effect of all capital movements will cost a huge raft of manpower and energy and prolong the audit cycle. Therefore, under realistic conditions, only when there are well-defined problems of capital movements can this method be used in the audit course. The main steps are as follows: first, determine the source and sectors of using of construction funds, then track the whereabouts of funds and calculate the amount of money spent for different purposes, and finally verify the truth of fund utilizing.

Database Inquiry

Database inquiry, also known as SQL statement query method, refers to the method of screening, contrasting and analyzing the massive construction data by feat of the query system of computer database. With the development of science and technology, more and more data are stored by computers. When electronic data is submitted to audit institutions as audit information by auditees, whether auditors can process the relevant electronic data in a timely and effective manner becomes the first step to carry out the audit work normally. Carrying out audit works by virtue of computer has been an important audit method under the new situation. Allowing for the progress in engineering valuation software, the well-organized implementation of plans on investment project management and the exchange storage of a mass of data information through computers, auditees are gradually superseding traditional paper documents by electronic data, and all records reflecting investment management are stored in databases in different modes of data processing. Therefore, auditors must keep pace with the times by updating audit methods and keeping up with the trend of audit development. The main steps are as follows: collect the electronic data of auditees at first, screen the data to obtain destination data for audit activities secondly, then write SELECT inquire statements to search key information, and at last analyze the problems revealed by the query results.

Information Query

Information query requires auditors to browse written documents such as relevant accounts, meeting minutes and contracts of auditees with the purpose of collecting audit evidence. The documents include project proposals, project approvals, feasibility study reports, preliminary designs, initial budget estimates, financial information, bidding documents, meeting minutes, bills of quantities and design papers. Moreover, electronic and paper information of NDRC and departments of planning, finance, land and construction can also be good auxiliary reference. The effectiveness and validity of information query to collect audit evidence are based on the reliability of the sources of audit data. Hence, auditors must at first ensure the authenticity, reliability and validity of the audit information when collecting evidence, and all audit works shall be carried out within the scope of relevant laws and regulations.

Questioning

Questioning, also known as interviewing, refers to the method by which auditors put questions to the staff of auditees for specific information and make records of investigation. The form of query is not restricted to only personnel interview and telephone interview, but applying by letter and holding a symposium. The audit evidence collected by this method is in oral form, namely the evidentiary weight is not strong enough, thus other correlative evidence is needed to draw conclusions.

Investigation

Investigation requires auditors to identify audit tasks and topics according to characteristics of audit projects by questionnaire survey, panel discussion, mobile APP survey and internet questionnaire survey, so as to make pointed references for information in a wide range, and summarize as well as analyze the information to form audit evidence. When there are violations of laws and regulations in investment construction management, the internal control system formulated by managers would perform no function practically, and the audit data presented to auditors is "processed". Therefore, it is difficult for auditors to distinguish between the authentic ones and the fake ones, which brings great difficulties to the audit work. Based on audit experience and professional intuition, auditors may be able to point out the doubts, but more information and even evidence through investigation around investment projects are required to further verify their judgements. For instance, in the audit of effect of investment and construction projects, the most direct and effective feedback is usually obtained by visiting and inquiring the users. The sector universally criticized by the public can always be the audit focus which implies a lot of "inside information".

Observation

Observation is the method by which auditors can obtain the most intuitive audit evidence by field investigation on the scale of construction, progress of works, financial management system, use of funds, project management and construction quality of investment projects. The method is considerably common in audit. Auditors try to verify the authenticity of investment projects by means of on-site observation, so as to promote the understanding of the basic conditions of investment projects and obtain the most direct information. For instance, by verifying the work amount and checking the visual progress of the construction projects, auditors can have direct access to truth about the projects, such as the scale of construction, the possibility of lockout and the fund security.

Sample Check

Sample check, also known as audit sampling, is adopted as an audit method in consideration of restrictions of audit cost and audit cycle. Sample check saves a lot of manpower, material resources and time, but it also brings great audit risks. Because of the randomness and contingency of the samples, some problems may not be pointed out. In the practice of investment audit, auditors tend to conduct sample surveys mainly on project quality and material quality, that is because large-scale projects always involve many materials, and a comprehensive review will consume a lot of manpower and material resources, and the audit cycle will be prolonged. By sample check, the condition of local quality can be an effective evaluation for the quality of the whole project. One thing to note, auditors must take the audit risks into full account and reasonably determine the range of choice of sample check.

Follow-up Auditing

Follow-up audit is in de facto the combination of pre-audit, in-process audit and post-audit. Following the principle line of project approval—construction—acceptance check—use, auditors shall participate in the audit of decision-making of the construction of fixed assets investment projects, the audit of quality, progress and cost management, and the audit of evaluation after the completion of the construction in 3 different stages. Through the follow-up audit of each stage of the project, auditors can make audit evaluations on the decision-making of project investment, the use of funds, the management of projects themselves, the completion acceptance and operational benefits in the service period.

Audit Procedures and Programs for Investment in Fixed Assets

Audit Procedures for Investment in Fixed Assets

Audit procedures consist of the workflow, audit content, time requirements and personnel placement that audit institutions and auditors must stick to in the course of audit work. Audit procedures for investment in fixed assets include: the determination of audit objectives, the formation of audit programs, the necessary preparation before audit, the implementation of audit. the final report of audit activities, as well as the feedback and tracking of problems.

Determination of Audit Projects. Determining audit projects is the first and the most significant link of the audit of investment in fixed assets, because a reasonable project selection can bring the audit of such projects and the supervision on socioeconomic order with abundant results and guiding significance respectively. Therefore, audit institutions must determine the audit projects of investment in fixed assets on the strength of taking the economic development, macroeconomic policies of the state and the reform measures of the government into full account. A small number of audit activities of domestic investment projects are arranged in a unified manner by the State Audit Office, such as the audit of the investment in government-subsidized housings. On the contrary, most of the audit activities are carried out by local audit institutions themselves according to requirements of local governments, local economic climate and macroeconomic policies of the state. When determining audit projects, audit institutions are inclined to choose the use of large-value funds, the implementation of reform measures of the government and their effect. Generally speaking, audit projects of investment in fixed assets mainly focus on the following aspects: key areas of fixed asset investment projects of the state, such as the construction of railway transportation and water conservancy facilities; public service and social area of people's livelihood, such as the construction of urban rail traffic facilities and government-subsidized housings; and good-sized public works such as the construction of university towns, hospitals and museums.

With the remarkable development of China's national economy and the improvement of the investment climate, the number and scale of fixed assets investment projects have been increasing exponentially. Most fixed assets investment projects are involved in stable guarantee of abundant financial and human resources, but audit institutions are insufficient in not only manpower but budget by contrast. Therefore, audit institutions must pay more attention to how to achieve the best audit results possible under the circumstance of limited resources.

Formation of Audit Project Plans. Audit project plans refers to the schedule and arrangement made by audit programs at the beginning of the year for audit projects and investigation projects. Getting involved in the consumption of huge sums of money, fixed assets investment projects are characterized by complicated audit contents, wide audit scope and long audit cycle. Therefore, reasonable arrangement of audit projects, sound allocation of audit resources and well-organized job management can ensure the completion of audit activities on time on the premise of ensuring the audit quality of the investment projects. In addition, more attention shall be paid to 4 sectors when submitting audit reports and work plans: first, the management of public funds and state-owned resources should be taken seriously in order to promote the stable economic development, boost the reform, readjust the economic structure, protect the welfare of the people and prevent potential socioeconomic risks; second, major projects are considered as important issues, and the construction of major projects is actually the priority among priorities, so audit supervision over this sector is of great significance, and new conditions and problems shall attract more attention; third, audit programs should pay more attention to people's livelihood, focusing on people's most concerning, direct-acting and realistic problems, namely education, culture, insurance, rural cooperative medical service, and the construction

315

of Beautiful China and pilot towns, so as to promote the establishment of a sound and thorough social security system and a living environment for people's lives in peace and contentment; fourth, priority shall be given to the economic responsibility audit of leading cadres, and further standardize the exercise of power by combining the strategy of combating corruption and upholding integrity with the implementation of the Eight-point Austerity Rules.

Preparation before Audit. The pre-audit preparation serves as the initial point of project audit and the foundation point of carrying out the next step of audit. Whether the preparation is taken meticulously and carefully or not is immediately related to the smooth development of the whole project audit. To make adequate preparation, it is necessary to fully and extensively collect the financial and operational information and make pointed references on previous auditing files on the strength of actual situations, with the purpose of understanding the problems of auditees and making preparation for identifying the audit emphasis. In addition, staff participating in audit activities shall be organized to get familiar with the business process of auditees, so as to point out the unreasonable aspects.

Main tasks of the preparation for the audit of investment in fixed assets include: pre-audit study and investigation for audit teams consisting of auditors, on the basis of fully understanding the characteristics and requirements of investment projects; selecting reasonable audit methods after the pre-audit study and investigation; preparing audit programs.

First, carry out pre-audit investigation to get the picture of the projects. Adequate acquaintance is the prerequisite to start the work, and similarly, the beginning of project audit is also based on full investigation and understanding of the construction of the investment project. Only by fully understanding the investment projects can audit institutions carry out audit activities with clear purposes, namely determining the objectives, scope, content and key points of audit reasonably, and then providing the theoretical and practical basis for audit methods and further lying solid foundation for audit programs. This requires auditors to clearly understand the scale, content, background, sources of funding and operation of investment projects, as well as the organizational structure, personnel allocation, internal control system, financial management and construction project management, etc. Because of their unicity, characteristics of different construction projects vary, and it is not wise to blindly copy the fundamental state of other projects for convenience. Second, determine the objectives, scope and key points of audit. Audit of investment to fixed assets shall get the audit objectives clear at first, audit scope shall be selected appropriately, and the key points of audit should also be highlighted pertinently. The limited audit resources determine that instead of giving consideration to all audit aspects averagely, audit activities shall make the focal points stand out by determining the objectives, direction and focuses, so as to maximize the audit efficiency. Audit objectives refers to the audit results estimated by audit institutions and audit teams before carrying out their service. Without targets, there is no direction for action, and the determination of audit objectives shows the path for the development of the business of audit teams. When faced with choices, all decision made should be closely related to the audit objectives set previously. Audit activities should be carried out around audit objectives, in line with which audit directions shall be selected. Focusing on economic interests and social benefits, audit objectives of investment in fixed assets are mostly guided by macro investment policies, therefore, more attention should be paid to raising the service efficiency of constructional funds of the state after considering the background, construction content and sources of funds of the investment projects. Instead of blindly pursuing "being magnificent", the determination of audit objectives must be practical, and one objective can be broken down into several sub-targets for audit institutions' convenience.

Audit scope refers to the content that auditors shall review in order to achieve the audit objectives, such as the sources of funds. The audit scope should be determined reasonably by comprehensively evaluating characteristics of audit objectives and investment projects. Within limited time, auditors will struggle to cope with too many issues if the scope is exceedingly widespread, and many hidden problems cannot be pointed out or investigated thoroughly. If the audit scope is too narrow, on the one hand, many audit resources may be left idle, on the other hand, some audit work will be overlapped, leading to the mismatch between problems and investigation. As a result, audit objectives cannot be actually achieved, and audit risks will be increased greatly. When determining the scope, auditors shall take characteristics of construction, investment scale, construction procedures, sources of funds internal control system and regional policies into full account.

The audit focus of investment in fixed assets refers to "prone areas" of problems, which attract more attention from auditors, such as project bidding and equipment procurement. In determining the audit focus, auditors shall go through the impact caused by construction, risks brought by project management and manipuility of specific audit implementation.

Finally, prepare audit programs. Prior to the implementation of audit activities, audit institutions shall formulate appropriate audit programs. For instance, Changsha Municipal Auditing Bureau asks leaders of audit teams to be responsible for the preparation of audit programs, which must be reviewed by persons in charge of the office of audit teams and reported to the leading cadres of sub-management bureau for approval before being carried out. In the preparation of audit program, it is a prerequisite to do a good job of pre-audit investigation and data analysis in order to give full play to the role of scientific guidance. Audit teams should actively explore and innovate new audit methods, integrate audit resources and establish teams for data analysis, so as to adapt to the pre-audit data mining under the background of big data. Moreover, reference check of the internal control system and business process of auditees is necessary to auditors, with the purpose of preliminarily estimating the prone areas of problems, forming a set of clear audit opinions on the strength of mastering the overall situation, and determining the key points and difficulties of audit as matters needing attention in audit programs. In line with characteristics of audit projects, the efficiency and effects of audit activities can be greatly improved by making the audit task allocation well and identifying the audit load-points.

Conduct of Audit. The conduct of audit refers to collecting audit evidence, keeping audit records, making audit papers, investigating the economic activities and internal control management of auditees, and finally exchanging opinions with auditees in accordance with audit programs which are formulated and passed in advance under the guidance with relevant departments and audit institutions.

Major steps of the conduct of audit are as follows:

First, audit notice. Audit institutions shall, before formally starting the audit work, issue audit notices to auditees. Audit works starts as soon as auditees receive audit notices. Second, pre-audit meeting with auditees on audit sites. The meeting is the initial contact between the staff of audit teams led by leading cadres of audit institutions as well as the management layer and persons in charge of auditees, mainly in order to introduce the staff involved in the coming audit activities, discipline of audit work and matters needing attention. Auditors are obliged to any questions raised by auditees about the audit work. Third, audit evidence collection. Audit teams shall, in light of the information presentation and the needs of audit work, and in combination with the characteristics of audit projects, put forward requirement on the access to relevant information, and the appointed files, including evidence of inner housekeeping such as internal rules and regulations and contract text, and financial evidence such as financial accounting books, original certificates and bank statements, shall be submitted to auditors by auditees unconditionally. During the collection of audit evidence, both parties shall pay attention to handover and custody of the evidence and ensure that there is no loss or damage of the files. Before the collection, a list of evidence should be made, according to which relevant information will be collected item by item, so as not to leave any valid evidence. Fourth, working papers preparation. Members of audit teams analyze and evaluate the data collected, and make audit records by reorganizing and reprocessing the information with high values in use or close relationship with construction projects. Problems pointed out in the actual course of audit and their sources should be recorded in detail in a timely and accurate manner for subsequent inspection. Audit papers are the highly refined and reprocessed audit materials by auditors, which are inducted and reorganized on the strength of facts and simplified in a terse manner. Auditor should be careful about making audit records to truly reflect the entire process of the conduct of audit. In the meanwhile, some audit reports can be used as audit papers. Fifth, the exchange of audit opinions. The purpose of exchange of audit opinions is to initially explain the problems found in the course of audit to auditees and ask them whether they have any objection to such issues, so as to try to reach a consensus with the auditees on the actual situations. If discrepancies exist, auditees are given permission by audit institutions to provide supplementary materials or statements.

Reports and Rectification. An audit report is a written report that audit team summarizes and reports the actual situations and problems of audit to higher audit institutions after discussing tasks and issues on the spot. Audit reports shall be made open and transparent, and the results must be fair and credible, and only in this way can audit institutions demonstrate their transparency and public credibility. After issuing audit reports, audit institutions shall follow up the rectification of audit problems and the implementation of audit opinions mentioned in audit reports, and auditees are asked to report back the rectification situation to audit institutions within the required time. At the same time, audit projects without feedback shall further be analyzed to find out the reasons, and audit institutions will supervise the rectification again.

Audit Programs on Investment in Fixed Assets

As the guide to accomplish audit objectives and tasks, audit program is closely bound up to the effect and quality of audit projects. Audit teams shall. After investigation, evaluate the key issues of auditees, and formulate corresponding measures and audit programs according to the assessment results. The audit of investment in fixed assets is the "programmed" audit. The Enforcement Regulations issued by the General Offices of the CPC Central Committee and the State Council further made clear the use of audit results especially, thus the characteristics of audit of investment in fixed assets determine that audit programs are necessary in particular before carrying out audit works. Audit institutions shall pay close attention to the possibility of auditors' and auditees' potential problems in the management of investment projects, and evaluate how the investment projects are running in a comprehensive and objective manner. Before the formal enforcement, leading persons of audit institutions would make audit programs, highlight the key points, scope, time requirements and personnel allocation that need to be noticed, because the quality of audit programs is directly relating to the job content of audit of investment in fixed assets, and an audit program which is reasonable in arrangement and appropriate in measures can usually facilitate the quality and efficiency of audit work.

Determine Audit Objectives. Taking the use of funds of governmental investment projects as the main line, audit of investment can promote the well-organized construction of the project and give full play to the investment efficiency of capital by investigating the fund appropriation and procedures of project construction, revealing problems of violations of laws and disciplines, loss and waste and serious mistakes of management, and put forward advice and suggestions, so as to regulate the implementation management, ameliorate investment performance, boost the campaign of anti-corruption and make the investment work at full capacity.

Pre-audit Investigation on Audit Projects. In the

preparatory phase, audit institutions shall carry out pre-audit investigation to get a clear picture of basic situations of auditees. Pre-audit investigation is an activity to visit and inquire relevant units for basic information through internet and archival sources according to the content, scope, key points and methods of audit, so as to grasp the first hand information. A good pre-audit investigation is of significance to understand the background of project construction from a macro prospective, and establish key points of audit in a targeted way.

Determine Scope and Objects of Audit. The scope of audit is the collection, use and management of funds as well as the project implementation from the very beginning to the end, and the spot check on project cost and quality. The objects of audit include the construction units or investors of the project, and the fund allocation and use related to the project in previous years as well as relevant units involved in the project implementation can also be included in the scope if necessary.

Determine the Key Content of Audit. According to the objectives and scope of audit, key points are as follows: First, the audit of project entity and internal control system. project unit entities, registered capital and other factors as well as the implementation and effect of the internal control system shall be spot checked. Second, the audit of project implementation. The first is to examine the legitimacy of bidding process, focusing on whether there are problems of not tendering with due qualification or not tendering in the visible market, analyze the causes and responsibilities, and spot check whether the survey, design, construction and supervision of the project are conducted in line with provisions of tender. The second is to review the compliance of construction procedures, namely whether the project is implemented according to the basic national construction program, whether the necessary procedures are complete, whether the production drawing and design documents have been approved by the examining institutions, whether the permissions of firefighting and environmental protection have been obtained, whether the procedures of completion acceptance are complete. The third is to check the implementation of construction contracts, namely the audit of the authenticity and legality of the signing, performance, modification and termination of contracts of construction projects, and the audit on whether the all types of contracts are signed on the strength of bidding documents, whether the subjects of contracts are clear, and whether the winning bidders are consistent with contract units and collection units. The fourth is to audit the authenticity and legality of the executive conditions of budget estimates, investigate whether the implementation of the project is in line with the reply, and adjustments are necessary in case of inconsistency, and whether there is unplanned expenditure outside the budget estimates. Third, the audit of the sources and use of funds. The first is to examine the sources of funds, namely to audit check whether the project investment is raised as planned, whether the sources of funds conform to the relevant laws and regulations and the provisions of the contract, and whether there are fraudulent agreements signed with the purpose of swindling financial subsidies. The second is to examine the use of funds and verify whether the funds are used and managed in accordance with compliance purposes, whether the expenditures are made in line with contracts, whether there are problems of seizing, retaining, occupying and embezzling fund under various names. Spot check is demanded when it comes to the use of management cost by construction units in amortized investment, focusing on pointing out whether there are expenditures in violation against the Eight-Point Austerity Rules. Fourth, extended audit of relevant units participating in the construction. Audit in this aspect mainly checks the following contents: First, conduct a sample survey on relevant collection units to emphatically investigate whether there are problems of transferring or embezzling the funds of construction and benefit transfer, with the use of funds as a main line. Second, check whether there are problems of illegal subcontract, whether the subcontractors are qualified, and further track down the direction of fund flows by auditing relevant construction organization. Fifth, audit of the settlement of construction costs, turnkey project, pile foundation, furnish, weak current, scenery and part of the auxiliary projects within the redline. Audit supervision on links of transfer of engineering data, communication with auditees and major issues of decrease in accounting is necessary, with the purpose of pointing out whether there are problems of over-evaluation, settlement no in accordance with the prices determined in bidding documents and contracts, and inadequate or unreasonable settlement basis, and providing necessary audit trail for further audit activities.

Response Measures Determined for Audit Matters. First, evaluate the degree of dependency on internal control to determine the effectiveness of the test internal control. Second, determine main audit steps and methods. Investment audit generally adopts on-site audit, and asks for relevant information by verifying the detailed accounts, examining relevant construction units and some of the construction sites on the spot, inquiring and observing personnel concerned as well as other professional auditing means. Third, determine the time of on-site audit and arrange the schedule reasonably according to audit tasks. Fifth, adjust audit programs and extended audit of relevant units in line with the needs.

Schedule of Audit. First, the pre-audit phase. Auditors shall read engineering files, inquire peripheral information, conduct pre-audit investigation, protocol audit programs and issue audit notice 10 to 20 days before the formal on-site audit. Second, the implementation phase. According to the difficulty level and the amount of money involved, the audit cycle should be determined, mostly 2 to 6 months. Third, the phase of audit reports. After the on-site audit, audit teams shall write audit reports and issue audit documents within 15 to 30 days according to audit evidence.

Reasonable Arrangement of the Audit Staff Division. According to work characteristics and professional proficiency, audit teams can be divided into financial audit teams and engineering audit teams. Financial teams are mainly responsible for the audit of the use and management of project funds, the establishment of units of project entity, the performance of registered assets and internal control system, and the use of management cost of construction units, and also participate in the extended audit of relevant units. Engineering teams are mainly answerable for the audit of project cost management, the implementation of basic procedures of the construction and the executive conditions of the bidding system, as well as the random inspection and audit of project quality.

Chapter Eight: Conclusion-Problems in China's Government Audit and Countermeasures

China's system of government audit was formally launched relatively late compared with western developed countries. During the development of several decades, audit institutions, together with the cooperation and guidance of party committees and governments at all levels, have fulfilled their duties of audit supervision and continuously expanded the breadth and depth of government audit in line with laws and regulations, making remarkable achievements in supervision and restriction of power, maintaining the state economic security and boosting the campaign of anti-corruption. However, what cannot be neglected is that there are still many loopholes in audit system, audit quality, audit information disclosure, accountability mechanism and performance audit.

Defects in Administrative Government

Audit

Established on the ground of its own political, economic and social conditions, the government audit system of any state shall out of question evolve with changes in such determinants. Determined by the specific national conditions during the current historical period, China adopts the administrative government audit, but allowing for the deficiencies exposed in audit courses, the system cannot adapt to the political and economic development at the current stage anymore.

Lacking of the Independence in Audit Institutions

Under the circumstance of administrative government audit, the lack of independence has been the most principal factor hindering audit supervision. At the inception stage, administrative government audit was designed to strengthen the cooperation between central and local audit institutions, ensure the implementation of policies and wills of the state, and chip away at the influence of local governments on audit institutions at the corresponding levels. With changes in economic and political condition, disadvantages of the system have incrementally loomed large in practical work, and the independence as well as objectivity of audit work have also been crippled. First, from the perspective of institution setting, China's audit institutions are under the dual leadership of audit institutions at the next higher level and local governments at the corresponding level, leading to the problems of "divided policies from various sources" and "multiple administrative instructions". Therefore, audit institutions are trapped in a dilemma of "obeying the superior" or "placing emphasis on the subordinate", or in other words, shall audit institutions report the situation to the superior as it stands or deliver the report according to the administrative instructions of the local government? Second, judging from interest game, there are both accordance and contradictions in the interest relationship between the local and the central. When faced with policies adverse to local interests, local governments are more inclined to be ostensibly obedient instead of implementing the policies faithfully, while it is the important responsibility of the government audit to supervise and audit the financial revenues and expenditures and operating activities of the government. As a pig in the middle, audit institutions have always been caught in the dilemma when faced with conflicts of interests, and the audit effects have also suffered major setbacks. Third, from the point of effect of supervision, audit institutions are subordinate to administrative departments, indicating that being part of the government, the government audit is also responsible for the supervision over financial revenues and expenditures of the government in the meanwhile. It is crystal clear that the nature of internal supervision to a large extent undermines the objectivity and independence of the audit work, and audit institutions are vulnerable to the intervention and disturbance of all powers and departments. As a result, the function of supervision cannot be fully performed.

Independence is the principle of the most significance in audit work. Influenced by the dual leadership system in China, the intrinsic contradictions of the government audit have seriously hindered the independence of audit institutions. whether in terms of institutional setup, interest game and the effect of supervision, audit institutions have not been equipped with the necessary independence, which directly impacts the consequence of the government audit. That is also the largest drawback of administrative government audit.

Lacking of the Independence among Auditors

The Auditing Standards set clear requirements for the independence of auditors. It is clearly stipulated in the Organization Law that the appointment and removal of persons in charge of audit institutions are mainly determined by the governments and People's Congresses at the corresponding levels. Article 15 of the Audit Law and Article 13 of the Enforcement Regulations of the Audit Law provide that "local audit institutions at various levels shall seek for opinions from audit institutions at the next higher levels in advance when it comes to the appointment and removal of persons in charge". Such regulations stress that audit institutions have some power over the appointment and removal of auditors, but in practical work, the power of personnel appointment and removal, especially those of main persons in charge, is still held by local governments. At this rate, auditors are very likely to be controlled and restrained by local governments during the course of audit supervision, and the independence of government audit cannot be ensured. Meanwhile, auditors themselves are also "economic men", who may also be tempted by interests and have economic interest relationships with auditees, which disenables the objectivity and independence of the audit work.

Lacking of the Independence of Audit Funds

Subordinate the administrative departments, audit institutions at various levels in China's administrative government audit system have to obtain funds from local financial budgets, which means that the funds of audit institutions are examined and approved by financial departments at the same level. According to the features of organization of China's government audit, local audit institutions shall exercise the power of supervision over the financial revenues and expenditures and operating activities of local government sectors. Therefore, there is a supervision relationship between local audit institutions and financial departments in essence. However, on the other hand, audit institutions and auditor are very likely to be constrained during the auditing process once the independence of source and use of audit funds—the economic guarantee of all necessary activities of audit institutions—cannot be ensured, and the quality of audit supervision would be inevitably impacted. At the same time, the needful funds of audit institutions cannot always be guaranteed in some economically underdeveloped areas allowing for the embarrassing fiscal situations of local governments, which would to a large extent deter audit institutions from carrying out the work and responsibility normally.

Unsatisfactory Quality of Government

Audit

Insufficient Competence of Auditors

Together with audit institutions, auditors constitute an important subject of the government audit, playing an important role in audit supervision. Therefore, the competence of auditors matters a lot to improving audit quality, fairness, authority and the function of audit supervision. China's National Auditing Standards explicitly stipulate that auditors shall have decent professional competency, namely relevant occupational knowledge, vocational ability and work experience, in performing audit services. However, throughout the team of government audit at present, there have still been insufficiencies.

Professional Competence of Auditors. Being highly professional, the government audit involves in comprehensive knowledge of various disciplines, including economics, auditing, law, statistics, accountancy, information technology, engineering, etc. Meanwhile, with the development of the government audit, some specific industries and key issues, such as government procurement and air pollution prevention and control, have incrementally been cynosures. Thus, the government audit has put forward higher requirements on the vocational competence of auditors. Under such circumstance, auditors shall not only master the systematic knowledge of auditing and economics, but an abundant knowledge reserve of other relevant disciplines. At present, China has an audit team of more than 10,000 auditors, the vast majority of whom are accounting and auditing professionals, while talents in other fields are scarce. When it comes to the audit of some specific fields, the audit team has to suffer the lack of trained personnel. In new fields such as performance audit, what prior to professional knowledge is the ability of comprehensive analysis. However, the shortcomings in knowledge system and overall quality of auditors have still been deficiencies of China's government audit, and therefore the quality and effectiveness of audit cannot reach a satisfactory level.

Professional Ethics of Auditors. In addition to professional competence, auditors shall also abide by the professional ethics. In the course of auditing, auditors shall carry out the work in line with relevant provisions in the Auditing Standards, stay away from the temptation and coercion of external interest and power bodies, make audit evaluations in a serious and objective manner, and safeguard the national economic security. The abidance by professional ethics mainly hinges on the self-discipline of auditors. On the one hand, the insufficient personnel training and follow-up education of the current auditors in practical work have contributed to the gradual attenuation of professional ethics, and on the other hand, auditors are very likely to be exposed to the temptation and coercion of power and interest because of the lack of independent status, responsibility investigation mechanism, reward and punishment mechanism and other constraining force that strengthen the moral sense of auditors. With the absence of professional ethics, there is a good chance for the government to fall into the crisis of credit and moral.

Backward Audit Methods and Approaches

Government Audit is Based-on Post-Supervision. The function of supervision of the government audit has been continuously strengthened as the political and economic development. Currently speaking, China put an emphasis on post-audit, and on most cases the problems pointed out have already caused substantial losses. The lack of pre-prevention and in-process control in auditing hold back the government audit to play the role of "immune system". Fail to run through the whole process of administrative actions, the time-lag puts the audit work into a passive situation.

Low Informatization Degree in Audit. With the evolution of information technologies, the vast majority of units have abandoned the traditional manual accounting and introduced the computerized accounting information system, which achieved the automatic processing via computers in the whole course. Compared with the traditional one, audit trails in the advanced system are more complex and covert. This has raised new challenges for the government audit, and the traditional methods can no longer meet the needs. In recent years, the State Audit Office has committed to strengthening the construction of informatization of the government audit. The Development Program on Informatization 2008-2012 explicitly stipulated that audit institutions shall explore new audit methods under the new circumstance of informatization, construct network centers and data centers of audit institutions all over the country, primarily establish the information system of state audit, and encourage the widespread use of computer technologies in the audit business. The Development Program during the 12th Five-Year Plan issued by the State Audit Office takes the construction of informatization of audit work as one of the overall targets, indicating that advanced technologies must be applied to actively innovate the information of audit methods. So far, the construction of audit informatization has recorded some achievements. For example, GPS position indicator was used to spot the specific locations of land when the Agent Office of Beijing, Tianjin and Hebei subordinate to the State Audit Office conducted the audit of the implementation of farmland protection policies. In the actual work process, however, the construction of informatization is still inchoate, and the degree of audit informatization is relatively low. Due to unbalanced development and other reasons, conditions of informatization is not ripe, and in many places, traditional methods, such as manual auditing and accounting, are dominating the audit work notwithstanding. Also, some of the auditors and leaders in less developed regions do not pay enough attention to this issue, affecting the level of audit informatization.

Insufficient Disclosure of Government

Audit Information

According to the principle-agent theory and the public accountability theory, the government is entrusted by the public to manage the public resources and funds, and the fulfillment of such fiduciary duties requires supervision and restriction of the audit work. Audit institutions shall audit the fiduciary duties of governments at all levels and produce audit reports, and finally disclose relevant information to the public. The full disclosure of government audit information and perfect announcement of audit results can promote the government transparency, improve the government credibility, boost the development of democracy, and in the meanwhile give full play to the function of audit supervision, which is of great practical significance to anti-corruption. For a variety of reasons, audit information disclosure is usually faulty and questionable in practice.

For the past few years, the number of announcements of audit results has been on the rise. According to the data on the website of the State Audit Office between 2010 and 2013, a total of 132 announcements, involving the audit of special funds, annual assets and liabilities of financial institutions, government debts, results of enforcement of financial budgets, financial revenues and expenditures of SOEs, and trial of cases violating laws and disciplines, were issued. Specific data is shown in the following table. As can be seen from the table, the content of audit announcements has been enriched in recent years, but the disclosed information is still limited and vague, and there is a lack of follow-up audit of specific audit items.

Unsound Government Audit Announcement System

Announcement of audit results means that audit institutions release the reports, opinions, decisions and other contents of important audit matters to the general public through media such as specialized publications, radio broadcasts, newspapers, internet and press conference. Currently speaking, a vast majority of countries in the world have established the government audit announcement system. In the trial measures issued in 2003, the Chinese government made explicit provisions on the contents, methods, approval procedures, required conditions and forms of announcement of audit results, and the system has been constantly developed. However, there are still many defects in the audit announcement system in practice. First, from the perspective of announcement procedures, China's relative laws and regulations stipulates that audit reports, especially those related to important matters, of different levels and types shall be approved by relevant persons in charge or the government. It can be seen that neither the State Audit Office nor local audit institutions are commissioned to directly publish the audit results, and both of them shall be subject to the State Council, local governments at the corresponding levels and their persons in charge. This is related to China's administrative government audit system. Second, in terms of the scope of audit announcement, audit institutions may, in line with the approval procedures, make some of the audit contents public, including those required by governments at the corresponding levels and audit institutions at the next higher levels to make public, those concerned by the public, and those shall be announced to the communities. However, the definitions of major items and audit items that need to be published are obscure, and specific scope of audit publication and important audit matters are not clearly indicated. Finally, audit institutions also have the responsibility of confidentiality. Contents involving with the secrets of the state and auditees shall not be made public without permission, and laws and regulations fail to effectively explain the defined scope of the contents "not suitable for publishing". Therefore, the loopholes in the audit announcement system become the hotbeds of black case work.

Limited Disclosure of Audit Information

The objects disclosed in the audit announcement include three aspects: first, auditees and their competent departments; second, governments and

People's Congress at the corresponding
levels; third, the public. Citizens have the right to be
informed, so they can supervise over the performance
of the government's fiduciary duties through audit
information. In this process, the full disclosure of audit
information guarantees the basic right. In the foreign
experience of audit announcement, the publicity of
audit information is also something of significance.
Although relevant laws and regulations in China have
stipulated the objects and contents of audit
announcement, the disclosure of audit information is
still considerably limited in practice. On the one hand,
in actual operation, current legal provisions have not
formed institutional constraints on the content of audit
information disclosure. Under the new social
circumstance, partial protection still exists in some local
governments. Once things go wrong on audit issues,
local governments are often inclined to repel the
information disclosure and try to cooperate with audit
institutions through "abnormal means". Consequently,
audit institutions can hardly do anything to settle the
matters through normal audit punishment after
pointing out problems. On the other hand, audit
institutions must present the audit reports about the
implementation of annual budget and relevant financial
revenues and expenditures to People's Congress at
various levels under the administrative audit system.
As audit institutions themselves are also subordinate to
administrative departments, there would be inevitably
the defect of "internal audit". Before submitting to the
People's Congress, the audit results must be "audited"
by local governments in advance. For the sake of
protecting local interests, local governments are very
likely to interfere the information disclosure wantonly.
As a result, the published audit results usually keep
silent about major charges while admitting minor ones,

and even ignore some significant issues. Because of the certain ambiguity of the content of audit reports, the depth and strength of the disclosure of problems pointed out in audit activities are booked for shrinking, and the degree and effect of audit announcements is also unsatisfactory. Finally, the disclosure of audit information must take the social impact into account. Audit institutions must expunge or modify the contents that are not suitable for disclosure, leading to the one-sidedness of some audit announcements and the impaired authority of audit reports.

Unsound Accountability-Seeking

Mechanism of Audit

Audit accountability-seeking mechanism refers to the system in which audit institutions find out cases of violations against laws, regulations and disciplines and lack of responsibilities of audit objects, hold relevant persons in charge accountable, and impose sanctions on them. As a restricted and supervisory mechanism of public power, government audit can promote the honest administration and clean government and improve the governance capacity through audit accountability. The report at the 18th Party's Congress clearly pointed out that the CPC shall encourage the exercise of power in a public and normative manner, optimize the openness of party affairs, government administration, judicial issues and other affairs in relevant areas, improve the systems of inquiry, accountability-seeking, economic responsibility audit, blame-taking resignation and recall, potentiate the inner-party supervision, democratic supervision, legal supervision and public opinion-based supervision, accredit the people to supervise over the power, and make the exercise of power more transparent. With the deepening and widening of government audit in recent years, more problems have been pointed out. China has been strengthening the audit accountability-seeking by persistence, but in practice some departments and areas are just incorrigible due to some reasons.

Lacking of the Audit Accountability System

The storm of audit rose suddenly in 2003, but the storm of accountability which should have followed did not come as expected. At present, China's relevant laws and regulations on the audit accountability system are still defective, provisions and articles are not detailed enough, and are not operable in practice. For the cognizance of the economic responsibility audit in China at the present stage, laws and regulations such as Regulations on the Economic Responsibility Audit of Major Leading Cadres of the CPC and Government Administration and Leading Personnel of SOEs, the Civil Servant Law of the PRC, and Temporary Provisions on the Implementation of Accountability of Leading Cadres of the CPC and Government Administration. Carried out by audit institutions, discipline inspection and supervision organs, organization departments and personnel departments, there are mainly 8 ways of accountability of leading cadres, including instructing open apology, to stop work and make a public self-criticism, to take the blame and resign, and to resign or relieve relevant personnel from office (this shall be made in line with the specific methods of laws and regulations of the state, for instance, the Interim Procedures of Economic Accountability of Leading Cadres in Hubei Province provides that instructing a paper self-criticism is also one way of economic accountability), circulating a notice of criticism, persuasion and admonition, open apology, stopping work and making self-criticism, taking the blame and resigning, instructing an resignation, and removing relevant personnel from the post. However, in terms of specific content, local regulations and provisions made by the central government are nearly the same, failing to take local audit characteristics into account. In the meanwhile, the audit responsibility partition is still obscure, existing laws cannot establish specific requirements on matching conditions and methods of audit accountability. In addition, the lack of specific methods of responsibility partition, straightforward measures for the implementation of accountability and the mechanism of accountability-seeking also contributed to the formation of a battery of specialized normative documents of audit accountability. When it comes to the stage of settling matters, the problems pointed out in auditing are usually solved by economic means such as imposing fines and confiscation, ignoring the correction of the overall problems.

Weak Allogeneic Accountability

According to subjects, audit accountability can be divided into single-subject accountability and allogeneic accountability: the former, as an internal supervision to a certain extent, mainly refers to the accountability of administrative officials within the administrative system, while the latter, different from single-subject accountability, emphasize the accountability of government officials by non-administrative systems such as People's Congresses at various levels, social media and the public. Currently speaking, single-subject accountability dominates China's administrative audit system. Once problems are identified, the superior usually calls the junior to blame, and the National People's Congress fails to play its due role as China's organization of supreme power. For the past few years, the State Audit Office and local audit institutions have successively introduced many laws and regulations on audit accountability, but the content is mostly provisions on internal accountability of audit institutions. At present, China's government audit accountability gives priority to single-subject accountability, focusing on internal treatment, while audit institutions have not taken maximum advantage of external supervision because of the relatively weak allogeneic accountability. In contract, since the storm of audit in 2003, the responses of public opinion have been tremendous after the announcements of audit results. Allogeneic accountability, as a force of external supervision, has played an active role in promoting the government audit accountability. However, its effect has still been quite limited thanks to various reasons such as insufficient audit transparency and administrative intervention.

Slacking Supervision over Follow-up Rectification

Audit rectification refers to the process in which audit institutions, after pointing out violations against laws and regulations of the auditees in accordance with the law, make decisions on coping with problems through delivering audit reports and offering suggestions so that the auditees can correct the problems in due course. Occupying an important position in the whole process, audit rectification and its effectiveness concern the public credibility and authority of the government audit, the positive operation of auditees, and even the objectives and significance of the government audit. for the time being, the cases of "focusing on audit and neglecting rectifications" have still been widespread in China's

343

audit work, and rectification is still a vulnerable spot, directly leading to the torpid process of solvement. Consequently, no institution can guarantee the effect of audit, and that is the chief cause of incorrigibility and repeated adjudication.

First, auditor, who have not realized the importance of audit results themselves, fail to equally juxtapose audit rectification to audit work and the treatments as well as solutions of problems. Auditors subjectively believe that the missions are accomplished after delivering the audit reports and voicing their opinions, and whether auditees will carry out the rectifications is none of their business. It is out of question that audit institutions cannot get timely feedback on the use of audit results under the circumstances of ignoring the tracking and supervision on follow-up situation, especially for those that take some time to be finished. Second, in the framework of administrative government audit in China, the authority of judicial departments and discipline inspection and supervision departments of administrative penalty in line with laws predominate China's audit supervision, while administrative audit penalty, because of the lack of compelling legal provisions supporting its behaviors and vague binding, cannot always smoothly punish auditees for rejecting or delaying the rectification according to law. The implementation of audit results and audit decisions lacks of relevant institutional constraints, and worse still, audit opinions and suggestions themselves are also optional. As a result, the follow-up supervision is weak and cannot be easily put into practice, failing to be a major method of punishment of violations against laws and regulations.

Unsound System of Performance Audit

In addition to financial audit, the audit on the process and effect of the management of public resources shall also be included into the government audit. According to the definition of the INTOSAI, performance audit is a review and evaluation on the economy, efficiency and effectiveness of the resources used by auditees in the course of performing their duties. Different from traditional audit, performance audit emphasizes on the performance responsibility, focusing on the extent to which government departments achieve the expected targets, and whether the expenditures give consideration to economy and efficiency at the same time. With the evolvement of democracy, the public has been paying more attention to the government performance. In recent years, China has witnessed a groundswell of opinions on government performance audit, but faced with many problems, performance audit in China is at the inchoate stage in terms of both practice and theory.

Inadequate Awareness of Auditors

As a nascent area in China, government performance audit starts relatively late and develops slowly, and the academic circle has not formed a systematic theoretical research on performance audit so far. With all institutional changes in the political restructuring and the development of China's government audit over the past 3 decades, audit institutions, as an integral part of the administrative department, have been inclined to the financial audit focusing on the authenticity and legitimacy of auditees under the administrative audit system. In this case, auditors have only limited knowledge of the performance audit concentrating on efficiency, effectiveness and responsibilities. First, theoretical guidance on the neonatal area is quite limited because the theoretical cycle has been at the stage of exploration, and a mature theoretical basis has not been formed yet. Second, China is apt to invest the audit resources to economic and financial audit in practice, while performance audit is just a spot project on some issues. Lack of popularization and publicity of performance audit, auditors in local audit institutions, especially the ones in economically underdeveloped areas, cannot have a good idea of performance audit. Finally, performance audit requires higher professional skills and comprehensive quality of auditors, which conflicts with the current situation that China has not launched training programs on a large scale for qualified auditors. Therefore, performance auditor has not enjoyed popular support.

Defective Laws and Regulations on Performance Audit

Attaching great importance to government audit performance, most developed countries have established impeccable systems of relevant laws and regulations. For instance, the Washington State of the United States issued the Act of Performance Audit of Government Departments, and the National Audit Office of the United Kingdom issued the Manual of Performance Audit and the Operation Guidance on Investigation Methods, which set out the principles, capital source, implementation, quality control and information distribution of performance audit in detail. While China, in turn, only mentioned performance audit in the Audit Law and National Auditing Standards, an no special laws and regulations have been issued. Worse still, even the existing laws and mostly formalistic, lacking special operational guidance in procedures, methods, assessment indicators and result utilization of performance audit.

Lacking of the Effective Assessment Indicator System of Performance Audit

Performance audit itself is kind of tricky. So far, China has not formulated special laws of detailed regulations on the principles, standards and procedures of performance audit. As far as it goes, China's assessment indicators of performance audit are very limited, lacking guidance in practical operation. In a nutshell, there are more financial indicators than non-financial indicators and more aggregative indicators than single indicators in the system, and other indicators such as "early warning" are also scarce. Lacking unified objectivity, standards of performance audit are relatively single, and as a result, being stuck in ambiguity, auditors have to evaluate the auditees by indicators in other areas or self-defined indicators. It is out of question that the embarrassing situation of no compelling valid provisions will both greatly increase the difficulty of the work of performance audit and lower the quality of work, and even discredit audit results.

Countermeasures and suggestions of China's Reform of the Government Audit

Transform the System of Government Audit to Legislative Audit

According to Article 91 and 109 of the Constitution of the PRC, China established the system of administrative government audit. This system is the inevitable choice for China allowing for multiple political and economic influences. However, the dual leadership system of the government audit can hardly even guarantee the independence and authority of audit institutions, China is bound to transform the audit system. when considering the future audit system in the shortlist, the final choice must conform to the specific national conditions. In the process of transformation, one important aspect is to ensure the independent status of audit activities. A blunt fact is that other types of government audit all have advantages over the administrative one in terms of audit independence. However, both the transformations to judicial or independent government audit may entail lengthy structural reform and enormous risk. As legislatures in China, the National People's Congresses themselves bear the responsibility of supervision, and the transformation to legislative government audit is in line with the reality.

Strengthen the Oversight by People's

Congresses

In the framework of China's administrative government audit, audit institutions are subordinate to administrative departments, which is closely related to China's political system, social and economic development, legal system and other factors. In the discussion of audit in the future, most scholars advocate the transformation to legislative government audit. According to China's national conditions at the current stage, some scholars raised the idea of "audit guided by legislatures", which refers to the audit work led or guided by legislatures and related to the function of budget supervision (centering on the budget audit including investment audit). Different from legislative government audit, in which audit institutions are affiliated with legislatures, audit institutions in this system are still part of administrative departments. In light of the leadership and organization structure of China's audit institutions, the administrative government audit system is too inveterate to be changed within a short period, but under such circumstances the People's Congress can still play its role in supervision by setting up institutions with some audit functions inside legislatures and engaging in the audit work with special meanings.

Audit institutions, as government departments, are characterized with internality in terms of supervision, while the People's Congresses and their standing commissions, as China's legislative bodies, represent an external force of political supervision, which is more authoritative in the restriction and supervision of governmental powers. According to China's political and economic conditions at the present stage, it is unsubstantial to put audit institutions under the administration of legislatures completely, so the keep running of dual-track audit system is still of practical

349

significance, namely specialized supervisory organs could be newly established under the standing commissions and Financial and Economic Committees of People's Congresses on the premise of retaining the existing audit institutions. For example, Budget Audit Commissions or Budget Investigation Commission affiliated to the Standing Commission of the People's Congress could be appropriate choices, through which budget audit can be assigned to the People' Congress. As working bodies subordinating to and directly responsible for the People' Congress, no other institutions shall interfere their works, and thus their independent status and personnel allocation of professional auditing teams can be ensured, so as to supervise over the budgets and final accounts of the government. To a large extent, institution setting in this way can avoid the drawback of the lack of independence in the current audit system, maintain the objectivity and impartiality of audit work, and effectively supervising over the power.

Listing Audit Funds into the General Budget of National Finance

It is difficult to carry out the audit work without sufficient audit funds – the necessary material guarantee. In the administrative audit system in China, audit funds are guaranteed by auditees, namely financial departments at the same levels. Therefore, audit work would be unavoidably restricted by various conditions. After reforming the current audit system, audit funds can be all listed into the general budget of national finance, and most of all, the funds of local audit institutions will no longer be included in the financial budgets of local governments. As a result, without interference and restriction from local governments, audit institutions can enhance the independence of audit work by directly reporting the implementation of budgets to superior institutions and the People's Congress at the corresponding level. without doubt, before putting the foregoing assumptions into effect, China shall at first further hoist the status of the government audit by amending the Constitution and the Audit law, and make detailed provisions on the system, independence and funds of audit and audit institutions.

Further Consolidating the Construction of "Staff, Laws and Techniques"

Strengthening the Construction of Audit Teams

First, improve the quality of leading cadres of the audit team. For the most part, the political theoretical attainment and professional skills of leading cadres of the audit team affect the direction of audit work. Therefore, for ameliorating China's present situation of audit, it is necessary to constantly strengthen the education of professional ethics and anti-corruption for leading cadres, so as to withstand external sugar-coated bullets in the aspect of ideology and politics; attach importance to scientific personnel allocation of leading cadres, adopt multi-candidate allocation and the system of open-review, broaden the channel of cadre selection, pay attention to the accumulation of grassroots experience, and actively train outstanding young cadres in terms of cadre selection; improve the assessment system of leading cadres, reinforce the supervision, effectively enhance their working competence and quality, and intensify the overall level of audit.

Second, take the introduction and training of audit talents seriously. What is known to all is that the smooth development of audit work always profits from a multitude of well-qualified auditors. Different from the internal audit of some enterprises, the government audit involves a wide range of knowledge. With the continuous development of government performance audit in recent years, in particular, audit institutions have demanded more from their employees in the aspects of professional skills and the ability of judgement. When it comes to the introduction of audit talents, professional skills and work experience shall be taken into account. Forming an unbalanced structure, a vast majority of auditors in China at present comes from auditing, accountancy and economic background. Selected by civil service examination, most of the auditors are rookies without work experience. Therefore, in terms of talent introduction, audit institutions shall lay emphasis on bringing in talents with professional backgrounds besides auditing and accountancy, such as law, computer science and other applied subject, with the purpose of counterbalancing the knowledge, rationalizing the personnel allocation of the whole audit team, and improving the quality and level of audit work; incrementally adjust the structure of talents of each region and each post, so as to optimize the allocation of staff and establish a sophisticated and well-qualified audit team; utilize the external human resources rationally, allow full play to expert consultation, and enhance the mechanism of talent introduction; intensify the training and education for auditors, and actively innovate new approaches of educational training and business training; establish and improve the system of audit training, carry out training programs of audit business and professional ethics such as special skill training courses, symposiums and analysis of audit cases, so as to improve the working competence and professional code of conduct from both theoretical and practical aspects. Only by this way can China establish an audit team with solid political quality, excellent professional proficiency and clean hands, so as to support the development of audit work in the future.

Third, improve the incentive mechanism for audit talents. With its incentive effect, external mechanisms can mobilize the enthusiasm of auditors and boost the effect and efficiency of audit work up to the hilt when it comes to the management of audit talents. First, it is important to establish the incentive mechanism with spiritual motivation as the main the material incentive as the auxiliary factor, so as to establish an audit team with honesty and integrity and correctly guide the values of auditors. Auditors who make remarkable contribution shall be awarded with opportunities of promotion. In addition, a reasonable salary system consisting of basic salary, performance pay and special-purpose fund shall be established, in order to build the relationship between the remunerations of auditors and audit projects. Second, ameliorating the reward and punishment mechanism also makes a big difference in audit work. For violations against laws and regulations, relevant departments shall punish the responsible persons with due severity in line with laws. Finally, with the purpose of invigorating the whole audit team, a system of the metabolism for audit talents shall also be set up to gradually achieve the exchange and movement of auditors, so as to ensure the reasonable personnel allocation.

Improving the Legal System of Government Audit

In China's current legal system, in addition to

piecemeal legal provisions in the Constitution and the Budget Law, special laws on audit are merely the Audit Law and the National Auditing Standards. At present, China is the at crossroad of economic transition and political restructuring, and the reform of government audit is bound to spread over multiple levels including the content, rights and liabilities, organizational relationship and personnel administration. On this occasion, China shall establish and improve the legal system of government audit with Chinese characteristics and promote the legislation and standardization by combining overseas experience and the actual situation of the Chinese society; improve the system of auditing standards and make detailed provisions the criteria, objects, scope, and methods of quality control of audit as well as the professional competence of auditors; ameliorate the system of audit techniques and methods by bonding advanced techniques from foreign countries with effective methods, so as to provide the audit work with theoretical foundation and guidance; refine the system of government decision-making, such as the supervision over major decisions and responsibility investigation relating to the government as well as the announcement of audit results; public hearings shall be held when it comes to the decisions concerning the immediate interests of the people, and corresponding procedures and mechanisms shall also be made with the purpose of seeking for opinions from all walks of life and informing the people of the decisions in due course. What is noteworthy at the same time is the consistency among laws, which will contribute to the scientificity, fairness and validity of the government audit.

Innovating Methods of Government Audit

and Increasing the Level of Informatization

Methods of audit have been continuously expanded with the application and popularization of information technologies, and informatization has been an irresistible trend of the government audit at home and overseas. The means and methods can directly affect the quality and effect of the audit work. The informatization of innovative audit methods is mainly accomplished through ameliorating the information-based system centering on the informatization of audit business and digitization of audit administration, and realizing the resources sharing online audit by constructing the national database for audit and connecting the fiscal system, financial system and taxation system by internet, so as to effectively monitor the economic operation, prevent potential risks beforehand, and better bring into play the function of audit supervision. In simple terms, to improve the scientificity and authority to the audit work, it is important to explore new methods in the aspects of control and evaluation of audit risks as well as analysis and processing of audit data by dint of computer technologies.

Improving the Mechanism of Audit Result Announcement and Audit Transparency

Improving the Mechanism of Audit Result

Announcement

Article 36 of the Audit Law explicitly stipulates that requirement on audit result announcement, that is, audit institutions shall keep the secrets of the state and auditees when issuing audit reports on their problems and opinions. It is apparent that the announcement of audit results is the power of audit institutions rather than the obligation. To improve the system of audit result announcement, rigid requirements shall be put forward at the legal level first of all. Relevant laws shall list the disclosure of problems pointed out in audit as a general requirement, so as to check whether the government has accomplished the fiduciary duties and whether there is room for improvement, and all stakeholders violating the regulation shall bear corresponding legal liabilities. At the same time, special provisions may be added to further refine the subjects, guiding ideas, contents, forms and specific requirements of audit announcement. For classified contents that are not suitable for disclosure, such as those involving national defence, foreign affairs, public security, business secrets of enterprises or those explicitly stipulated by national laws that should be dealt with cautiously, audit institutions shall generally follow the international convention of "disclosure is normal, while confidentiality is an exception". Audit institutions shall take the following issues into account when disclosing the data and information of audit projects: the feasibility of disclosure, namely whether the capacity of the media is enough; the consequence of disclosure, namely the impact on auditees; and the necessity of disclosure, namely whether the public is demand it. Therefore, for improving their fairness and authority, it is necessary to offer audit institutions with appropriate disposition.

Rather than focusing on the announcement of audit

results, audit disclosure shall be a normalized administrative act. Besides the disclosure of the basic information on the personnel allocation, institution setting and funds management, other materials such as the tracking information of phased objectives of audit projects as well as the investigation and rectification of major cases shall also be available at the request of the public, so as to promote the audit information disclosure in breadth and depth.

Broadening Channels for Social Supervision

Involving multiple subjects including the People's Congresses at various levels, audit institutions, auditees, the public and media, the audit result announcement shall realize its role in supervision as a third-party force to protect the citizens' right to be informed. Because of the serious information asymmetry between audit institutions and the public, the people are short of understanding on the work content and nature of government audit, which weakens the effect of supervision. For this reason, audit institutions shall make full use of media including the internet, news and newspaper in order to, on the one hand, constantly promote the propaganda about the government audit by, for instance, carrying out publicity campaigns regularly, printing and distributing pamphlets and making promotional videos, so as to acquaint the public with audit psychologically and strengthen the power by public opinions; on the other hand, broaden the channels for the disclosure of government audit information and potentiate social supervision. Subordinating to administrative departments, audit institutions have the nature of internal supervision somewhat, and the participation of social forces can availably boost the openness and transparency of the government audit as well as improve the level of government audit and administration. Traditional channels for audit publicity in China include bulletin of government audit, sitting in on audit meetings, magazine, news report, hearing and notification. Along with the development of e-government and new media, government audit can be combined with modern information techniques while further expanding the influence of traditional channel. Audit institutions shall establish uniform portal websites of government audit to make the audit service public and inform the people of hip-off hotlines, and hold press conference on projects of public concern in due time, so as to provide channels for participation of social forces. Public communication platforms such as microblog can also be employed with the purpose of effectually integrating audit into social supervision, giving full play to the positive role of public opinions, and broadening the channels for social supervision.

Improving the Auditing Accountability Mechanism

Supervision is an important function of government audit, the fulfillment of which would not only discover violations of laws and regulations, but play a crucial part in rectification and punishment. Therefore, the establishment of audit accountability is an indispensable requirement on building a government of responsibility. By establishing and improving the accountability mechanism, the government can enhance the authority as well as public credibility of the government audit and encourage the audit subjects to better perform their fiduciary duties.

Improving the Legal System for Audit Accountability

On this issue, China shall establish and improve the system of audit accountability, make uniform and operational methods for the identification and implementation of audit accountability, so as to remove obstacles of the accountability from institution aspect; make clear the subjects and objects of responsibility, divide the jurisdiction and responsibility among subjects of responsibility including the departments of discipline inspection, supervision and judicature, and limit the deadline of accountability and approaches of reporting relevant results; improve the operability of the accountability system by setting out the content, procedures, criteria and basis, and measurable indicators of working efficiency in detail; improve the corresponding supporting systems such as the scope of official duties of posts of leading cadres and methods of accountability investigation, ameliorate and upgrade the current audit accountability centering on inquiry, potentiate the power of audit institutions to dispose and punish, refine the criteria for punishment and put the targets of audit accountability into practice.

Coordinating the Rights and Liabilities of Accountability Subjects

Involving administrative departments, judicial departments and legislative branches at the same time, the audit accountability merely relying on audit institutions not only plays a limited role, but contradicts the development of democracy. Only by coordinating all accountability subjects and establishing a reasonable order can audit accountability make a real difference. Instead of working each for itself, all accountability subjects shall be brought all together and form a system of multi-department joint accountability covering submission, transfer, processing, implementation and feedback. Allogeneic accountability shall keep pace with single-subject accountability, and the People's Congress at various levels shall form the legal basis for accountability, so as to provide full support for budget supervision, regular communication and post-supervision. Judicial, discipline investigation and supervisory organs should cooperate with audit institutions to cope with violations of laws and regulations unearthed in the process of audit, hold relevant stakeholders responsible in line with law, and make the rectification carried out in real place. As the bridge between government and the people, the media shall make use of all kinds of resources to timely deliver the audit information to the public, and expose the audit accountability to the supervision by the society and public opinions. In a word, whether audit accountability can play a real role in supervising the operation pf public funds and power rests with the full cooperation among all subjects.

Strengthening Accountability. After pointing out problems of auditees, audit institutions always put forward audit treatment suggestions and inform relevant units and departments. In de facto, however, audit institutions are in lack of effective control over whether or to what extent the corrective recommendations have been implemented, leading to an inevitable result of "focusing on audit while neglecting rectification". In most cases, the "storm of accountability" never ensues after the "storm of audit". Instead of launching administrative accountability or judicial accountability, accountability incurs internal rectification under most circumstances, and the follow-up supervision is considerably limited. Audit institutions shall strengthen the responsibility investigation, and adopt appropriate methods according to discrepancies in responsibilities and natures. Compared with administrative accountability, which emphasizes the performance of statutory duties, legal accountability is more mandatory and normative. Therefore, the transformation of working mode from centering on traditional administrative means to laying equal stress on administrative means and judicial means is conducive to ensuring the authority of audit accountability. With regard to the implementation of audit results, a system of follow-up check shall be established and improved to strengthen the supervision over the rectification of audit results as well as the handling and transfer of cases, and audit institutions can promote the implementation of remedial measures and strengthen the post-supervision by follow-up audit and return visit.

Promoting the Construction of Performance Audit

Fiduciary duty is an important prerequisite for the emergence and development of government audit. Government performance audit is just the review and evaluation of the economy, efficiency and effectiveness of the use of public resources and powers by auditees in the process of performing fiduciary duties, which is also known as "3E" audit. Therefore, performance audit is the inevitable trend of the development of modern government audit. Audit of economy focuses on the degree of resource conservation, namely whether the allocation of human resources, materials and property is reasonable, and whether there are problems of extravagance and waste; audit of efficiency centers on the input-output ratio and the cost-income ratio of resources, quantifies the effectiveness of economic activities, and evaluates the structure and functions of management of government departments in order to look for new approaches and measures to improve efficiency; audit of effectiveness places emphasis on the comparison between the expected and actual results, with the purpose of reflecting the realization of the established goals and benefits. However, the development of performance audit based on the foregoing three core values is still at the inchoate stage, and there is still a long way to go to promote it.

First, China shall progressively enact relevant laws and regulations for solid legal support and basis for performance audit. currently speaking, a vast majority of auditing laws in China aims at financial audit and economic audit, while standards and regulations on performance audit are relatively scanty, and the discrepancies between the two parties in terms of objectives, methods and contents are huge. On the strength of the existing Audit Law, the Constitution and other laws, China shall enact operation guides and standards of government performance audit as soon as possible, in order to make detailed regulations on the subjects, objectives, scope, procedures and methods as well as the determination and use of evaluation indicators and establish a complete battery of system of performance audit with operability. In the process of improving the legal system, China shall pay enough attention to the effective connection between new laws, existing laws and local regulations for maintaining the consistency of policies and laws, for fear that laws may overlap or contradict with each other.

Second, China shall attach importance to the cultivation of special talents in performance audit. Performance audit place great demands on the professional competence and comprehensive quality of auditors. Based on the current professional skill training, more personnel in law, computer science, economics and other areas shall be introduced for a compound and high-level audit team. In addition to setting up training bases for auditors in colleges and universities, hiring external experts and dispatching auditors abroad for studying advanced experience when appropriate also contribute to improving the working competence of auditors and the quality of audit work.

Finally, China shall improve the assessment indicator system of government performance audit. Assessment indicator system is the core content of performance audit, without which performance audit cannot even move a single step. At the current stage, with the purpose of promoting the development of performance audit, China may combining multiple evaluation criteria such as qualitative indicators and quantitative indicators, profitability indicators and non-profitability indicators as well as financial indicators and non-financial indicators in accordance with different subjects of evaluation, and set clear standards for projects of specific indicators.

Bibliography:

A

Ai-Dong, L. , Cheng, D. , & Lin-Rong, C. . (2007). The public resource auditing of china:a review of quantitative research. On Economic Problems.

Ai-Dong, L. , & WANG-hui. (2003). Research on the effects of auditing credibility system on chinese capital market efficiency. Journal of Central South University(Social ence).

Ai-Qin, C. . (2007). Understanding of formulating the internal auditing standard in china. Sci-Tech Information Development & Economy.

Ai-Qun, L. I. , Zhao-Dong, Q. , Energy, X. N. , & Exchange, S. S. . (2017). Suggestion on constructing china's environmental auditing standards. Journal of Hunan Finance and Economics University.

Alqahtani, S. M. , Gamble, R. , & Ray, I. . (2013). Auditing Requirements for Implementing the Chinese Wall Model in the Service Cloud. IEEE Ninth World Congress on Services. IEEE.

Amp, B. Q. , & Ping-Zhi, W. . (2012). Announcement system in china's national auditing and effect analysis. Journal of Beijing

Technology and Business University(Social Science).

Amp, L. M. , & Shoucheng, W. . (2008). The evolution of china's independent auditing system in 30 years of reform and opening up. Accounting Research.

Amp, L. M. , & Xiaoxia, L. . (2012). Environmental auditing research in china:a literature review. Academia Bimestrie.

Auditing, G. , & En-Feng, L. . (2001). Comparative research in intosai auditing standards and chinese. Economy & Audit Study.

B

Bank, T. W. . (2008). Huangtai thermal power plant, shandong, china : auditing report.

Bin, J. X. , Hai, L. R. , Heng, H. L. , Nanjing, & China. (2003). The research for construction project land using auditing indicator in jiangsu province. Journal of Nanjing Forestry University.

Bing, W. , & Qing-Quan, X. . (2009). Independent auditing demand deficiency in china:contract execution analysis. Economic Theory and Business Management.

Bo, H. . (2010). Risk-oriented auditing in china: reflection and enlightenment. Contemporary Economy & Management.

Bo, H. U. . (2010). A discussion on the major features of auditing specialty in chinese general universities. Journal of China Women's University.

Bo, J. Y. . (2013). Comments on auditing risk and prevention of registered accountants in china. Coal Economic Research. by Professor

Bing Ling. (0). Auditing state secrets in china. Publications Office.

C

Canling, & Zhou. (1997). Internal auditing work at sino-china petrochemical corporation (sinopec). Managerial Auditing Journal, 12(4/5), 227-234.

Carey, P. , Liu, L. , & Qu, W. . (2017). Voluntary corporate social responsibility reporting and financial statement auditing in china. Journal of Contemporary Accounting & Economics, S1815566917300310.

Chang, S. , Chang-Xin, Z. , & Lei, H. . (2009). A study of the audit results announcement of the local auditing organs in china. Contemporary Finance & Economics.

Chang, S. . (2010). A research on the system of performance auditing with chinese features. Journal of Audit & Economics.

Changdong, W. . (2010). On improving control mechanisms of corruption risk by chinese national auditing——thinking based on un convention against corruption about control mechanisms of corruption risk. Jianghai Academic Journal.

Chang-Jiang, Z. . (2011). Ten years of review of environmental auditing research in china:track,problems and prospect. China Population,Resources and Environment.

Chang-Ping, S. , & Jun-Yao, J. . (2009). Present problems in chinese local budget auditing. Journal of Shanxi University of Finance & Economics.

Chao, W. J. D. . (1998). On setting up china internal auditing standards.

JOURNAL OF JIANGHAN PETROLEUM INSTITUTE.

Chen, & X.-M. (2012). Internal auditing systems and method in china: reform and improvement. Communications in Computer & Information Science.

Chen, J. , & Geng, X. . (2014). Auditing the management of technological innovation in chinese companies. International Journal of Innovation and Technology Management, 01(02), 0400015.

Chen, S. , Su, X. , & Wang, Z. . (2010). An analysis of auditing environment and modified audit opinions in china: underlying reasons and lessons. International Journal of Auditing.

Chen, W. , Smieliauskas, W. J. , & Liu, S. F. . (2010). Performance assessment of online auditing in China from the perspective of audit cost control. Systems Man and Cybernetics (SMC), 2010 IEEE International Conference on. IEEE.

Chen, W. . (2007). One continuous auditing practice in china: data-oriented online auditing(dooa).

Chen, W. . (2007). One continuous auditing practice in china: data-oriented online auditing(dooa).

Chen, Wei, Smieliauskas, Wally J, & Liu, Sifeng. (2010). Performance assessment of online auditing in china from the perspective of audit cost control.

Chen, Wei, Smieliauskas, Wally J, & Liu, Sifeng. (2010). Performance assessment of online auditing in china from the perspective of audit cost control.

Cheng Huanling. (0).

Research on Integrated Auditing of Listed Companies in China.

Chien, Minh, Dang, Neil, Fargher, & Gladys 等. (2017). Audit quality for us-listed chinese companies. International Journal of Auditing.

Chong, & Gin. (2000). Auditing framework in the people's republic of china and the international auditing guidelines: some comparisons. Managerial Finance, 26(5), 12-20.

Chong, G. . (2009). Legal cases and auditing in china.

Chong, G. . (2009). Legal cases and auditing in china. Handbook of Business Practices & Growth in Emerging Markets, 19(6), 49–54.

Chong, Gin. (1998). Chinese auditing systems. Management Accounting Magazine for Chartered Management

Account(July).

Chong, H. G. . (2008). Auditing in china. , 19(6), 49-54.

Chong, H. G. . (2008). Auditing in china. Journal of Corporate Accounting & Finance, 19(6), 49-54.

Chow, Lowell. (2009). Challenges of social auditing in china: from the social auditors' perspective.

Chuanlian, S. , & Xiaoan, Q. I. . (2013). The positioning of the auditing environment supervision in china from the perspective of independence. Ecological Economy.

Chun-Hua, P. , & Bao-You, S. . (2005). Current situations and measures in auditing of government performance in china. Journal of Zhanjiang Teachers College.

Cooper, B. J. , Chow, L. , & Yun Wei, T. . (2002). The development of auditing standards and the certified public accounting profession in china. Managerial Auditing Journal, 17(7), 383-389.

D

Dan, A, Simunic, Xi, & Wu. (2009). China-related research in auditing: a review and directions for future research. China Journal of Accounting Research(2), 1-25.

Davidson, R. A. , & Chang, S. . (2001). The importance of auditing topics to chinese auditors. , 5(2), 127-139.

Davidson, R. A. , & Chang, S. . (2010). The importance of auditing topics to chinese auditors. International Journal of Auditing, 5(2), 127-139.

Defond, M. L. , Zhang, F. , & Zhang, J. . (2020). Auditing research using chinese data: what's next?. Accounting and Business Research, 1-14.

Deng, S. M. , & Macve, R. H. M. . (2018). How china has built an accounting and auditing profession with potential global impact. Social ence Electronic Publishing.

De-Yin, L. . (2007). Probing into environmental auditing in china. Ecological Economy.

Dianhua, Z. . (2018). Military auditing system of socialism with chinese characteristics in new era:achievements,inadequacies and suggestions. Fiscal ence.

Ding, S. , Qu, B. , & Zhuang, Z. . (2011). Accounting properties of chinese family firms. Journal of Accounting Auditing & Finance, 26(4), 623-640.

Ding, Shengyan. (2012). Auditing quality in china.

Dong, L. , Yaowu, W. , & Lidan, Z. . (2009). Follow-up auditing of chinese infrastructure project based on earned value auditing theory. Journal of Northeast Agricultural University(Social ence Edition).

E

Ellis, R.K, Weihua, J, & Warren, L. (1996). The feasibility of an environmental auditing system for chinesemanufacturing industry: a systemic approach.

Enyue, & Zhuang. (2013). Development trends of internal auditing in china. Managerial Auditing Journal, 12(4/5), 205-209.

F

Fa-Jun, Y. . (2013). Analysis on the effectiveness of accounting firm performance auditing in china. Journal of Jiyuan Vocational and Technical College.

Fang, J. . (2009). Regulated changes in audit fee disclosure and improvement of audit environment:evidence from china's auditing market. China Accounting Review.

Feng. G (2012). Study on performance auditing of public fiscal poverty-alleviation project fund in china. Advances in Applied Economics & Finance, 3(4).

Feng, L. . (2002). Auditing market in china and auditor s selection: a case analysis. Accounting Research.

Feng, L. I. , & Rong, Y. . (2009). Game analysis of nongovernmental auditing independence in china. Journal of Audit & Economics.

Feng, Q. . (2008). Reflections on auditing environment in china. Journal of Nanjing

Forestry University(Humanities and Social ences Edition).

Feng-Li, D. , & Guo-Rui, R. . (2009). Preliminary discussion on announcement system of auditing findings in chinese government. Business Economy.

Fu, S. . (2007). International practice of tax auditing and its implications for china. International Taxation in China.

Fu-Kang, Z. . (2004). On the deficiency of cpa auditing professional ethicsin china and reconstitution of its supervisory mechanism. Journal of Yangzhou Polytechnic College.

Fu-Kang, Z. . (2005). Chinese independent auditing: problems,causes and countermeasures. Journal of Yangzhou University the Humanities & Social ence Edition.

Fukang, Z. . (2007). Problems and countermeasures of chinese independent auditing. Journal of Shanghai Economic Management College.

G

Gong, Y. , Zhu, J. , Chen, Y. , & Cook, W. D. . (2018). Dea as a tool for auditing: application to chinese manufacturing industry with parallel network structures. Annals of Operations Research, 263(1-2), 1-23.

Graham, L. E. . (1996). Setting a research agenda for auditing issues in the people's republic of china. International Journal of Accounting, 31(1), 19-37.

Guang-Hong, Z. , & Ying-Xin, D. U. . (2002). Discussion on the development of countermeasure of enterprise internal auditing in china. Journal of Yuzhou University.

Guangli, Z. . (2019). Evolution of china's government auditing system:institutional change and reform direction. Auditing Research.

Guo-Ai, N. , Ting-Ting, F. , & University, T. . (2014). The improvement of china's auditing report. journal of tongling university.

Guohua, C. , Chuan, L. , Banghan, C. , & Jiayu, B. I. . (2011). Auditor switching and auditing quality:a comparative approach based on the listed companies in china and the united states. Journal of Audit & Economics.

Guozhu, Z. , & Jinghua, C. . (2008). The research on the financial fraud of listed companies in china and auditing countermeasure. Journal of Wuhan Institute of Technology.

H

H., Gin, & Chong. (2008). Auditing in china. Journal of Corporate Accounting & Finance.

Hai-Jing, W. U. . (2004). A discussion about problems over chinese enterprise internal-auditing with illustration of case of worldcom. Journal of Huaiyin Industry College.

Haimei, Z. . (2009). Research on quality control over auditing of accounting firms in china. Journal of Nanjing University of Finance and Economics.

Hai-Yan, G. . (2004). The development trend of china's internal auditing and the countermeasures. Journal of Heb University of Economics and Trade.

Haiyan, J. , Department, F. , & University, L. N. . (2014). Realistic problems in performance auditing in chinese colleges and universities and their solutions. Journal of Liaoning Normal University(Social Science Edition).

Han, X. . (2018). A commentary on the evolution of auditing thoughts in ancient china. Auditing Research.

Hao, P. , & Zhen. (1999). Regulation and organisation of accountants in china. Accounting Auditing & Accountability Journal, 12(3), 286-302.

Hao, X. , & Youmei, Z. . (2007). The audit firms dependence and audit fee under duplicate auditing arrangements: evidence from chinese a b-share market. Journal of Nanjing University of ence and Technology(Social ences Edition).

Hao, X. , & Youmei, Z. . (2007). The audit firms dependence and audit fee under duplicate auditing arrangements: evidence from chinese a b-share market. Journal of Nanjing University of ence and Technology(Social ences Edition).

Haw, I. M. , Qi, D. D. , & Wu, W. . (0). The market consequences of voluntary auditing: evidence from interim reports in china. Social ence Electronic Publishing.

He, G. , & Perloff, J. M. . (2012). Does customer auditing help chinese workers?. Ilr Review, 66(2), 511.

He-Xiong, Y. . (2009). Auditing opinion shopping in china a-share markets. Journal of Audit & Economics.

Hong, G. U. . (2004). A study on three question of "ludependent auditing criterion for chinese registered accountant".

Journal of Xichang Teachers College.

Hong, J. . (2006). Brief analysis on the improvement in china's internal auditing systems in modern enterprise system. Journal of Chongqing Institute of Technology.

Hong, L. . (2006). On the relations of government auditing in china. Journal of Yangtze University(Social ences).

Hong-Xia, J. . (2007). Causes and preventive resolution of private auditing risk in china. Journal of Jiyuan Vocational and Technical College.

Hongzhou, L. . (2006). Internal IT Auditing for Chinese Commercial Banks. Proceedings of the 3rd International Conference on Innovation & Management vol.1. College of Management, Henan University of Technology, Zhengzhou 450052, P.R.China.

Hu, K. H. , Jianguo, W. , & Tzeng, G. H. . (2017). Risk factor assessment improvement for china's cloud computing auditing using a new hybrid madm model. International Journal of Information Technology and Decision Making, 16(03), 737-777.

Hu, Y. , Luo, J. , & Fan, H. . (0). An Empirical Study on the Acceptance of the Government Performance Auditing in China.

Hua, Q. . (2005). Internationalization coordination analysis on china's independent auditing. Journal of Guangdong Business College.

Hua, Y. . (2008). Demonstration study of factors affecting auditing fee in china's listed companies— —take a-share market in shanghai and shenzhen stock exchanges. Journal of Lianyungang Technical College.

Huai-Liu, G. . (2005). On performance auditing and the mode of performance auditing with china's features. Academic Exploration.

Hui, N. , & Shu, L. I. . (2018). Online course teaching team building in the open university of china——taking auditing as an example. Journal of Tianjin Radio and Television University.

I

I, David, & Dong, Yi. (2011). China - report on the observance of standards and codes (rosc) : accounting and auditing. World Bank Other Operational Studies, 32(1), 25–29.

J

Ji, XuDong, & Ashgate. (2017). Development of accounting and auditing systems in china. Accounting & Business Research, 33, 86-87.

Jia, H. U. . (2002). A discussion about restructuring the state auditing modal in china. Journal of Shanxi Finace and Economics University.

Jianfei, X. . (2008). An analysis of the current situation of digital-based auditing development in china. Journal of Inner Mongolia Finance and Economics College.

JianWua, & Jou. (1997). The present situation and developing trends of chinese internal auditing. Managerial Auditing Journal, 12(4/5), 235-242.

Jianxin, G. , & Zhijian, L. . (2018). Explorations on the situation and future of water auditing in china. Auditing Research.

Jiayi Liu. (2015). Study on the Auditing Theory of

Socialism with Chinese Characteristics, Revised.

Jiayi Liu. (2017). Basic Framework of the Auditing System of Socialism with Chinese Characteristics. Study on the Auditing System of Socialism with Chinese Characteristics. John Wiley & Sons, Inc.

Jie, C. , & Xiao-Hong, Z. . (2011). Analysis of social demand status of china's auditing talent training——perspective from the questionare suevey. Journal of Huaiyin Teachers College(Natural Science), 22(9), 932-933.

Jing, L. . (2009). An analysis of risk-oriented auditing and its application in china. Journal of Inner Mongolia Finance and Economics College.

Jingfen, Z. . (2006). A study on the quality cost auditing in china. Audit & Economy Research.

Jinhua, Li. (1998). China's governmental auditing system. International Journal of. (Apr).

Jin-Tian, L. , & University, F. J. . (2016). The present situation of off- office auditing research of chinese natural resources and suggestions. Journal of Inner Mongolia University of Finance & Economics.

Juan, T. U. , & Kai, X. U. . (2008). Orientation shift of china's "non-monetary assets exchange" and its effect on the statement auditing. audit & economy research.

Jun, Z. , & Dongwei, Z. . (2015). The establishment of performance auditing standards in china. Finance & Economics.

Ju-Zi, X. . (2008). The enlightenment of the study on risk-oriented internal auditing in foreign countries to china.

Journal of Anhui Business College of Vocational Technology.

K

Ke, Z. . (2014). Implication on japanese environmental auditing development to china. Environment and Sustainable Development.

Kenny Z Lin and K.Hung Chan. (2000). Auditing standards in china—a comparative analysis with relevant international standards and guidelines. The International Journal of Accounting.

Kenny Z Lin and K.Hung Chan. (2000). Auditing standards in china—a comparative analysis with relevant international standards and guidelines. The International Journal of Accounting.

Kun, Y. I. . (2007). Reforms on internal auditing systems of state-owned medium-large enterprises of china. Tunnel Construction.

L

Lan Wan Hua, Georgios Georgakopoulos, Ioannis Sotiropoulos, & Ekaterini Galanou. (2010). Main principles and practices of auditing independence in china: a multifaceted discussion. Asian Social ence, 6(7), 3-11.

Len Jui, & Wong, Jessie. (2015). The past, present, and future of auditing in china. Cpa Journal.

LI Qingyun. (2002). Edp system auditing in china: necessity and approaches. Journal of Xian Petrdleum Institute.

LI Xun , LinChuan , HuMing. (0). An empirical exploration on regional relations influences auditing pricing in china. 财经论丛.

LI Zhen, LU En-ping, & WANG Lei. (2017). On the development of enterprise internal auditing in china based on risk-oriented auditing. Value Engineering.

Li, & Qun, T. . (2011). Problems and countermeasures for chinese government performance auditing. Advanced Materials Research, 268-270, 721-725.

Li, & Qun, T. . (2011). Study on the auditing problems of the private universities in china and its internal audit improvement policy. Advanced Materials Research, 268-270, 726-731.

Li, L. . (2016). Chinese and american comparison research of government auditing and its inspiration for china.

Journal of Shanghai Business School.

Li, R. . (2011). On the regulation optimization of china's securities auditing market under the system of larger departments. Contemporary Finance & Economics.

LI, Xiaofeng, Senior, Engineer.Professional, Auditor, & of 等. (2007). Effects of the beijing subway accident on engineering monitoring and auditing. China Standardization.

Li, Y. , & Wang, P. . (0). A Review of the Independence of CPA Auditing in China.

Lian, H. U. . (2007). Ceo duality effect on the auditing price——based on chinese a-stock market using panel data from 2001 to 2003. Journal of Shanxi Finance & Economics University.

Lianglin, L. . (2007).

Stralegic options for internationalization of china's auditing standards:assimitation & distinction. Communication of Finance and Accounting(Academy Version).

Li-Fang, Z. . (2002). Development of evidence collection for auditing and a realistic choice for auditing in china. Journal of Inner Mongolia University.

Limei, C. . (2003). On the charge for auditing of chartered accountants in china. Journal of Southwest University For Nationalities.

Limin, Y. . (2013). The current development and suggestions of environmental auditing in china. Journal of Chongqing College of Electronic Engineering.

Li-Min, Z. , & Yang-Yang, H. . (2004). Involuntary auditor change and auditing supervision — — evidence from china's audit market in 2001. Economy & Audit Study.

Lin, C. , Yue, W. , & Accounting, S. O. . (2019). Thoughts on cpa auditing rent-seeking in china's capital market. Taxation and Economy.

Lin, C. , & University, X. . (2018). Problems and countermeasures to implementing ecological auditing on chinese rural tourism development. Journal of Changsha University of ence and Technology(Social ence).

Lin, J. , Z., Xiao, Jason, Z. , & Tang, Q. . (2008). The roles, responsibilities and characteristics of audit committee in china. Accounting, Auditing & Accountability Journal.

Lin, K. Z. , & Chan, K. H. . (2000). Auditing standards in china--a comparative analysis with relevant international standards and guidelines. The International Journal of Accounting, 35.

Lin, Kenny Z., Chan, & K. Hung. (2000). Auditing standards in china--a comparative analysis with relevant international standards and guidelines. International Journal of Accounting.

Lin, Z. Jun. (1998). Accounting and auditing in China /. The pronunciation of English in Australia /. Angus and Robertson.

Ling, L. . (2006). Discussion of turning inside auditing into outside auditing in china. Journal of Qiqihar University(Philosophy & Social Science Edition).

Ling, Lei, Lisic, Sabatino, (Dino), & Silveri, et al. (2015). Accounting fraud, auditing, and the role of government sanctions in china. Journal of Business Research.

Lingli, L. U. , & Xiaomei, Z. . (2005). New developments of international standard on auditing 260 and revelation for china. Economy & Audit Study.

Li-Qun, F. . (2005). Study on corporate ethics auditing in china. Journal of Nanchang Institute of Aeronautical Technology.

Litian, G. . (2001). China's auditing reform and development in face of knowledge economy epoch. Journal of Heb University of Economics and Trade.

Liu, Chunhui, Yao, Lee J., Nan, & Ling. (2011). The impact of ifrs on accounting quality in a regulated market: an empirical study of china. Journal of Accounting, Auditing & Finance.

Liu, D. . (2011). On the relations between China and the auditing commission. 2011 2nd

International Conference on Artificial Intelligence, Management Science and Electronic Commerce (AIMSEC). IEEE.

Liu, F. , Su, X. , & Wei, M. . (2010). The insurance effect of auditing in a regulated and low litigation risk market: an empirical analysis of big 4 clients in china. Social ence Electronic Publishing.

Liu, J. . (2017). Features, Effects, and Experience of the Auditing System of Socialism with Chinese Characteristics. Study on the Auditing System of Socialism with Chinese Characteristics. John Wiley & Sons, Ltd.

Liu, J. . (2017). Foundation of the Auditing System of Socialism with Chinese Characteristics. Study on the Auditing System of Socialism with Chinese Characteristics. John Wiley & Sons, Ltd.

Li-Ying, F. U. . (2008). Coordination between internal and external auditing in china enterprises. Audit & Economy Research.

Lou, Jianbo. (2014). Introducing environmental auditing at the closure of business in china. Journal of Biological Chemistry, 264(18), 10327-30.

Lu, L. I. . (2012). On the theory and practice of water environmental auditing in china. Journal of Zhongnan University of Economics and Law.

Lu, Z. , Lin-Yu, X. U. , Kai, W. , Environment, S. O. , & University, B. N. . (2017). Corporate environmental auditing in china:literature review and research suggestions. China Population,Resources and Environment.

Lu, Z. . (2009). On developing chinese government auditing

information publicity system. Journal of Zhongzhou University.

M

McMahon, Dinny, Rapaport, Michael, Feng, & Sue 等 . (2011). Challenges auditing chinese firms. Wall Street Journal Eastern Edition.

Md.Tajuddin, & K.China Busi. (2013). An enhanced dynamic auditing protocol in cloud computing. International Journal of Engineering Trends & Technology, 4(7).

Mei, C. , & Jun-Ning, C. . (2003). An analysis on the theoretic foundation of establishing internal auditing department in china. Science-technology and Management.

Men,Qing. (2002). A study on chinese auditing standerds. Kwansei Gakuin Shogaku Kenkyu, 51, 109-124.

Michael, A. , Alexander, K. , & Vasarhelyi, M. A. . (2003). Lessons for china and other developing economies from the crisis in us auditing. The International Journal of Digital Accounting Research, 3, págs. 33-60.

Min, Z. , & Xiao-Ping, Z. . (2010). Study on the assoeiation between internal control quality and auditing pricing——evidence from the cross-section data of china a-share quoted company. Economic Management Journal.

Ming-Zeng, Y. , Hao, F. , & Ming-Hao, X. . (2004). The regulation about the Improvement of auditing for fraud in china. Journal of Sdtvu Editorial Board.

Mmg-Quan, S. , & Zai-Hua, J. . (2003). China's auditing innovation in the 21st century. Commercial Research.

Mmg-Quan, S. , &

Zai-Hua, J. . (2003). China's auditing innovation in the 21st century. Commercial Research.

Q

Qiang, W. , & Marxism, S. O. . (2018). On the internal auditing mechanism of banking industry in modern china. Historical Research in Anhui.

Qin, C. , & Xiu-Lan, L. . (2002). Problems and countermeasures existing in computerized auditing in china. Theory Observe.

Qing, Y. . (2006). Structure optimization and developing strategy of china's auditing market. Journal of Anhui Agricultural ences, 34(2), 390-392.

Qing-Hua, P. , & Business, S. O. . (2017). On function expansion of china's internal auditing under economic new

normal. Journal of Hunan University of ence & Technology(Social ence Edition).

Qinglong, Z. . (2013). Study on the design of general competency framework for internal auditing in china——analysis based on a survey. Accounting Research.

Qing-Shui, L. I. . (2007). He analysis of the government performance auditing in china. Journal of Sanming University.

Qu, W. , & Leung, P. . (2006). Cultural impact on chinese corporate disclosure – a corporate governance perspective. Managerial Auditing Journal, 21(3), 241-264.

Quan-Min, C. , Ru-Ying, G. , & Juan, Z. . (2012). A survey on auditing government performances in china from the perspective of gagas. Journal of Bjing Jiaotong University(Social ences Edition).

Quan-Min, C. , Ru-Ying, G. , & Juan, Z. . (2012). A survey on auditing government performances in china from the perspective of gagas. Journal of Bjing Jiaotong University(Social ences Edition).

R

R.K. Ellis, J. Weihua, & L. Warren. (2002). The feasibility of an environmental auditing system for Chinese manufacturing industry: a systemic approach. IEEE International Conference on Systems. IEEE.

Richard Henry Macve. (2015). The future structure of the global accounting and auditing profession: western and chinese perspectives.

Ronald A. Davidson, & Stanley Chang. (2001). The importance of auditing topics to chinese auditors. International Journal of Auditing.

Ronald A. Davidson, & Stanley Chang. (2001). The importance of auditing topics to chinese auditors. International Journal of Auditing.

Rong-Bing, H. , Tianyue, W. U. , Auditing, D. O. , University, N. A. , & Management, S. O. . (2016). Research on state audit quality and public financial irregularities. China Soft Science.

Rongsheng, Q. . (2008). Some thoughts on the china state auditing development strategy. Auditing Research.

Rui-Qin, W. U. . (2007). The review performance auditing in america and english and the thought of performance auditing in china. Journal of Zhejiang Wanli University.

Ruiqing, S. , & Lijuan, C. . (2006). An analysis on

the auditing opinions of uncertainty of china's listed companies' sustainable operation. Audit & Economy Research.

Run, T. , & University, N. A. . (2019). The role of auditing socialist countries with chinese characteristics in promoting the modernization of state governance. Jiangsu Commercial Forum.

S

Sami, H. , Wang, J. , & Zhou, H. . (2011). Corporate governance and operating performance of chinese listed firms. Journal of International Accounting Auditing & Taxation, 20(2), 106-114.

Samir. (2009). Auditing and accounting in the people's republic of china: review of research accomplished and prospects for additional research.

Shaikh, N. , Ummunissa, F. , Hanssen, Y. , Al-Makki, H. , & Shokr, H. M. . (2010). Thoughts on countermeasures of performance auditing development to china's public environment projects. Chinese Public Administration.

Shao-Jun, C. . (2006). Auditing rent-seeking and its counter-measures on china capital market. Audit & Economy Research.

Shao-Jun, C. . (2006). Discussion on the auditing rent-seeking in china capital market. Journal of Shijiazhuang University of Economics.

Shao-Jun, C. . (2007). Auditing leasing-seeking in china's capital market. Commercial Research.

Sheng-Yong, Z. , & Ling-Zhi, Z. . (2012). The research on legal risk of independent auditing in chinese listed company. Journal of Hub Financial and Economic College.

Shiqiao, Z. , & University, N. A. . (2017). On ten issues of perfecting the government auditing system in china. Finance & Economics of Xinjiang.

Shu, W. . (2007). Research on fair value auditing standards in china based on international auditing standards. Communication of Finance and Accounting(Academy Version).

Shuang, L. . (2002). The china's independent auditing standards: the establishment, implementation and development. Journal of Central University of Finance & Economics.

Shuang, L. I. , Xiao, L. I. , Yaozhong, Z. , & Na, S. . (2011). Cpa firms' industry specialized investment and its

auditing pricing: from the perspective of china's auditing market for initial public offering and listing stacks. Journal of Audit & Economics.

Shuhuan, S. . (2004). The comparative and enlightenment of state auditing with china and uk. Journal of Guangzhou Radio & TV University.

Sihai, L. , & Yueqiao, L. . (2012). Auditing quality, debt financing and investment:empirical evidence from the listed companies in china. Review of Investment Studies.

Sihu, H. . (2007). On internal auditing of china's listed companies. Journal of Guangdong Polytechnic Normal University.

Simunic, D. A. , Wu, X. , Sauder School of Business, The University of British Columbia, Accountancy, S. O. , & Central University of Finance and

Economics. (2009). China-related research in auditing: a review and directions for future research. China Journal of Accounting Research.

Song, J. I. , & Zhi-Fa, D. . (2001). The influence of china's entry into wto on the auditing risks and the risk prevention. Journal of Wuhan University of ence and Technology.

Song, J. I. , & Zhi-Fa, D. . (2001). The influence of china's entry into wto on the auditing risks and the risk prevention. Journal of Wuhan University of ence and Technology.

Song-Nan, L. . (2008). Contribution of performance auditing system in chinese government. Journal of Dalian Maritime University(Social ence Edition).

Su, Xijia, Chen, Shimin, & Wang, Zhenglin. (2006). An Analysis of Auditing Environment and Modified Audit Opinions in China: Underlying Reasons and Lessons. International Journal of Auditing.

T

Tang, & Qingliang. (2018). Institutional influence, transition management and the demand for carbon auditing: the chinese experience. Australian Accounting Review.

Tang, Q. , Chow, C. , & Lau, A. . (1999). Auditing of state-owned enterprises in china: historic development, current practice and emerging issues. International Journal of Accounting, 34(2), 173-187.

Tang, Q. , Chow, C. W. , & Lau, A. . (1999). Auditing of state-owned enterprises in china: historic development, current practice and emerging issues.

Tang, Q. , & English, L. M. . (2019). Institutional influence, transition management and the demand for carbon auditing: the chinese experience. Australian Accounting Review, 29.

Tang, Q. . (2017). Institutional influence, transition management and the demand for carbon auditing: the chinese experience. Social ence Electronic Publishing(3).

Tao, L. , & Lin, Y. U. . (2010). A strategic study of china's tax auditing for handling financial crisis. Journal of Yunnan University of Nationalities(Social ences).

Ting Sun, Michael Alles, & Miklos A. Vasarhelyi. (2015). Adopting continuous auditing: a cross-sectional comparison between china and the united states. Managerial Auditing Journal, 30(2), 176-204.

Ting, C. , & Accounting, S. O. . (2018). The construction thinking and framework of china's environmental auditing standards and guidelines. Communication of Finance and Accounting.

Tuanye, Y. . (2002). The comparative study of social auditing standards in china and america. Journal of Tongji University Social ence Section.

W

Wakasugi, A. (2000). On the auditing system in mainland china. Accounting, 158, 1-15.

Wang, J. (2007). On international convergence of china's auditing standards. Journal of Hunan Financial and Economic College, 4(1), 1-13.

389

Wang SL. (2012). Study on problems of economic accountability auditing in china and countermeasures. Innovation.

Wang Y, & Xie YJ. (2005). On auditing system of china in terms of constitution. Journal of North University of China.Social ences.

Wang, F. , & Zhou, H. . (2014). Types of guarantees and their relation to external auditing:evidence from the chinese bond market. China Journal of Accounting Studies, 2(4), 264-293.

Wang, X. . (2019). The national ecological accounting and auditing scheme as an instrument of institutional reform in china: a discourse analysis. Journal of Business Ethics, 154(3), 587-603.

Wang,Yu. (1999). Independent auditing in china. Ryukoku University the Bulletin of the Graduate School Social ence, 13, 26-34.

Wanting, Z. . (2007). The economical analysis of the folk auditing independence in china. Communication of Finance and Accounting(Academy Version).

Watch, C. L. . (2011). Auditing Giant Intertek Sued In Relation to Auditor Bribery. Neutral Current Sheets in Plasmas. Springer US.

Wende, H. , & Baozhang, F. . (2015). Study on ancient chinese legislation on audit. Auditing Research.

Wu Qian. (2016). Research on performance auditing of public crisis management— —evidenc e from china's audit results announcement. Jiangsu Commercial Forum.

X

Xia, C. . (2003). On the establishment of china's credibility mechanism for independent auditing. Journal of Inner Mongolia Normal University.

Xia, T. . (2011). The existing problems and countermeasures study on performance auditing of chinese government. Logs Engineering and Management.

Xiangsen, L. I. , Law, S. O. , & University, N. A. . (2019). On the independent auditing system in modern china and its historical enlightenments. Journal of Nanjing Audit University.

Xiang-Xia, M. , & Cheng-Ai, L. I. . (2008). Harmonizing the law conflict in china agricultural auditing. Audit & Economy Research.

Xiang-Zhen, X. U. ,

Wen-Hui, C. , Management, S. O. , & Jinan, U. O. . (2014). On the auditing of agricultural policy in china:from the perspective of public policy. Journal of South China Agricultural University(Social ence Edition).

Xiang-Zhen, X. U. . (2013). Study on the construction of chinese government auditing system. Journal of Xi'an University of Finance and Economics.

Xiao, & Jason Zezhong. (2004). The chinese government auditing aystem: issues and reform.

Xiao, & Jason Zezhong. (2008). Issues in the Chinese government auditing system: empirical investigation and theoretical analysis. International Conference on Natural Computation. IEEE Computer Society.

Xiao, J. Z. , Yang, S. , &

Zhang, X. . (2010). Chinese government auditing: audit storms, institutional arrangements, and audit independence. American Accounting Association Annual Meeting.

Xiao, J. Z. , Zhang, Y. , & Xie, Z. . (2000). The making of independent auditing standards in china. Accounting Horizons, 14(1), 69-89.

Xiao, J. Z. , Zhang, Y. , & Xie, Z. . (2000). The making of independent auditing standards in china. Accounting Horizons, 14(1), 69-89.

Xiao, Jason Zezhong, Yikuan Zhang, & Zhihua Xie. (2000). The making of independent auditing standards in china. Accounting Horizons.

Xiao, Jason Zezhong, Yikuan Zhang, & Zhihua Xie. (2000). The making of independent auditing standards in china. Accounting Horizons.

Xiao, Z. . (2019). Comparison of the financial system auditing practice between china and the u.s. − −from the perspective of financial risks prevention. Auditing Research.

Xiao-Dan, Y. E. . (2008). Research of legislation on chinese environmental auditing. Journal of Yangtze University(Social ences Edition).

Xiao-Fei, D. . (2009). Model design of government performance auditing with chinese features. Science-Technology and Management.

Xiaofeng, Liu, Hanxiu, Cheng, Xiaoling, & Wu. (2018). Study on the Systematic Logic and Realizing Path of Chinese Cooperative Environmental Auditing.

Xiaolin, L. . (2006). A new probe into auditing history in zhou dynasty and han dynasty− −a concurrent review on volume 1 of china's auditing history. Journal of Bjing Technology and Business University(Social ence).

Xiaolin, L. . (2006). A new probe into auditing history in zhou dynasty and han dynasty——a concurrent review on volume 1 of china's auditing history. Journal of Bjing Technology and Business University(Social ence).

Xiao-Ling, X. . (2006). An analysis on china's cpa independence from the perspective of auditing relationship. Journal of Wenzhou Vocational & Technical College.

Xiaoman, S. , & Chucan, C. . (2014). Research on accounting firm's external governance effectiveness:evidence from panel data analysis of ipo auditing in china's growth enterprise market. Journal of Nanjing Audit University.

Xiao-Yuan, H. . (2011). Problems,reasons and countermeasures of chinese independent auditing. Journal of Jiangsu Vocational and Technical Institute of Economics and Commerce.

Xi-Hui, C. , Zhuo, Z. , & Xiang-Juanb, X. . (2012). Research on implementation framework of sustainable energy auditing in china. East China Economic Management.

Xin, Y. . (2002). On the effect of "enron event" on china's auditing practice. commercial research.

Xing-Fen, W. . (2011). Internal governance of auditing firms in china:empirical study on management decision-making for clients' portfolio risk. East China Economic Management.

Xin-Yan, W. , &

Department, A. . (2015). How to increase the value of the internal audit organization in hospitals under the new medical reform. China Health Industry.

Xinyu, J. . (2006). A study on risk-based auditing in china. Journal of Changchun University of ence and Technology.

Xiu-Ling, C. . (2014). Thinking on improvement of internal accounts auditing in china. Hunan Agricultural Machinery.

Xun, L. I. , Chuan, L. , & Ming, H. U. . (2013). An empirical study on regional relations' influence on auditing pricing in china. Collected Essays on Finance and Economics.

Xusheng, L. I. . (2009). Resources environment auditing research in china. Inner Mongolian Environmental ences.

Y

Yan, Z. . (2002). Mandatory disclosure and cpa auditing in china's securities market. Journal of Sichuan University(Social ence Edition).

Yang, & David Chie-Hwa. (0). Accounting and auditing in China /. Ashgate.

Yang, A. . (2012). The technical platform support to continuous auditing in enterprise groups of china. 598-601.

Yang, S. , Xiao, J. Z. , & Pendlebury, M. . (2008). Government auditing in china: problems and reform. Advances in Accounting Incorporating Advances in International Accounting, 24(1), 119-127.

Yang, Suchang, & Xiao, Jason Zezhong. (2008). Issues in the chinese government auditing system: empirical investigation and theoretical analysis. Journal of East China Shipbuilding Institute, 24(25), 3676–3688.

Yanjuan, M. . (2002). The enlightenment of american corporate governance reform act to china --discussing the role of internal auditing in the corporate governance. Journal of Nanjing Institute of Economics.

Yanru WAN. (2005). Main defects of cpa auditing system in china. Cross-Cultural Communication, 1(1), 735-44.

Yan-Ru, W. , Sheng, B. I. , Prof, Z. H. , Management, S. O. , WUT, & Wuhan, et al. (2002). Fraudulent financial statements of listed companies and dissimulation of auditing function. Journal of Wuhan Automotive Polytechnic University.

Ya-Rong, Z. . (2008). Theoretical research and practical conditions of government performance auditing in china. Audit & Economy Research.

Yi, G. , & University, N. A. . (2019). Research on the perfection and application of policy effect auditing in china. Jiangsu Commercial Forum.

Yi, L. . (2011). Auditing chinese higher education? the perspectives of returnee scholars in an elite university. International Journal of Educational Development, 31(5), 505-514.

Yi-Gang, L. , Xiao-Yan, Y. , & Jie, H. . (2012). Debt governance,high quality auditing and company value: empirical evidences from china's a-share listed companies. Journal of Jiangxi University of Finance and Economics.

Yiming, Hu, Jifeng, Luo,

Hui, & Fan. (0). An Empirical Study on the Acceptance of the Government Performance Auditing in China.

Yin-Qiang, H. , & Ye, L. I. . (2015). Study on convergence of chinese auditing standards and international auditing standards. ence & Technology Vision.

Yongbing, Z. . (2009). Discussion on the path of developing risk-oriented auditing in people's bank of china. Journal of Financial Development Research.

Yong-Chun, S. , & Jia-Ling, Y. . (2002). On marketization of china's nongovernmental auditing after entry into wto-audit marketing. East China Economic Management.

Yu, H. , Xinpei, Z. , Qian, L. , & Yaping, C. . (2016). Auditing the immunization data quality from routine reports in shangyu district, east china. International Journal of Environmental Research & Public Health, 13(11), 1158.

Yu, L. . (2010). Auditing quality,earning management & stock price − − performance of securities market in china. Journal of Shanxi Finance and Economics University.

Yu-Dong, S. , Zhe, L. , & Chun, C. . (2013). On the establishment of warning indicator system of fiscal risk in chinese fiscal auditing. Journal of Nanjing Audit University.

Yue, C. , Jing, L. I. , Zhong-Xin, W. U. , School, B. , & University, H. . (2016). Evolution of china's national auditing institution:history & logic sketch. The Theory and Practice of Finance and Economics.

Yujuan, L. . (2009). The

choice of performance auditing mode in china. Auditing Research.

Yuming, H. . (2003). The institutional arrangement and audit quality in china' s auditing market. Journal of the Graduates Sun Yat-Sen University(Social Sciences).

Yun, Z. . (2005). On cpa' responsibility of fraud auditing in china. Commercial Research.

Yun-Guo, L. , & Jian-Qing, M. . (2006). On auditing quality of four giant accounting firms: preliminary evidences from china's capital market. Journal of Sun Yatsen University(Social ence Edition).

Yun-Xuan, L. . (2008). Building the assess index system of economic responsibility auditing for china commercial banks. Audit & Economy Research.

Yu-Ping, L. I. , &

Zhong-Ying, Y. . (2006). Investigation and analysis of the auditing efficiency of the chinese government. Womens Academy at Shandong.

Yurong, W. . (2009). Empirical study on influencing factors of modern risk-oriented auditing quality − − based on the empirical evidence of china's stock market. Communication of Finance and Accounting.

Yuting, S. , & University, N. A. . (2019). Research on announcement of audit results of local auditing organizations in china. Jiangsu Commercial Forum.

Yu-Ying, Y. U. . (2006). The role of american government auditor and enlightenment for china in performance auditing. journal of henan institute of financial management.

Yuze, L. . (2017). A study on the concept and

application of off-site auditing in china. Auditing Research.

Z

Ze-Bin, W. U. , & Wei-Dong, L. . (2009). Auditing the performance of china's local governments on preserving farmland. China Land Science.

Zhang Xue-mei. (2009). On the internal auditing of stock company in china. Journal of Tianjin Institute of Financial & Commercial Management.

Zhang, J. , & Han, J. . (2016). Adoption of sarbanes-oxley act in china: antecedents and consequences of separate auditing. International Journal of Auditing, 20(2), n/a-n/a.

Zhang, W. , & Wu, Z. X. . (2012). A study on establishing low-carbon auditing system in china.

Low Carbon Economy, 3(2), 35-38.

Zhaohui, Y. . (2014). Research on the related problems and countermeasures of environmental auditing in china. Journal of Environmental Management College of China.

Zhaoliang Wang. (2011). Study on the problems and countermeasures of interior auditing of enterprise groups in china. International Business Research.

Zhaoliang, W. . (2011). Study on the problems and countermeasures of interior auditing of enterprise groups in china. International Business Research, 4(2).

Zhaorui, G. . (2011). International big four accounting firms and high auditing quality——evidence from china's securities market. Auditing Research.

398

Zhen, X. . (2013). U. s. biodefense strategy implementation auditing and enlightenment to china. Auditing Research.

Zhenchang, W. , & Zeyin, Y. . (2012). An analysis of government budget auditing game of china:from the perspective of stakeholder theory. Journal of Audit & Economics.

Zhenfei, Y. . (2010). Discussion on auditing function and role of china's government. Business Economy.

Zhengdan, X. , Rong, X. , & Chunyuan, H. . (1997). Due professional care of certified public accountants in the people's republic of china. Managerial Auditing Journal, 12(4/5), 214-218.

Zhi-Hua, M. . (2011). On the current environmental perfrmance auditing research in china. Journal of Zhengzhou Institute of Aeronautical Industry Management.

Zhong-Sheng, Z. . (2008). Does corporate governance quality affect external auditing efficiency——evidence from chinese listed companies. Journal of Shanxi Finance and Economics University.

Zihong, G. . (2006). Reflections on countermeasures for pushing chinese internal auditing development in the context of economic globalization. Audit & Economy Research.

This book is the result of a publishing agreement between Northeast Asian Studies College, Jilin University (CHINA) and Paths International Ltd (UK)

This book is published with the financial support by the project of Center of integrity studies at Jilin University (2018LZY008)

Government Audit: An Effective Tool for the Anti-Corruption Struggle in the New Era of China's Governance
Authors: Zhao Yang, Zhang Yanzhe, Zhang Jian, Zou Bowen
ISBN: 978-1-84464-606-7
Ebook ISBN: 978-1-84464-607-4

Paths International Ltd
www.pathsinternational.com

Published in the United Kingdom

CPSIA information can be obtained
at www.ICGtesting.com
Printed in the USA
LVHW060234210521
688034LV00001B/1